The Life of the Author: Jane Austen

Life of the Author

new series aims to transform literary biography from its status as a resource
acts and details to that of a dynamic, innovative aspect of teaching, criti-
n and research. Outside universities, lives of writers are by far the most
pular genre of books about literature, but within them they are neglected as
focus for interpretation and as frameworks for advanced research. *The Life of
1e Author* will reverse this imbalance by exploring new questions on how and
why our conception of the author frames our evaluation and understanding of
their work.

New books in this series

The Life of the Author: John Milton
The Life of the Author: Maya Angelou
The Life of the Author: William Shakespeare
The Life of the Author: Jane Austen

The Life of the Author: Jane Austen

Catherine Delafield

WILEY Blackwell

This edition first published 2023

© 2023 John Wiley & Sons Ltd

The right of Catherine Delafield to be identified as the author of this work has been asserted in accordance with law.

Registered Offices

John Wiley & Sons, Inc., 111 River Street, Hoboken, NJ 07030, USA

John Wiley & Sons Ltd, The Atrium, Southern Gate, Chichester, West Sussex, PO19 8SQ, UK

Editorial Office

The Atrium, Southern Gate, Chichester, West Sussex, PO19 8SQ, UK

For details of our global editorial offices, customer services, and more information about Wiley products visit us at www.wiley.com.

Wiley also publishes its books in a variety of electronic formats and by print-on-demand. Some content that appears in standard print versions of this book may not be available in other formats.

Library of Congress Cataloging-in-Publication Data

Names: Delafield, Catherine, author.

Title: The life of the author : Jane Austen / Catherine Delafield.

Other titles: Jane Austen

Description: First edition. | Hoboken, NJ : Wiley-Blackwell, 2023. |
   Series: The life of the author | Includes bibliographical references and
   index.

Identifiers: LCCN 2022010791 (print) | LCCN 2022010792 (ebook) | ISBN
   9781119779346 (paperback) | ISBN 9781119779353 (adobe pdf) | ISBN
   9781119779360 (epub)

Subjects: LCSH: Austen, Jane, 1775-1817. | Austen, Jane,
   1775-1817–Correspondence. | Novelists, English–19th
   century–Biography. | Women novelists, English–Biography.

Classification: LCC PR4036 .D45 2023 (print) | LCC PR4036 (ebook) | DDC
   823/.7 [B]–dc23/eng/20220728

LC record available at https://lccn.loc.gov/2022010791

LC ebook record available at https://lccn.loc.gov/2022010792

Cover Design: Wiley

Cover Image: © Wikimedia Commons

Set in 9.5/12.5pt STIXTwoText by Straive, Pondicherry, India

Printed and bound by CPI Group (UK) Ltd, Croydon, CR0 4YY

C114699_030922

Contents

List of Figures

A Note on Texts and Abbreviations

References to the works of Jane Austen are to *The Cambridge Edition of the Works of Jane Austen* (2005–2006). General Editor: Janet Todd. Cambridge: Cambridge University Press. They are abbreviated as follows:

> J *Juvenilia*, edited by Peter Sabor
> NA *Northanger Abbey*, edited by Barbara Benedict and Deidre Le Faye
> S&S *Sense and Sensibility*, edited by Edward Copeland
> P&P *Pride and Prejudice*, edited by Pat Rogers
> MP *Mansfield Park*, edited by John Wiltshire
> E *Emma*, edited by Richard Cronin and Dorothy McMillan
> P *Persuasion*, edited by Janet Todd and Antje Blank
> LM *Later Manuscripts*, edited by Janet Todd and Linda Bree (including *Lady Susan*, *The Watsons*, and *Sanditon*)

The cover illustration is reproduced from the frontispiece of James Edward Austen-Leigh's *A Memoir of Jane Austen* (1870). The engraving by William Home Lizars was based on a watercolour by James Andrews that was itself based on Cassandra Austen's unfinished sketch (c. 1810) now in the National Portrait Gallery.

References to the letters of Jane Austen are to Deirdre Le Faye (2011). *Jane Austen's Letters*. Oxford: Oxford University Press.

Two other works of reference are abbreviated in the text:

> AP *Austen Papers, 1704–1856* (1942). Edited by Richard Austen-Leigh. Colchester: Spottiswoode Ballantyne.
> C *A Chronology of Jane Austen and her Family* (2013). Edited by Deirdre Le Faye. Cambridge: Cambridge University Press. 2nd ed.

Acknowledgements

I would like to express my gratitude to participants and staff on the People and Places and Country House in Literature modules at the University of Leicester where some of the early research for this book was unwittingly conducted. Mapping the *Mansfield Park* universe and writing a postcard from Bath seem long ago in the teaching process. More recently I have benefited from the efforts of Devon Libraries and of the resources at Internet Archive when so much material seemed unavailable.

Parts of this book have been rehearsed in "Jane Austen and the letter" in *Jane Austen and the Arts* (Edinburgh University Press, forthcoming) and I am grateful for the feedback provided by its editors Joe Bray and Hannah Moss. I would like to thank Julian North for suggesting that I might take on both projects and Series Editor Richard Bradford for his support. I would also like to remember the much earlier encouragement of Park Honan, my dissertation supervisor at the University of Birmingham, and to record my gratitude to the late Deirdre Le Faye for sharing and making accessible so much of her Austen information. Closer to home, George has once more shouldered the task of providing feedback and encouragement in trying times.

Select Chronology of Letters

17 December 1775	Austen born 16 December (Reverend George Austen to Mrs Walter)
September 1783	Typhus fever at school in Southampton (Jane Cooper to Mrs Cooper who died 25 October 1783 in Bath)
9 January 1796	First extant letter (Austen to Cassandra at Kintbury)
15 January 1796	'flirt my last with Tom Lefroy' (Austen to Cassandra at Kintbury)
1 September 1796	Wedding clothes presumed (Austen to Cassandra from Rowling)
23 August 1796	First letter from the 'vortex' of London (Austen to Cassandra from Cork Street)
18 September 1796	Last letter to Cassandra until 24 October 1798
1 November 1797	'Manuscript Novel . . . about the length of Miss Burney's Evelina' (Rev George Austen to Cadell)
11 December 1797	Austen has written from Bath (Eliza de Feuillide in London to Philadelphia Walter at Seal)
8 April 1798	Letter on death of Mr Walter (Austen in Cassandra's stead to Philadelphia Walter at Seal)
24 October 1798	Writing-box and £7 rescued from trip to West Indies (Austen to Cassandra from Dartford)
27 October 1798–3 January 1799	Nine letters to Godmersham (Austen to Cassandra)
28 December 1798	'Frank is made' commander (Austen to Cassandra at Godmersham)
8–9 January 1799	First reference to '<u>first impressions</u>' (Austen to Cassandra at Godmersham)
17 May 1799	First of four letters from Bath visit with Edward and Elizabeth (Austen to Cassandra)
2 June 1799	Sketch of lace (Austen to Cassandra from Bath)

25 October 1800–11 February 1801	Eleven letters to Godmersham (Austen to Cassandra)
1 November 1800	Austen wears Mrs Cooper's 'band' to 'a pleasant Ball' (Austen to Cassandra at Godmersham)
1 December 1800–3 January 1801	Letters on Bath removal presumed missing
5–6 May 1801	House-hunting from Paragon, Bath (Austen to Cassandra at Ibthorpe)
26–27 May 1801	Topaz crosses from Charles (Austen to Cassandra from Bath to Kintbury)
27 May 1801–8 April 1805	Gap in letters
August 1802	Austens in Dawlish (see 10–18 August 1814)
14 September 1804	Single "gap" letter from Lyme Regis (Austen to Cassandra at Ibthorpe)
27–28 January 1805	'our dear trio' after George Austen's death (Henry to Frank)
30 August 1805–7 January 1807	Gap in letters
13 August 1806	Austen 'trio' at Stoneleigh (Mrs Austen to Mary Lloyd Austen)
22 February 1807–15 June 1808	Gap in letters
15 June–1 July 1808	Four letters to Cassandra (Austen from Godmersham)
1 October 1808–30 January 1809	Twelve letters to Godmersham (Austen to Cassandra)
7–9 October 1808	Fanny Knight 'almost another sister' (Austen to Cassandra)
13 October 1808	Elizabeth Austen died 10 October; Martha Lloyd is 'Sister under every circumstance' (Austen to Cassandra at Godmersham)
5 April 1809	Manuscript of 'Susan' recalled (Austen to Crosby from Southampton)
26 July 1809–8 April 1811	Gap in letters
25 April 1811	'sucking child' *Sense and Sensibility* (Austen to Cassandra)
6 June 1811–24 January 1813	Gap in letters
18 August 1811	Philadelphia Walter married (Cassandra to Phylly at Pembury)
29–30 November 1812	Letter in gap; Knight name change and Mrs Dundas (Austen to Martha Lloyd at Barton Court, Kintbury)
24 January 1813	Eleanor Jackson, niece to the Papillons, is 'rejected Addresser' (Austen to Cassandra)

Introduction

A Life in Letters

'Short and easy will be the task of the mere biographer' announced failed banker clergyman Henry Austen in his 'Biographical Notice' (Austen 1818) of his sister Jane. Two hundred years after Austen's death, Austen scholar and House Museum Trustee Kathryn Sutherland has nonetheless pronounced both sister and author 'richly unknowable' (2017a, p. 12). Neither of these statements of transparency and opacity has deterred the rise and rise of an industry devoted to Austen's biography in many incarnations beginning with James Edward Austen-Leigh's *Memoir* (Austen-Leigh 1870, 1871) and much supplemented in the bicentenary year (Byrne 2017; Clery 2017; McMaster 2017; Sutherland 2017b; Worsley 2017). This is also in spite of the fact that the available record of Austen's life is markedly representative of that 'notable disproportion between meagre new biographical fact and . . . tremendous literary reputation' noted recently by Dale Salwak (2019, p. 117).

It is biography's shared goals with fiction and its re-enactment of character and place (Nadel 1984, p. 8) that allow lives to be told and retold. Michael Benton has suggested that biography is about 'writing back to the future' (2011, p. 69) and animating historical data using the techniques of fiction (p. 70). Biography is in its own way a letter from the past. One of Austen's noted biographers has suggested that it is the biographer's task to attach established biographical facts in a 'linear string' to approximate emotional experience (Honan 1990, p. 15). Honan's 1987 *Life* begins with Austen's brother Frank riding home to Steventon, enacting Honan's 'key requirement' of devising 'new, adequate forms for presenting evidence that one comes to know closely' (1990, p. 16). Any reading of the biographies discussed in this Introduction, however, amply demonstrates that Austen's life also enacts Hermione Lee's warning that biography is 'not neutral ground' (2009, p. 100).

This life of the author makes Austen's letters its focus in order to examine the voice created by the letters and honed in the novels. As explored below, Austen's

The Life of the Author: Jane Austen, First Edition. Catherine Delafield.
© 2023 John Wiley & Sons Ltd. Published 2023 by John Wiley & Sons Ltd.

life has been addressed in a wide range of linear biographies partly by the reassembly of her letters into a chronological sequence. This biography takes a non-linear approach by building a life from the letters using the themes of family, correspondent, and fiction. This Introduction briefly previews the chosen themes by discussing women's letters and Austen's letters, collected and in biography. There are then three pairs of chapters exploring the letters, correspondents, and novels. Chapter 1 reads the life from the surviving letters and Chapter 2 reviews the family treatment of the life. Chapter 3 reorients the mirror to look into the role of Cassandra Austen as absent correspondent and editor, and Chapter 4 discusses the 'sisterhood' of correspondents in surviving and missing letters. Chapter 5 rereads both the Juvenilia and the mature novels for their letter content and structure based on Austen's own lived experience of epistolary fiction and communication; and Chapter 6 reads the fiction again as representations of place refined from the experience of letter writing. Chapter 7 takes a different stance by examining surviving scraps with links to the letters that together make up a patchwork of the life in recipes, accounts, and needlework, and in the gentry networks of Austen's family.

In the ninth chapter of Volume 2 of *Mansfield Park* Fanny Price receives 'the only thing approaching to a letter which she had ever received' from her cousin Edmund with whom she is secretly in love: 'Two lines more prized had never fallen from the pen of the most distinguished author – never more completely blessed the researches of the fondest biographer' (*MP*, p. 308). Jane Austen might have been anticipating the keenness of biographers to find evidence of her life when she recorded this slightly hysterical response to a casual note. Austen's relatively few surviving letters have been positioned as new work both to supplement her fiction and to substantiate her life but the volume of material is slight by comparison with other novelists such as Frances Burney and Charlotte Brontë. Austen's sister Cassandra has become notorious for her decision to destroy many letters in the 1840s. The letters are limited in volume and suggestive in their voids and gaps. The letters represent the life by being part of a responsibility to communicate and their existence is weighted by survival and absence. For Austen, the letter is not an autobiographical tool but a conversation on paper where commonplaces and rules are mocked as they were in the burlesques of her Juvenilia. If a reliance on letters creates a life out of absence and lack of evidence, the re-collected letters perform both a service and a disservice to biography.

Unlike the writing of novels, writing letters was ostensibly a neutral act and part of women's duties and occupations. Patricia Meyer Spacks has pointed out, however, that Austen 'understood letters as voice and as action and understood conventions as capable of manipulation' (1989, p. 75). One source of such manipulation was the letter advice manual that presented model letters for all occasions.

The manual was a site of crossover with the fictional letter. The manual also authorised the familiar letter as conversation aligning the domestic economy of exchanged information with creative composition even in the absence of news.

Letter IX of a sequence for separated friends in *The British Letter-Writer or Letter-Writer's Complete Instructor* (1760) bemoaned the lack of material as Austen often does: 'News, the life of Correspondence has no Existence here' (p. 30). By Letter XI the fictional and semi-fictional letter-writers are elided: 'You and I write like *Clarissa Harlowe* and *Miss Howe*, only not totally in the same strain but in this, I believe we all four agree, that next to the Conversation of a Friend is her Correspondence' (pp. 36–37). *The Complete Letter-Writer* agreed, advising 'Let your words drop from your pen, as they would from your tongue' (1776, p. 39). In the introduction to another much reissued manual, Charles Johnson used the exact words of Samuel Johnson's *Rambler* essay of 31 August 1751 to propose 'Ease and Simplicity', 'unlaboured Diction', and 'an artless Arrangement of obvious Sentiment' (1779, p. iii): 'The Purpose for which Letters are written when no Intelligence is communicated, or Business transacted, is to preserve in the Minds of the Absent, either Love or Esteem' (p. iv). Words are to be like pebbles polished into diamonds to stand in for things (p. iv). Several biographers have used this polishing analogy to describe Austen's letters although her economies are also those of someone buying paper out of her allowance while avoiding the burden of extra postage costs for her recipient.

The filled paper and the associated economics of composition mean that the letters speak for themselves about relative poverty and the costs of correspondence. Most of Austen's letters took the form of a single sheet of paper folded to make four sides and folded again into thirds so that the centre section of the fourth page could accommodate the address (Modert 1990, p. xix). The letter was sealed with a wax wafer which would leave its own vacant space on the completed document (Figure I.1). Austen often wrote around and above the original text layout to maximise the use of space since the cost of postage was paid by the recipient and charged by the page. The so-called epistolary pact thus included paying for receipt of a letter and consequent value for money. These economics of transmission were occasionally supplemented by the franking privilege of an MP or, in Austen's case, the shared channel of business communication within Henry's banking network. Eliza de Feuillide, both cousin and sister-in-law, provides Austen with a frank for 30 April 1811 but in her own letter to their half-cousin Philadelphia she complains on 22 September 1797 of being deserted by 'franking Friends'. She tells Phylly, 'I am vexed to make you pay postage for so stupid a letter' (Le Faye 2002, p. 148). Eliza refers on 11 December 1797 to a letter from Austen no longer extant. She fears missing the post and concludes that it 'grieves' her 'to leave so much Paper [unem]ployed' (p. 150). The very end of this letter from Lowestoft is missing suggesting unshareable content about Eliza's pursuit of Henry Austen whom she

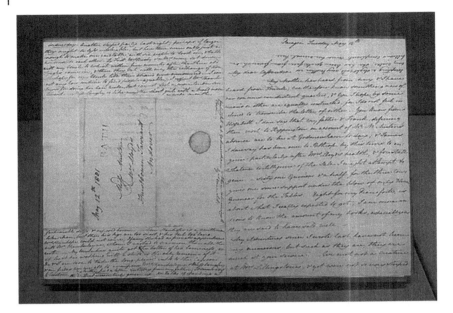

Figure I.1 Austen to Cassandra Austen, 12 May 1801; detail of folding, address, and seal. Pierpont Morgan Library.

married on 31 December; or the nearly blank paper was perhaps merely reused by the unmarried Phylly caring for her parents in Kent.

In addition to the valuation of their content, the ability of letters to recirculate was a gift within the epistolary pact. The manipulation of fabric and fashion discussed in the letters is akin to the manipulation of letter contents. The layout of Austen's 30 November 1814 with its advice to Fanny Knight, for instance, allows selective reading because pages 2 and 3 are concealed inside the folded quarto sheet and so the ongoing discussion about Fanny's suitor John Plumptre can be more easily withheld from reading out loud. Such layout and sharing were planned. Austen herself asks Fanny in the same letter to 'write <u>something</u> that may do to be read or told'. The letter was a textual space designed to accommodate a women's economy of news, family information, and entertainment. As explored in Chapter 5, *Emma* is a novel structured around letters that are discussed without ever appearing in the text until Frank Churchill's long explanation is addressed to Mrs Weston and read by Emma and Mr Knightley (*E*, pp. 476–488). We can share the experience of this circulation of women's letter writing and reading when Emma leaves Miss Bates's 'very moderate sized apartment' (p. 166) having 'heard the whole substance of Jane Fairfax's letter' but escaped 'the letter itself' (p. 173).

The theorisation of letters crosses generic boundaries spanning literature, history, and social science (Delafield 2020, pp. 8–11). The work of Liz Stanley explores social science's suspicion of the value of letters, their originals fragmented and dispersed (2004, p. 204) but ambiguously present as shadows in transcribed versions (p. 222). Other critics in other disciplines identify issues of societal obligation in letter writing (Earle 1999, p. 8), fact at the borders of fiction (Cook 1996, p. 19), and letters as a textual representation of the self (Bigold 2013, p. 14). In light of these issues, Austen's letters have been critiqued since first publication with varying appreciation of her social status and obligations. Critics have identified a perceived discrepancy with her fiction and a need to excuse her when she uses own voice as a correspondent.

The status of letters as life evidence must be part of any reading of correspondence where letters are collated as life writing, and the seminal 1986 issue of *Yale French Studies* differentiates between the letter read and the letter sent (Porter 1986, p. 7), debating the role of collaboration between correspondents (Bossis 1986), and describing publication as 'reinscription' (Altman 1986, p. 19). Stanley has more recently addressed the question of letters as marginalised documents in social science, pronouncing them dialogical, perceptival, and emergent (2004, pp. 202–203). This biography follows Stanley's lead in discussing the reciprocity of letters emerging from their own conventions and from the passage of time. Stanley (2011) has expanded the original epistolary pact derived from Lejeune's autobiographical pact to include the 'epistolary gift' where letters reach new recipients as Austen's did through Cassandra. Stanley fruitfully explores other characteristics such as cross-hatching, interrupted presence, recirculation, and reasons to close as features of an 'epistolary system of exchanges' (pp. 138–139). For Austen this system was derived not just from letter manuals but directly from Samuel Johnson (31 August 1751), quoted in her 8–9 February 1807 letter, and from the lived experience of her own correspondence (Brant 2006, p. 10).

This correspondence has helped to supplement the bare details of her life. Jane Austen biography began with Henry Austen's 'Notice' (Austen 1818) revised in 1833. The family's *Memoir* (Austen-Leigh 1870, 1871) and *Letters* (Brabourne 1884a, 1884b) were followed by a Leslie Stephen DNB entry in 1885. In 1913, the later Austen-Leighs' *Life and Letters* effectively amalgamated the *Memoir* and *Letters* taking account of the Hubbacks' *Sailor Brothers* (Hubback 1906) and referencing Constance Hill's *Homes and Friends* (Hill 1902). A copy of Brabourne's *Letters* accompanied Hill as a guide for her pilgrimage to places where Austen had lived but she nonetheless observed that Austen 'was not amongst those authors who have unveiled in their letters their innermost thoughts and feelings' (1902, p. vi). After appearing in a collected works (Johnson 1912) and a selected letters (Johnson 1925), the letters were collected into a scholarly edition by R.W. Chapman (1932). Elizabeth Jenkins makes use of this edition in her biography and declares the letters 'a treasury of interest and delight' (1938, p. 135) in their 'racy careless perfection' (p. 136) but a 'sidelight only on Jane Austen's character' (p. 135). Joan

Rees points out that the letters appear 'through the medium of the family filter' (1976, p. 13) which she nonetheless uses to eavesdrop on Austen's life through these 'natural, spontaneous, often hurried bulletins' (p. 52). Rees was criticised by Park Honan for creating a 'shallow portrait' (1986, p. 21) out of the letters. In his account of Austen biographies, Honan approved the *Memoir*, finding James Edward Austen-Leigh's approach 'alert, revealing and charming' in its 'intelligent family piety' (p. 18) and in agreeing with Honan himself that the letters are 'trivial' (p. 18). Honan's survey had found David Cecil's account 'good-tempered' and 'cautious' (Honan, 1986, p. 21) and Cecil in turn had thought Austen not a great letter-writer (Honan 1978, p. 72) despite her other charms and partly because she wrote as a woman without a man's public persona to maintain. Honan's own expansive biographical social history categorises Austen's letters to Cassandra as 'casual' with their 'smart, witty' and 'bright polished remarks' (1987, p. 94). He agrees on the letter as an influencing medium for a woman, outside the ballroom at least (p. 101) but, like D.W. Harding in his 'Regulated hatred' essay (1940, p. 351), suggests Austen behaved well in public in exchange for her brutal jokes in private (Honan 1987, p. 255).

This was a period in criticism when women's letters were becoming more valued as readings of their lives. In her biography of Austen as a professional writer, however, Jan Fergus finds the letters inaccessible and 'as unrevealing as possible' (1991, p. 1). She sets them aside because they need translation and sees them as mundane or harsh (p. 75). Claire Tomalin reads the letters as defensive, emotionally distant, and avoiding intimacy (1997, pp. 6–7). This view provides a context for Tomalin's overall treatment of Austen's early rejection under the family's childhood dry-nursing arrangement. For Tomalin, the letters become 'safety valves', the 'sharpening stones against which she polished the small knives of her prose' and 'closer to the deliberate boyish bad taste of the juvenile stories' (pp. 144–145). Jon Spence (2003) animates both the earliest letters and the memorandum of Austen's ancestor Elizabeth Weller (1671–1721), widow of Austen's great-grandfather John Austen IV, into origin stories for authorship. More recent research now suggests that inheritance issues were even closer in time than John Austen III's West Kent will (Ballard 2017). The film resulting from Spence's book, *Becoming Jane Austen* (2007), elaborated still further on the role of Tom Lefroy from the rickety evidence and speculation of two or three letters. Carol Shields's brief and impressionistic account points out that biography indeed clothes a rickety skeleton with speculation (2001, p. 10) but concludes that 'the point of literary biography is to throw light on a writer's works, rather than combing the works to recreate the author' (p. 164). By the end of the twentieth century, biographers had thus decided that Austen's letters were variously rehearsals for fiction, brief, organised, polished, guarded, untranslatable, valueless, and workaday while not hesitating to quote from them to support the chosen trajectory of their life writing.

Popular and academic appreciations of Austen are not disconnected despite some snobbery on both sides. The Austen brand (Harman 2009) and the life-writing industry (Sutherland 2005a; Dow and Hanson 2012) are both thriving, and valuable work on factual and interpretative matters continues to be done across all sections of Austen fandom. In the background, the facts recoverable have been retranslated by Deirdre Le Faye from *Life and Letters* into an updated *Family Record* (Austen-Leigh, Austen-Leigh and Le Faye 1989) itself updated in Le Faye (2004) when the Austen-Leighs were detached from its authorship. In Le Faye (2004), revised in 2013, Le Faye made available in published form the full range of her research in *A Chronology of Jane Austen and her Family* which amalgamates many sources of family history including banking records and pocket-books. The information is supplied with a studious neutrality that demands some of the closer reading of the letters attempted in this biographical study. The facts are only one part of the narrative construction of a literary biography. Although the existence of the *Chronology* has made research and the checking of matters of fact easier there is, of course, still a case for seeing items in their original form. For this, the *Letters* are well-served in facsimile by Modert (1990) in conjunction with Le Faye's twice revised edition (2011).

A letter does not set out to tell a life story. Collected letters are re-contextualised over time and their text made serial by the reversed plot of the life. The use of letters as life writing was a feature of nineteenth-century biography into which *Memoir* and *Letters* made an uneasy entrance (Delafield 2020, pp. 115–136). Richard Altick suggests that 'Biographers found a self-conscious virtue in letting their subjects speak for themselves' (1966, p. 196). Not surprisingly, Honan is suspicious of the 'single epistolary perspective' that he regards as inward-looking rather than contextualising the subject (1990, p. 13). Only a few years later, the letters of Elizabeth Gaskell were seen conversely by her biographer as a continuation of 'the narrative of her outer life' (Uglow 1993, p. 98). Letters themselves are also far from 'neutral ground' as evidence of a life. A letter reconsidered as a life-writing document is not only a text to be re-sequenced, recovered, and reprinted as evidence. The logistics of production, physical appearance, the place of writing, and composition process are all part of the life. The correspondence itself is modulated within temporal networks such as planned arrival and elapsed time within the communication, and some gaps that are now the source of endless speculation were engineered to avoid double communication and double cost.

The afterlife of Austen's letters in print extends from the Austen 1818 'Biographical Notice' to the fourth modern edition (Le Faye 2011). From the first, readers have identified a clash between the author and the individual read from within her letters. Biographers have found it necessary to apologise for the letters in the context of the authorship of the novels (Brabourne, 1884a, p. 2; Favret 1993, p. 133). When Roger Sales reclaimed the letters as 'important literary texts', he described them as 'a historical source rather than as a collection that always has to be read with disappointment' (1994, p. 31). A biographical reading of the letters must also, however, read them as women's texts in a women's context written for a women's circle as counter-cultural expressions of their inverted power.

In the period after the Austen-Leighs' *Life and Letters* (Austen-Leigh 1913), critics found different ways to deny and excuse the letters. Reginald Farrer's perceptive centenary essay extracted the 'dry bones of her facts' (1917, p. 246) concluding that Austen 'lived remote in a great reserve' writing 'pleasant little empty letters' (p. 247). R.W. Chapman turned to the letters in 1932 as part of his Oxford complete works, making considerable efforts to complete and update the existing material. He struggled, however, with the referential frame of the letters and betrayed some irritation about the difficulties of compiling them from the dispersals of the late nineteenth century. His introduction damned the 'pious destruction' of Austen's first editor Cassandra but he was soon squirming to excuse the content, suspecting that the destruction 'has not materially affected the impression we should have received from a richer survival' (Chapman 1932, p. xxxix). In his later work, tellingly entitled *Facts and Problems*, he reiterated that 'The letters . . . were deliberately robbed of their significance' (Chapman 1948, p. 90). According to Chapman's edition the letters were 'the small change' of Austen's life and he offered contrasting interpretations of, on the one hand, an amusing correspondent and on the other, the letter-written betrayal of her 'cold heart' (1932, p. xliii). He was looking for a coherent narrative and plot, and condemned the letters as 'inconsequent' (p. xlii). He makes two transparently time-bound comments that should put any reader of women's letters on alert. He thinks the themes of the letters 'accidental' and brief (p. xlii), and he identifies 'us her unlicensed readers' (p. xliii) as the fourth wall around the surviving materials. The letters thus attained the status of a scholarly edition but were devalued as merely women's letters contextualised within an unsatisfactorily autobiographical frame.

The edition led, however, to two important breakthroughs in critical thinking that benefited from the letters and editions of the novels: Elizabeth Jenkins's biography (1938) and Mary Lascelles's critical study (1939). With Austen's own words unlinked from the family framework of the *Memoir* and *Letters*, D.W. Harding found 'unexpected astringencies' (1940, p. 347) in the novels. For Harding, Austen's fictional writings become like letters needing to keep on terms as part of 'the means for unobtrusive spiritual survival, without open conflict' (pp. 11–12).

Mary Favret distinguishes Austen's letters as 'a mirror of the surrounding community' rather than a 'lens through which one scrutinised the writer' (1993, p. 136). Marilyn Butler explains that Austen's letters are neither subjective (1985, p. xxii) nor photographic (xxiv). Deborah Kaplan sees them emerging from a women's counterculture that used letters to re-value the trivia of life (1988, p. 224). Kaplan's later book-length study identifies the enactment of self-effacement in the letters (1992, p. 49) within which women used a private discourse to represent their separate selves (p. 74). In the same vein, Susan Whealler suggests that letters offered a space for private control 'as well as the constant and contrasting knowledge of subordination' (1993, p. 193). Carol Houlihan Flynn adds that the opportunity for criticising the powerful was balanced with social control through surveillance (1997, p. 112). Letter writing and letter sharing were duties but at least the logistics of travelling and laundry could be brought to the attention of those with power. In her edition, Vivian Jones points out the shaping of the letters (2004, p. xiv) but suggests that most have 'no immediate function other than communication itself' (p. xiii). For Susan Allen Ford the letters put information 'to narrative account' as a result of 'narrative thrift' (2008, p. 220) and Sutherland describes 'a continuous if unsynchronized conversation' (2009, p. 21) using 'a shared idiolect with its private mechanisms for recalibration' (p. 22). Deidre Shauna Lynch sees 'semi-public documents of sociability' (2017, p. 79). The letters are not a diary or descriptive work. They are mobilised to critique the life and to offer the value of that life to a circle of women and other family members. They are both duty and outlet, and they manipulate the resources and conventions of the social circle and level occupied by Austen as an unmarried daughter of the lower gentry.

The letter has been used to narrate the linear progress of Austen's life from the beginning. Henry Austen quoted from two letters in 1818. The post-Victorian Austen-Leighs, two further generations beyond James Edward, call their memoir *Life and Letters* but adopt the tone of his *Memoir* by asking the letters along for a delightful journey to accompany the life. As discussed in Chapter 2, the family biographies were paradoxically using her letters to deny Austen a voice and rewriting her for their new age. In binding her to them, the family bound Austen to a time and place. Austen-Leigh insisted that Austen's life was 'passed in the performance of home duties, and the cultivation of domestic affections, without any self-seeking or craving after applause' (1871, p. 165) and as late as 1989 his great-granddaughter Joan Austen-Leigh argued that *Life and Letters* was the 'definitive' text 'on which all subsequent biographies are, or should be based'. Kathryn Gleadle (2018) writing about the diaries of Lord Brabourne's daughter, Austen's great-great-niece Eva Knatchbull-Hugesson, points out, however, that a family archive is subject to 'sentimentality, chance, and inclusive or neglectful practices of curation'. Jane Austen's life was memorialised within the family and given a factual basis by *Life and Letters* before the later twentieth-century emergence and re-evaluation of women's stories, and there is thus a danger that patriarchal suppression has denied us readings of the letters and of the missing archive (Beizer 2009).

If the medium of biography imposes meaning on the life as lived and the letter is part of historical data, biography can also play a role in rereading the letter as written. Some 'truths' have taken hold in the tale of Austen's life and a biography must deal with the pros and cons of evidence compiled with another agenda. Any use of the letters as evidence should, as this book aims to do, remain conscious of the logistical and physical elements of the letters both at the time and in the course of their preservation. News will appear as a linear production that is also timed to fit both the day of actual posting and the volume of paper at hand. A reading of multiple aspects of the letters within the life will therefore reanimate this latest round of collaboration with the family archive of Jane Austen. This book concentrates on the letters, inflecting them against other techniques (or sub-genres) applied to biography. The organisation of the letters by correspondent in Chapters 3 and 4 is partially modelled on *The Clear Stream*, a biography of Winifred Holtby in which Marion Shaw takes a 'prismatic approach' (1999, p. 4) to her subject. The letters as a medium in parallel with novel writing owes something to the work of Jenny Uglow in *Elizabeth Gaskell: A Habit of Stories* (Uglow 1993), and the exploration of the Papillon and Jackson families in Chapter 7 nods to the extended footnote deployed by Rebecca Stott in *Darwin and the Barnacle* (Stott 2003). The life of objects structures Deborah Lutz's non-linear group biography *The Bronte Cabinet* (Lutz 2015) and also Paula Byrne's *Real Jane Austen* (Byrne 2013), and the final chapter of this biography revisits valued scraps of texts and textiles as biographical bridges with the letters.

Austen's Fanny Price would have been less enthusiastic to find that letter collections have become subject to the 'fondness' for speculation demanded of celebrity biography. Through Cassandra and Chapman, we have words originally in Jane Austen's voice, allowing us to reconsider her as a woman writer and not just as an aunty construct of a woman. It is essential, however, that we read these letters like Cassandra and not like Chapman. The letters as a sequence provide one biographical construct but can also be inflected across other biographical approaches. We can read a life in context without the letters becoming merely incidental. Jane McVeigh has suggested that the way a biography is written becomes part of the life (2017, p. 1) and the aim of this biography is to unearth the plot of a correspondence. The letters are reflections on Austen's own epistolary practice and a commentary on that of the reader-recipient-correspondent. This biography offers several journeys through her chronological life using the letters, their readers, and recipients. The later chapters explore letters as devices within her fictional writing and then the parallel scraps reread in letters. First, however, the letters themselves must be examined and their plot revealed.

1

Austen's Life in Letters

This chapter traces the life recoverable from Austen's letters and discusses the role of letters in the life-writing cycle. It follows a number of themes within Austen's life readable in the letters and then tracks the publication of the novels. The shape of this correspondence as a whole has been altered by the events of the life and by preservation and publication. The first section therefore considers how the distribution and weighting of the surviving letters shape an understanding of Austen's life. The chapter goes on to situate the novels in the life using the letters. Austen is sister, aunt, author, and letter writer adopting and acting out both conventional and unconventional roles.

The letters inform the outline of Austen's life in progress. She lived in Steventon Rectory from 1775 to 1801 having spent brief periods at school in Oxford and Southampton (1783) and in Reading (1785–1786). She also visited family in Kent and friends in Ibthorpe, and stayed in Bath (1797 and 1799). In May 1801, the family relocated permanently to Bath taking up the lease on a house for a few years but visiting the seaside in the summer including Lyme Regis (1804) but also Dawlish (1802). After the death of the Reverend George Austen in January 1805, the Austen women – or as Henry called them 'our dear trio' – were reliant on financial support from Austen's brothers and lived in Bath lodgings in between trips to see family in Kent and in Warwickshire. Having been joined by their friend and sister-in-law Martha Lloyd, in 1806 they united their domestic arrangements with brother Frank Austen and his wife Mary and lived in Southampton. In 1809 the four women were provided with a cottage by Edward Austen Knight in Chawton near Alton where Austen lived until her removal to Winchester for medical treatment in May 1817. There were trips to London to oversee the publication of the four novels that appeared in Austen's lifetime as well as to nurse both Henry and his first wife Eliza.

The Life of the Author: Jane Austen, First Edition. Catherine Delafield.
© 2023 John Wiley & Sons Ltd. Published 2023 by John Wiley & Sons Ltd.

The reordered modern edition of the letters (Le Faye 2011) has a well-established pattern of its own. As demonstrated chronologically in Figure 1.1, there are 92 letters to Cassandra, 16 to Anna Lefroy, 10 to Caroline Austen, eight to Frank Austen, six to Fanny Knight, five to John Murray, four to Martha Lloyd, three to James Edward Austen-Leigh, and three to librarian James Stanier Clarke. There is one letter each to Alethea Bigg, Anne Sharp, Cassy Esten Austen, Frances Tilson, and Charles Austen all dating from 1817, and three letters to individuals (Catherine Prowting, Charles Haden, and the Countess of Morley) relating to the publication of *Emma*. There is evidence of letters being written to James, Edward, and Henry but none to them from Austen survive. James and Henry were themselves survived by their wives who may have made any final decision about preservation and Henry had a wandering life even after his ordination in 1816. No letters survive to any of the sisters-in-law other than Martha and none to Austen's parents. There is the possibility that the letters to and from Cassandra were shared with them, of course, and that Cassandra had the final say over survival when putting her affairs in order as she reported she was doing to Charles in 1843 (Modert 1990, p. xxi). Austen also names in the surviving letters a number of other correspondents including the other Bigg sisters, her mother's friend Mary Newell Birch, the Cookes in Great Bookham, and the Bullers in Devon.

The modern edition contains 161 letters of which two are poems, one is Austen's will, and one is in backward writing for an eight-year-old niece. Four are scraps with limited or no content probably redistributed for autographs, and one (29–30 November 1812) is a spoof fan letter whose original was rediscovered and sold for £162,000 in Austen's bicentenary year (Le Faye 2017, pp. 26–27). One is in Austen's hand dictated by Henry (20–21 October 1815) and another merely protests at the gift of a turkey (December 1816). Of the other 150 letters there are briefer communications with the 12-year-old Caroline, as well as negotiated epistolary spaces on paper shared with others. Some letters were intentionally shorter and others have been preserved with leaves missing. The greatest concentration by number of letters on one subject and with various correspondents concerns the publication and distribution of *Emma* in late 1815. The physical appearance and layout of the letters has biographical import as does the coding of internal references. The letters reveal factual details but at the same time the medium of the letter with its detailed language and narrative economies supplements our knowledge of Austen's life and methods as an author.

Figure 1.1 charts the distribution of available letters without weighting their length or biographical significance. There are not just four-page bulletins to Cassandra but also the shadows of letters in scraps, and notes with a single purpose. Of the total, 34 were written during Austen's residence at Steventon and 86 during her time at Chawton. It is notable that there are no surviving letters until 1796 and none for 1797. There is only one letter (from Lyme) between May 1801

Year	Letters(no.)	To CEA	To Others
1796	7	7	
1797	0		
1798	9	8	Philadelphia Walter (1)
1799	6	6	
1800	6	5	MLA (1)
1801	10	10	
1802	0		
1803	0		
1804	1	1	
1805	8	5	FWA (3)
1806	0		
1807	3	3	
1808	12	12	
1809	7	4	FWA (2), Crosby (1)
1810	0		
1811	6	6	
1812	2	0	AL (1), MLA (1)
1813	19	15	MLA (1), FWA (3)
1814	20	6	CMCA (1), FWA (1), AL (9), FCK (2), MLA (1)
1815	19	4	JM (5), JSC (2), AL (4), CMCA (2), Countess of Morley (1), C Haden (1)
1816	12	2	JM (1), JSC (1), AL (2), CMCA (3), JEAL (2), C Prowting (1)
1817	13	0	FCK (3), CMCA (4), JEAL (1),CJA (1), A Bigg (1), F Tilson (1), Cassy Esten (1), A Sharp (1)

Key:

AL	Anna Lefroy
CEA	Cassandra Austen
CJA	Charles Austen
CMCA	Caroline Austen
FCK	Fanny Knight
FWA	Frank Austen
JEAL	James Edward Austen-Leigh
JM	John Murray
JSC	James Stanier Clarke
MLA	Martha Lloyd Austen

Figure 1.1 Letter chronology by recipient.

and January 1805, and of the eight letters in 1805 three are to Frank about George Austen's death. The 1807–1809 letters from Southampton shared domestic and family news as Austen and Cassandra alternated at Godmersham particularly after the death of Elizabeth Austen, wife of Edward. In April 1809 Austen wrote to the publisher Crosby requesting the return of her manuscript of 'Susan' and there is then a further gap until April 1811 when Austen was in London to proof-read *Sense and Sensibility*. The two surviving 1812 letters are to Anna Lefroy and Martha Lloyd, suggesting that Cassandra stayed at Chawton keeping house while Austen redrafted *Pride and Prejudice* and began *Mansfield Park*. The volume of surviving letters between 1813 and 1817 reflects the adoption of nieces and nephew as correspondents; about one third, 33 of the letters, are to James's children Anna, (James) Edward, and Caroline, and to Edward's eldest daughter Fanny. Eleven letters concerning the publication and dedication of *Emma* constitute more than half of the 20 dated 1815. Austen had gone with Cassandra in May 1816 to take the waters in Cheltenham. The last two letters to Cassandra were written in September that year to Cheltenham when Cassandra was accompanying Mary Lloyd Austen. The more numerous letters of 1817 suggest memorial preservation since these include Austen's last letters to James Edward, Fanny, and Caroline. Anna lived within walking distance. The 1817 letter borrowed by Henry for his 'Biographical Notice' is the only letter to Frances Tilson, a friend from London. Alethea Bigg, Anne Sharp, and even Charles Austen are noted as regular correspondents and yet have preserved only their last letters from Austen written in 1817.

The letters as they now appear have a deducible pattern based on travel and visits; their survival and preservation emerge from other imperatives. Figure 1.2 presents the sequences of letters initially preserved by Cassandra herself as records of her separation from Austen. It is notable that 57 of these letters were received by Cassandra when she herself was away from home. These letters would have had to be transported after the completion of Cassandra's visit even before being considered for preservation between residences in Hampshire and Bath. These letters and other single missives were evidently doubly removed and valued. On 23 August 1796 Austen writes from Cork Street *en route* to Kent when Cassandra is presumed to be at home since there are four subsequent letters to her from Austen (1–18 September 1796) from their brother Edward's first marital home at Rowling. Cassandra was away from home on 8 April 1798 but unusually there are no letters written during this visit during which Austen wrote, from Steventon, her only surviving letter to their half-cousin Philadelphia Walter. From 27 October 1798 to 23 January 1799 Austen was at Steventon having returned from Godmersham where Cassandra remained after the birth of their nephew, Edward's fourth son William. Austen, along with her parents, had travelled back via Dartford, as evidenced by another letter written on the road (24 October 1798).

Year	Letters	JA	CEA
Jan 1796	2	Steventon	Kintbury
Sept 1796	5	London/Rowling	Steventon
Oct 1798–Jan 1799	10	Dartford/Steventon	Rowling
May/June 1799	3	Bath	Steventon
Oct 1800–Feb 1801	11	Steventon/Ibthorpe	Godmersham
May 1801	4	Bath	Ibthorpe/Kintbury
April 1805	2	Bath	Ibthorpe
Jan/Feb 1807	3	Southampton	Godmersham
June 1808	4	Godmersham	Southampton
Oct 1808–Jan 1809	12	Southampton	Godmersham
April 1811	6	London/Chawton	Godmersham
Jan/Feb 1813	3	Chawton	Steventon/Manydown
May 1813	2	London	Chawton
Sept–Nov 1813	9	London/Godmersham	Chawton
Mar 1814	3	London	Chawton
June 1814	2	Chawton	London
Nov/Dec 1815	3	London	Chawton
Sept 1816	2	Chawton	Cheltenham

Figure 1.2 Letter sequences.

The letters of 17 May to 19 June 1799 were written as a tourist from Bath on a visit for Edward to take the waters.

Between late October 1800 and late January 1801 Cassandra was at Godmersham and Austen at Steventon until the end of November when she was at Ibthorpe but back at Steventon on 3 January. It was on this return that Austen was informed of her parents' decision to move to Bath. A gap in correspondence between 1 December 1800 and 3 January 1801 is assumed to be the result of destroyed letters criticising the move to which Austen had apparently become more resigned in five letters between 3 and 25 January in which preparations were in an advanced state. In February 1801 Austen was visiting their friends the Bigg sisters at Manydown while Cassandra was in London returning from Godmersham. The four May 1801 letters from Bath are Austen's first as a resident. Cassandra was at Ibthorpe visiting the Lloyds and at Kintbury with the Fowles, brother and sister-in-law of her deceased fiancé Tom. Farewell visits may have made the letters more treasured but at the same time their preservation would have been more difficult among the sparse movables of the two women.

Their peripatetic life may also explain that sizeable gap in letters up to their settling in Southampton. The sisters were together at the death of the Reverend George Austen described in the three January 1805 letters to Frank. The period of the Southampton residence found Cassandra at Godmersham from 7 January to 10 February 1807 and then again from 1 October 1808 to 30 January 1809 at the time of Elizabeth Austen's unexpected death. Austen wrote to Southampton from Godmersham between 15 June and 1 July 1808. In all there are 15 letters over this period, the majority dealing with the aftermath of Edward's becoming a widower.

The period of the Chawton letters begins with three letters from London between 18 and 30 April 1811. In all there are 30 letters from London, and half of these were written to Cassandra. The early 1813 letters report from Chawton on their reading aloud the recently published *Pride and Prejudice*. In May 1813, letters show that Austen was in London and there again in September on her way to Godmersham where she remained until early November. For three letters in March 1814 Austen was again in London with Edward's family at Henry's new reduced home in Henrietta Street and she signalled the publication of *Mansfield Park* in a scrap to Frank on the same visit. In June 1814, it was Cassandra's turn to be in London and Austen at Chawton but 24 August and 17 October are again from London to Chawton with letters also passing to Fanny on her love life in November and to Anna about novel writing from July onwards. For letters between November and December 1815, *Emma* is going through the press superintended from Henry's new Hans Place address where his business is faltering. The two letters of early September 1816 are the last epistolary evidence of the sisters being apart. Austen claims in 8–9 September to have been nursing herself up into 'beautiful' better health for a doctor's visit: 'my Back has given me scarcely any pain for many days. – I have an idea that agitation does it as much harm as fatigue, & that I was ill at the time of your going, from the very circumstance of your going'. This is a tortuous explanation of her inability to cope with Cassandra's absence, and she is pressing for Cassandra's return on the 23rd: 'I shall grudge every half day wasted on the road. If there were but a coach from Hungerford to Chawton'. Perhaps Cassandra returned earlier in response to this letter or she may have destroyed evidence of Austen's deterioration in the letters that must be missing.

Letters have much to offer the logistics of a life. The next section of this chapter explores one chronological segment of Austen's letters using the first year of extant correspondence before moving onto a broader thematic approach. Reading the letters back into the life demands an awareness of the immediacy of the written context tempered by future-proofed knowledge that the 'new' reader now holds. In between these two poles, in the middle of the spectrum, stands the decision-making of the letter-holding survivor, in this case Cassandra.

Jane Austen's chronological life reflected in her letters begins on 9 January 1796 when she is 20 years old wishing her older sister a happy 23rd birthday. She jokingly declares Cassandra and Tom Lefroy 'very near of an age' although Tom is actually three years younger all but a day. When the letter appears in a modern edition, the reader is now familiar with a scenario that was incomplete at the time of Austen's letter. A convenient footnote will provide the information that Lefroy lived to be part of the conversation about his supposed love affair with the novelist. This conversation took place when James Edward Austen-Leigh and his sisters were compiling the *Memoir*. Lefroy died during the same period aged 92 having reportedly confided his 'boyish love' to his namesake and nephew T.E.P. Lefroy (Le Faye 2004, p. 278) who was by then married to the Austen sisters' great-niece Jemima, Anna Lefroy's eldest daughter. The reader will now also find that Cassandra herself was with the Fowles at Kintbury in 1796, staying with the family of her fiancé, also Tom, and will further know that neither of the Austen sisters married anyone. It will also be apparent that if Cassandra did not want future generations to know about Austen's 'profligate and shocking' behaviour with her 'Irish friend' then this letter, along with 14–15 January, would not survive. At the same time it might be that Cassandra was willing to take this risk of information passing to the next generation because a letter would thus be preserved relating to her own hopes of a happy married life that we now know would never be fulfilled. Her Tom is the brother of the Reverend Fulwar Fowle who is rector of Kintbury and married to Eliza née Lloyd, sister of future sisters-in-law Mary and Martha. Herein lies the danger of letters for both writer and recipient, and for the licensed and future unlicensed reader.

On 23 August 1796, Austen writes from Cork Street in London that she has reached 'once more . . . this Scene of Dissipation & vice'. This seems to be a shared joke about warnings against the metropolis by sermon-writers such as James Fordyce whose work will be read aloud to the Bennets by Mr Collins. In the Preface to his much reprinted *Sermons to Young Women* (Fordyce, 1766), Fordyce deplored the 'contagion of vice & folly' (p. viii) in the capital by comparison with the country. In Sermon IV, he warned his readers against 'the man that imprudently pleads for vice' with 'the appearance of honest frankness, drawing you to every scene of dissipation' (p. 98). In Sermon VII, the two concepts are more closely linked: 'that whorl of dissipation, which, like some mighty vortex, has swallowed up in a manner all conditions and characters . . . How quick the descent from thoughtlessness to vice' (p. 198). Austen counsels her niece (or 'neice' as this is her chosen spelling scorned by Lord Brabourne) against the inclusion of a 'vortex of dissipation' in her own work 18 years later; but only as over-used 'thorough novel slang' by the time of the advice in a letter to Anna (28 September 1814). The August 1796 London stopover is *en route* to Rowling in Kent from which we gain the earliest epistolary knowledge of the Bridges and later Knight families, and of the frequent frustrations for both sisters of having to make travel arrangements at the whim of their brothers. In August 1796, Austen is nonetheless going to Astley's Amphitheatre and cuts short her letter in order to seek out dissipation in the streets of the vice-ridden city.

On 1 September 1796, Austen commends Cassandra as 'the finest comic writer of the present age', reminding her how they joked about dying 'of laughter' at school. The reader of the modern edition knows that the sisters and their cousin Jane Cooper nearly did die of typhus fever in Southampton in 1783. The mirror image, sister alternate of the 'finest comic writer', 'diverted . . . beyond moderation' has been helping to make shirts for Edward and pronounces herself 'the neatest worker of the party'. Time and again there is a surface attention to the promotion of duties that Cassandra would have been decoding and probably performing out loud to her own audience whether her parents or her brother's family. The precarious state of the sisters within that family is announced in the next letter from Rowling (5 September 1796) when Austen asks for advice about tipping a servant five or ten shillings. Her 'Distress' over this, however, straddles with characteristic dashes the news of Richard Harvey's intention to marry a woman called Musgrove: 'but as it is a great secret, & only known to half the Neighbourhood, you must not mention it'. The second half, sides three and four, of this letter does not survive and was not available for the letter edition of 1884 meaning that either Cassandra did not retain this page at the time, lost it in a move, or destroyed it in 1843. It might also be that the paper was reused for something else leaving the scant hope that the two sides might resurface from another archive in the future.

The likelihood that Cassandra chose destruction leaves another gap for speculation since there seems to be another whole letter missing before Austen's next. In 15–16 September 1796 she jokes that Edward, who is due to change his name to Knight in return for an inheritance, is thinking about 'taking the name of Claringbould' if Cassandra can assist with 'five or six Hundred pounds' which of course she cannot. Austen is only just burlesquing the complexity of the inheritance system and its singular propensity to overlook them. The sisters live in a family full of inheritees changing their names for money including Uncle James Leigh-Perrot, Edward and the family of his adoptive parents, and finally James Edward Austen-Leigh. By 18 September 1796 the logistics of Austen's return take up most of her letter almost putting Frank's appointment to the *Triton* into the shade. Austen is embroiled in a plan to travel home to Steventon with Mary Pearson, Henry's then fiancée and is thwarted by the naval plans of Frank but could be helped by Edward who has his own carriage. Austen has to hope that her father will collect her from Greenwich otherwise she will have 'to walk the Hospitals, Enter at the Temple, or mount Guard at St James' as a medical student, lawyer or soldier; or at worst 'fall a Sacrifice to the arts of some fat Woman who would make me drunk with Small Beer' and so become a prostitute. The extremity of these professions, and the fact that the latter is the only one open to a woman of the time, is deliberately alarming in the context of travel arrangements and sisterly duties.

The chronology of the letters supplies an outline of Austen's life, gaps permitting. Even this first year highlights themes that will resonate in the letters of each year for which epistolary evidence survives. As the following section demonstrates, Austen embellished family news with topics to which she returned again and again especially gender-typed occupation, the act of letter writing, fashion economies and errands, social occasions, income, and dependence. The letters help to trace a themed as well as a chronological approach to the biographical documentation of a life.

The family and its 'important nothings' are a dominant ongoing strand for news tied into an oblique commentary to be read by Cassandra. Austen expects Cassandra's agreement when she dubs Charles, younger sibling to both of them, 'our own particular brother' (21 January 1799). He repays them with the topaz crosses that he can ill afford out of his £30 naval earnings on the *Endymion* (26–27 May 1801) and though Austen intends to 'scold' him these gifts were apparently treasured. They can be seen both at Jane Austen's House and in *Mansfield Park* where the gift of an amber cross becomes part of Fanny Price's dilemma in rebuffing Henry Crawford. Topaz was a cheaper alternative to amber. While Fanny has two chains from which she must choose one to wear with the cross for her coming-out ball, the Austen sisters perhaps shared their two slightly differentiated crosses and chains. The real-life crosses are believed to have been retained with the letter in which they are mentioned that was then bequeathed to Charles by Cassandra. A testamentary letter of 1843, however, originally leaves one 'topaz cross and gold chain' to Charles's daughter also Fanny (*C*, p. 664) who married Frank's eldest son Francis that year, uniting the naval brothers. As this marriage was childless and Fanny's elder sister Cassy Esten, Cassandra's executor, died unmarried, the crosses seem to have been passed down with the letter to Charles's granddaughters by his second wife Harriet. The objects were apparently purchased by a young librarian and future scholar/collector Charles Beecher Hogan in the 1920s and having been a wedding present to his wife, were given by him to the Jane Austen Society in 1974 (Harman 2009, pp. 208–209). In 1801 Austen writes more straightforwardly, 'We shall be unbearably fine'.

The crosses represented both affection and a competing offer of a gift from the youngest of the Austen siblings and the neediest other than the disabled George. The 26–27 May 1801 crosses-letter is part of the sequence written on first removal to Bath when the sisters were more dependent than usual on family favours. Jane is staying with the Leigh-Perrots and Cassandra has gone from Ibthorpe to Kintbury to visit the Fowles. James has effectively turned them out of the family home, Frank and their father are visiting Godmersham (21–22 May 1801), and Henry is suffering from a long-running chest complaint (Le Faye 2002, p. 160). Cassandra is waiting to be brought to Bath by the Reverend George Austen on 1 June and Jane adopts some of her breathless Tom Lefroy prose to announce an 'Airing in [Mr Evelyn's] very bewitching Phaeton & four' in a section of 26–27 May upside down between the lines of the original text of page 1. The initial news of the letter composed over two days was spaced out at only 26 lines per page. This journalised information was then effectively overwritten and crowded out by the phaeton and the crosses, announcing the themes of journeying and portable possessions so prevalent in the letters.

At the other extreme of brotherliness, 23 June 1814 succinctly notes 'Henry at Whites!' He was celebrating the end of the war at a Burlington House ball costing £10,000 and attended by the Prince Regent (Le Faye 2004, p. 213). 'Oh! what a Henry' is Austen's ostensibly indulgent exclamation but Cassandra would be reading it with long experience. The comment is characteristically sandwiched, and separated, by dashes, between a reported failure by Edward's Chawton steward to provide their mother with special wood for fire-lighting and a longer sentence, 'I do not know what to wish as to Miss B, so I will hold my tongue & my wishes', sharing a brief paragraph with the brief but pungent Henry comments. It is left to Cassandra to know the identity of 'Miss B', presumed in the modern edition of the letters to be Frances Burdett, sister of Sir Francis and possible love interest of Henry (Le Faye 2011, p. 438; p. 503; Le Faye 2004, p. 216). Although 'Miss B' is part of their epistolary exchanges, Austen leaves some doubt about the exact subject on which her tongue is nominally remaining silent.

The act and actions of letter writing are another constant theme reflecting the advice of the letter manuals as well as Austen's own particular relationship with her correspondent. In the letters preserved from the period of the Bath move, accommodation and income is a source of concern and letter writing, veiled and satirised by the comparison between their country and city pursuits. In 3–5 January 1801 a query about the future location of their bees in Bath is juxtaposed with the information that the Reverend George Austen has brought in tithes of £600 to maintain his income. By the end of the third page Austen claims to have 'attained the true art of letter-writing' by 'talking as fast as I could the whole of this letter' which justifies the bees and tithes becoming an upside-down pre-script postscript at the top of page 1. In the next letter Austen suggests two personal economies relating to letters and millinery as a consequence of their new arrangements. She recommends 'laying out a few kisses in the purchase of a frank' to save money and agrees to delay the purchase of cambric muslin in the next sentence 'with a kind of voluntary reluctance' (8–9 January 1801).

The sharing of letters then features in Austen's next because Mary Lloyd Austen's letter has already reached Steventon with Cassandra's news about the Chilham ball and its franking opportunities. Cassandra has danced with 'stupid' Mr Kemble instead of 'some elegant brother-officer who was struck with your appearance as soon as you entered the room' (14–16 January 1801). This is Austen the 'merciless Sister' oppressing Cassandra with her letter frequency and reading back into the news her own allusion to a potential novel scenario. Austen at the centre passes on other messages and proxy shopping requests from Martha Lloyd, who will write soon, and critiques a letter written by James to Edward filling 'three sides of paper, every line inclining too much towards the North-East, & the very first line of all scratched out'. A joke about James's style is perhaps intended in Austen's next remark that 'this morning he joins his Lady in the fields of Elysium & Ibthrop'. He is, of course, about to succeed Austen and Cassandra and their parents at Steventon Rectory and is not being very politic in his succession. The 8–9 January letter mentions possession being taken of the brown mare '& everything else I suppose will be seized by degrees in the same manner'.

After that 'merciless' letter frequency, there is a longer than usual gap between 14–16 January, when Mr Bayle has been valuing the house contents for auction, and 21–22 January. This may suggest editing by Cassandra or it may merely be that another letter from another correspondent stood in. The 21–22 January letter begins with a joke about the material for letters, deriving from the manuals: 'Expect a most agreable Letter; for not being overburdened with subject – (having nothing at all to say) – I shall have no check to my Genius from beginning to end' although there is news to digest about Frank. Austen comments on her cousin Edward Cooper's 'chearful & amusing letters' and on his wife Caroline's rapid recovery from lying-in. Her additional comments here reflect Austen's later opinions of Edward's published sermons: 'He dare not write otherwise to me – but perhaps might be obliged to purge himself from the guilt of writing Nonsense by filling his shoes with whole pease for a week afterwards'. His true style may perhaps be gauged from Austen's hope in a letter written after the death of Elizabeth Austen that 'he will not send one of his Letters of cruel comfort to my poor Brother' (15–16 October 1808).

By contrast with the 'Genius' of January, Austen writes 'long sentences upon unpleasant subjects' in 22 May 1801 from Bath when their potential residence in Green Park Buildings must be rejected on account of damp. Despite her report of 'putrifying Houses' of good size and situation, this is the street in which the Austens will be living by 21 January 1805 when Austen writes to tell Frank of their father's death, marking the degeneration of their status even before the loss of George Austen's income. The marked gap between this and the initial move to Sydney Place in 1801 includes only one letter, 14 September 1804 from Lyme. From their shabby comfort as travellers in cheapish lodgings, Austen tells Cassandra, who is in Weymouth with Henry and Eliza, about letter-reading within the family. Austen describes a 'puzzle' arising from letters including one from Cassandra to Miss Irvine in Bath that addressed the question of Charles's prospects 'with less explicitness & more caution' than a letter from Mrs. Austen to her sister-in-law Jane Leigh-Perrot written 'without restriction'. In survival terms this is the very next letter after the topaz cross purchase and Austen suggests that 'in your place I should not like' their aunt having 'the perusal' of Cassandra's letter to Miss Irvine. The whole provides an early sample of a situation created for another seaside location in *Sanditon* in which a letter 'chain' unravels when only one group of new residents emerges from Diana Parker's epistolary interference. Austen's 'fine sheet of striped paper' in 1804 is both closely written and crossed on the first page. It stands now in stark contrast with 21 January 1805 and the 'melancholy news' of George Austen's death told in half the number of lines per page and with no manipulation or mockery of epistolary conventions. Archival evidence, however, demonstrates that a second letter of 22 January 1805 had to be sent because of Frank's relocation from Dungeness to Portsmouth discovered by means of a letter from him to Cassandra. Austen was forced to write her news again and the modern edition now almost suggests that we unlicensed readers have received the news of George Austen's death before his own son.

For daily correspondence, however, letter processes such as regularity, epistolary debt, and composition in real time are all subject to Austen's humour and exaggeration. In 8–9 February 1807, she plans to ring 'the Changes of the Glads & Sorrys' but concludes: 'There, I flatter myself I have constructed you a Smartish Letter, considering my want of Materials. But like my dear Dr Johnson I beleive I have dealt more in Notions than Facts'. This is an allusion to Johnson's *Rambler* essay on correspondence (31 August 1751) that formed the basis of advice in the manuals. In 7–9 October 1808, Austen adds to her housekeeping responsibilities in Southampton while Cassandra is at Godmersham by taking 'complete possession of the Letter [from Edward's eldest son Edward] by reading, paying for, & answering it'. In the one surviving letter to Alethea Bigg, Austen literally draws up accounts for her correspondence when she seems to reproach her friend: 'I believe the Epistolary debt is on your side' (24 January 1817). The value of a letter calculated from its appearance is a regular observation. In 24 October 1808, Austen commends Cassandra for sending her 'a great deal of matter, most of it very welcome': 'Your close-written letter makes me quite ashamed of my wide lines'. In 14–15 October 1813, Austen prepares both to get and not to get a frank from MP Mr Lushington and so plans to 'write very close from the first, & even leave room for the seal in the proper place'. The letter shows this in practice with 43 lines per page. It extends unusually to a fifth page, however, because the letter travels under Mr Lushington's frank after all. Austen is both economising and settling her debts when she tells Cassandra, 'When I have followed up my last with this I shall feel somewhat less unworthy of you than the state of our Correspondence now requires'.

This debt was created by the planning of correspondence and the frugality of information to disseminate. The post seems to be collected less frequently from Godmersham and in 26 June 1808, Austen explains: 'As Fanny writes to Anna by this post, I had intended to keep my Letter for another day but, recollecting that I must keep it two, I have resolved rather to finish & send it now'. As readers of Austen's letters in their re-collected form, we find unintentional humour in Austen's practical considerations at the time that '[t]he two letters will not interfere, I dare say; on the contrary they may throw light on each other'. Five years later, Austen offers an even more complex negotiation for epistolary space. In 26 October 1813 she must write herself into 'a humour for writing' but has the opportunity of the letter's being taken to Cassandra in London by one of their nephews: 'It is throwing a letter away to send it by a visitor, there is never convenient time for reading it – & Visitor can tell most things as well'. The intervention of the visitor will change the nature of the communication particularly as other letters demonstrate her disapproval of the nephews' pastimes. She is very much writing 'a la Godmersham' (15–17 June 1808) if she can say to Cassandra in 1813, 'I <u>had</u> thought with delight of saving you the postage – but Money is Dirt.'

Austen uses her sphere of women's letter writing to pass on these economies of transmission. In 26 March 1817 she commends 11 year-old Caroline's 'pretty hand' but prepares her prophetically for her own epistolary life as a spinster. In her very last letter to her niece, Austen's energies seem almost spent when she calls herself 'a poor Honey', a term she has reserved for women like Edward's sister-in-law Harriet Bridges, who gains consequence from 'her spasms and nervousness' and is 'determined never to be well' (25 September 1813). Austen and Caroline have been exchanging letters through Henry, now curate at Chawton but standing in for James at Steventon and Austen is 'very sorry to think that opportunities for such a nice little economical Correspondence, are likely to fail now'. In fact, by the time of the next clerical substitution in May, Austen will have made her will.

Austen's last letter to Fanny debates logistics involving Henry too. In 23 March 1817, Austen tells the future Lady Knatchbull who can always afford her postage costs or later exchange kisses for franks from her MP husband: 'I have had various plans as to this letter, but at last I have determined that Uncle Henry shall forward it from London. I want to see how Canterbury looks in the direction'. It has been suggested that this route added an extra penny to the postage because there was a delivery route via Ashford that meant recipients (or their servants) did not have to collect mail from the Faversham post office (Le Faye 2011, p. 465). At the time this letter performed yet another function before taking on the status of treasured last letter. Still visible on the fourth page where the seal would be is a shopping list of which Austen would have approved for one of their shared trips to London. Fanny intended to buy India ink and 'Good Poetry' but also 'Calico&c', long gloves for her sister Louisa, and '1yd. Jac[one]t. mus[lin]' (Le Faye 2011, p. 464).

In defiance of Fanny's future disapproval of her aunts' social standing and refinement (23 August 1869; Le Faye 2004, pp. 279–280), this incorporation seems fitting since Austen's letters are interwoven with further strands of logistical discussion about the sisters' fashion economies and errands. Austen's tone of interest and her animation of various items of clothing into characters in their own right betrays that this was a fraught question for women of the gentry with little money to call their own. Seeking and imagining Cassandra's advice is part of the *raison d'être* for writing both to agree and to disagree as Austen will later do on the subject of novel writing. In 28 December 1798 Austen proposes an application to their father for 'washing & letter expences' in the wake of Frank's celebrated promotion. In 2 June 1799 commissions in Bath result in a sketch of some lace: 'My Cloak is come home, & here follows a pattern of the lace' along with the relative costs if Cassandra's is to be wider at threepence a yard more without going above an outlay of two guineas. Bath's shops provide the opportunity to buy decorative fruit and Austen is also comparing gauzes. The purchase of flat shoes in this letter is suggestive of Austen's above average height. She also announces that she has been given a hat by Elizabeth, in 'a pretty stile' half straw and half purple ribbon but nonetheless donated and representative of the need for contriving on a limited allowance. In 27–28 October 1798 Austen has previously bought Japan ink to begin operations on a hat on which '[y]ou know my principle hopes of happiness depend'. In 18–19 December 1798 Austen acknowledges £10 of her own likely to have been for Christmas but this previews a discussion of the economics of a shared fashion item: 'I took the liberty of asking your Black velvet Bonnet to lend me its cawl, which it very readily did' to improve a cap, After the next ball it will be 'entirely black' but Austen seeks forgiveness for diverging from Cassandra's 'advice as to its ornaments' with a silver band twice round, no bow and a feather in 'Coquelicot', a colour which is 'all the fashion this winter'.

During the same absence, 8–9 January 1799 seems casual in its range of subjects but there is actually a detailed description of a gown 'very much like my blue one' once again approved by Cassandra but with short sleeves, a fuller wrap with apron over, and completed with a band. At the same time, Austen claims to hate describing the fashionable 'Mamalouc cap' lent to her by James's wife leaving Cassandra to guess its appearance while the later mentioned 'Green shoes' and 'white fan' are familiar items. Such objects are in effect substitutes for presence. They are also associated in the letter with Catherine Knight's decision to give Godmersham to her adopted son Edward in her lifetime. Austen seems to be making a bitter joke out of Mrs. Knight's retention of an income: 'this ought to be known, that her conduct may not be over-rated. – I rather think Edward shews the most Magnanimity of the two, in accepting her Resignation with such Incumbrances'. The letters of this period are particularly anarchic but there is a more poignant post prescript reference in 1 November 1800 to 'Mrs Cooper's band' as an accompaniment to 'your favourite gown'. Austen is dressing with her absent sister's approval and in memory of the aunt who rescued them from typhus but the letters written in December this year are missing. The 8–9 January 1801 birthday letter is the first to survive after their parents' decision to relocate to Bath and postpones the acquisition of cambric muslin. Two weeks later in 25 January 1801, however, Austen tells Cassandra rather grumpily 'I write because you will expect to hear from me' and prepares for life in Bath with a lengthy discussion of the same fabric: 'I shall want two new coloured gowns for the summer, for my pink one will not do more than clear me from Steventon'. The 'very pretty yellow and white cloud' is to be bought in Bath but Cassandra is to buy 'plain brown cambric muslin' for morning wear in two different shades 'as it will be always something to say, to dispute which is the prettiest' between dresses worn by Austen and their mother. The lengths are also specified: 'one longer than the other – it is for a tall woman' and differentiated as seven yards for Mrs. Austen and seven and a half yards for Austen herself. In *Sanditon*, Charlotte Heywood's height advantage grants her the role of observer. Walking with Mary Parker, she is 'considerably the tallest of the two' and sees the white ribbons of Clara Brereton's seduction by Sir Edward Denham (*LM*, p. 208). The evidence of Austen's height in 25 January 1801 is clear but the letter itself may have been shortened. The manuscript of Austen's letter is missing, having appeared in Brabourne's *Letters*, so the usually distinctive dispersal of capitalisation and dashes cannot be recovered. Austen's insistence on cambric muslin is curious unless it is being emphasised by her mother or else acting as part of a now lost code. Austen is allotting herself the role of observer, and the prospect of thin conversational topics in Bath is a prophetically depressing commentary on the life to come.

The themes of fashion and dependence continue into Austen's thirties. In 20–22 June 1808 from Godmersham to Southampton Austen announces the receipt of 'a letter from Mrs Knight, containing the usual Fee, & all the usual Kindness'. This phraseology perhaps expresses some discomfort at her own gratitude for the 'very agreeable present' paid for by spending 'a day or two' with Edward's adoptive mother once the travel arrangements can be sorted out. Edward has Godmersham and Chawton Manor from the Knights, and Austen will have a pelisse with half her 'fee'. The term is suggestive of the subordination of a paid companion and there is some bitterness in the money's making her 'circumstances quite easy' although in context the acquisition of a pelisse was a significant outlay (Davidson 2017). The association of Godmersham with fabric and opportunism is reinforced in 31 May 1811 when Austen reminds Cassandra about pieces for patchwork, spare fabric being more readily available in the Kent house for projects at Chawton.

Austen's later visits to London in the capacity of author provide opportunities for a greater variety of shopping choices and the means to access them with her own earnings. In 15–16 September 1813 Austen accepts £5 from 'kind, beautiful Edward' regarding it this time as a 'Gift' but she is by now a published author who has 'written herself into £250' (3–6 July 1813). She is writing *Mansfield Park* and considering 'very pretty' poplins with a preference for the more expensive Irish variety (15–16 September). In 5–8 March 1814 she has been indulging 'pretty Caps in the Windows of Cranbourn Alley' for Cassandra's temptation and 'ruining herself in black satin ribbon with a proper perl edge', narrow with loops. In 9 March 1814, a gauze gown is adapted with possibly the same plaited black satin ribbon and is worn with some concern about the suitability of long sleeves. Finishing the letter after a visit to the theatre in her 'Costume of Vine leaves & paste', Austen reports that she has been reassured by Frances Tilson, wife of Henry's partner, that long sleeves are worn in the evenings. She is toying with the seriousness of being on view, dressing up to act the part of an audience member.

There are many such social occasions to be described. After control of dress and portable possessions, the news from balls and dinners, drives and visits is important trading material for the female letter writer. In 12–13 May 1801 Austen talks to the phaeton-owning Mr Evelyn in the Upper Rooms in Bath and observes the 'Adultress' Mary Cassandra Twisleton who 'was highly rouged, & looked rather quietly & contentedly silly than anything else'. Mrs. Badcock's drunken husband is also present. Austen compares the situation for Cassandra as 'shockingly and inhumanly thin for this place' although enough for 'five or six very pretty Basingstoke assemblies' with which they were long familiar before the move. The real value of the occasion, of course, derives from their family relationship with Miss Twisleton who resembles her sister Julia Judith Leigh. Julia was a cousin of the Austens twice over being both wife of James Henry (1765–1823) who was grandson to Mrs. Austen's uncle William (1691–1757) and great granddaughter of William through his daughter Cassandra Leigh Turner. The dispersal of the name Cassandra also comes through this line as illustrated in Figure 1.3. Mrs Austen's grandmother Mary Brydges Leigh was sister-in-law to Cassandra Willoughby Brydges, Duchess of Chandos named after her grandmother Cassandra Ridgway (1605–1675). The Duchess wrote travel journals and family history. After she becomes associated with the family, Cassandras are scattered throughout the Leigh and Austen family trees as shown. Mrs. Austen's aunt Leigh Wight (1695–1778) and cousins Turner (1723–1770) and Cooke (1744–1826) are followed

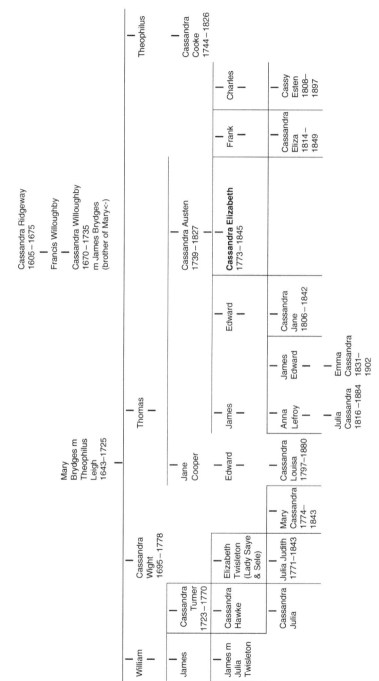

Figure 1.3 Cassandra connections: a selected family tree.

by Mrs. Austen and her daughter. Edward, Frank, and Charles will have daughters called Cassandra as will Mrs. Austen's nephew Edward Cooper. Austen is teasing Cassandra about family resemblance and the recognizability of both a Leigh and an adulteress with whom Cassandra shares a name.

In the longer term, this is a family connection that looms larger through the male line. In 1806 Mrs. Austen and her daughters visit the family seat at Stoneleigh in the company of James Henry Leigh's uncle Thomas, rector of Adlestrop who has inherited a life interest in the estate. Cassandra's godmother Elizabeth Leigh lives at Adlestrop with her brother and when he dies in 1813 Austen writes to Frank that 'the respectable, worthy, clever agreeable Mr Tho. Leigh . . . must have died possessor of one of the finest estates in England & of more worthless Nephews & Neices than any other private Man in the united Kingdoms' (3–6 July). Stoneleigh is destined for James Henry, one of these nephews but as a rector's spinster daughter Austen worries more about the living and the future home of Elizabeth.

There are no Austen letters from the 1806 visit but in much of her correspondence wealth and its responsibilities are treated with ambiguity. The 30 June–1 July 1808 letter is written after hearing a child reading in the Godmersham library 'in warm & happy solitude' continuing a letter but expecting to come home to Southampton to care for the orange wine. Although Austen proposes to 'eat Ice & drink French wine & be above Vulgar Economy' at Godmersham, the letter closes under the address panel: 'Luckily the pleasures of Friendship, of unreserved Conversation, of similarity of Taste & Opinions, will make good amends for the Orange Wine', homemade rather than French. The 'Elegance & Ease & Luxury' of Godmersham seems to come at the price of other comforts. There is enforced sociability and even if Austen was not writing concertedly at this time, solitariness was valued. This letter also refers to the settlement over Stoneleigh that has been drawn up to buy out Uncle James Leigh-Perrot's interests. Mrs. Knight has expressed concern for the Austens' 'Good' and reference to Edward's benefactress prompts Austen to comment: 'Indeed, I do not know where we are to get our Legacy – but we will keep a sharp look out'. In 26 June 1808 Austen has already pronounced a legacy as 'our sovereign good' in promoting a Christmas visit to Kent but this is an edgy comment in part directed at Elizabeth Austen who is casually assuming that the Southampton Austens can afford such a journey. In the same letter Austen must relinquish visits to the Walters and the Cookes *en route* because she is to be transported by Edward and has no 'travelling purse' of her own.

On her last visit to Godmersham in 1813 Austen is relieved that the billiard table draws people away from the library leaving five of them 'snugly talking' (14–15 October) with the prospect of numbers reducing to their, nonetheless large, family party. In 26 October she concludes that she finds 'time in the midst of Port & Madeira to think of the 14 Bottles of Mead very often', once again prizing homemade liquor over bought, and in 6–7 November her last letter from Kent, she luxuriates in writing in the half hour before breakfast '(very snug, in my own room, lovely morn^g, excellent fire, fancy me)'. In 11–12 October earlier in the same visit she hopes that dining on goose 'will secure a good Sale of my 2^d Edition'. Cassandra knows this is the second edition of *Sense and Sensibility* and can sense Austen's divided energies as sister and author. For Austen, Godmersham seems to be a duplicitous place in the context of dependency and the parallel Chawton life, offering ease without stability, transitory benefits that provide comfort only in the moment.

In the context of her life and letter writing, legacies, dependence, and mead production, it is not surprising that for Austen an income will tell its own story. When she finally gets to be an author, Austen is keen to ensure the believability of the Dashwoods' life in *Sense and Sensibility* as she notes to Cassandra in 25 April 1811 when letters resume from Chawton after the gap since 1809. The Austen women's variously derived income of £450 a year was now very close to that of the women in the novel. Mrs. Dashwood's £500 will not allow for a carriage and leaves the fictional foursome at Barton Cottage prey to Sir John Middleton's sociable schemes. Austen's letters under such strictures demonstrate the calculations of her outlay on things she can and must afford such as bonnet trimmings and postage. She is ironic over the two shillings and three pence (2/3) postage for a letter from Frank (25 September 1813) and in 26 November 1815 a parcel costing two shillings and ten pence (2/10) is carefully calibrated against the cost of replacing stockings and handkerchiefs in the same letter as she corrects the proofs of *Emma*. She gives Cassandra value on their own terms with news of rhubarb (8 September 1816), orange wine, naked Cupids (20 May 1813), Don John, cruelty, and lust (16 September 1813).

As the novels and the life cohere, the next section of this plot of Austen's letters reveals a consistent pattern of self-deprecation and counter-cultural references, alongside the importation of her characters into real life and a relish for profit. The life being lived to the moment in epistolary acts demonstrates how the novels become part of Austen's letter-writing occupation as communicator, sister, and aunt. Henry circulates in the background but periodic letters to Frank also add to the layering of Austen's representation of herself as an author. The more professional correspondence with James Stanier Clarke creates a new personality borrowed from her regular stance and given a creative outlet in 'Plan of a Novel'.

On 5 April 1809 Austen tried to reclaim the manuscript of her novel 'Susan' using the pseudonym 'Mrs Ashton Dennis c/o Southampton Post Office'. She was rebuffed if not threatened by the publisher Crosby (Le Faye 2011, p. 183). Austen's letter and its contents now act as an extraordinary bridge over that gap of 27 months between 30 January 1809 (from Southampton to Godmersham) and

18–20 April 1811 (from Sloane Street to Godmersham). The only other surviving text from this period is a poem dated 26 July 1809, including evidence of the removal to Chawton, whose main concern is the birth of Frank's first son Francis. No other letters survive. In 5 April 1809 Austen describes 'Susan' as a 'work of which I avow myself the Authoress' but her implication that the novel may have been published without her knowledge and her suggestion that the manuscript may have been lost convey feelings of lack of control within this avowal. *Northanger Abbey* can only appear once Austen has used her future profits to buy back the manuscript and, having renamed it, she tells Fanny in 1817 that 'Miss Catherine is put upon the Shelve, and I do not know that she will ever come out' (13 March 1817). When the novel was finally published after Austen's death it was elided with both *Persuasion* and Henry's 'Biographical Notice'.

Between April 1809 and April 1811, however, Austen goes from being 'MAD' with Crosby to correcting the sheets of her first published novel. In 25 April 1811 she 'can no more forget [*Sense and Sensibility*] than a mother can forget her sucking child' aligning the novel with the birth of Frank's second son Henry on 21 April. In brother Henry's absence, Eliza has a role to play in the circulation of the proofs and this is when Austen hopes the 'Incomes' can be altered. According to Cassandra's note on the dates of composition, the original version of the novel entitled 'Elinor and Marianne' was composed in epistolary format in 1795 but was being revised by November 1797 (Sutherland 2005b, p. 17). Income, status, and independence to marry are at the forefront of *Sense and Sensibility* and the alteration was presumably to reflect the worth of income against status by 1811. In 25 April 1811 Austen uses her technique of owning and identifying with her characters. She believes that Mrs. Knight 'will like my Elinor, but cannot build on any thing else'.

In 29–30 November 1812, Austen announces to Martha Lloyd that *Pride and Prejudice* has been sold for £110 rather than the £150 she had hoped for. The novel has a traceable provenance in the letters. Cassandra's posthumous memorandum dates the composition of the original 'First Impressions' to October 1796–August 1797 and Cadell's rejection of the novel occurred in November 1797. The manuscript continued to circulate in private, however, and the very first surviving reference occurs in a birthday letter to Cassandra who has requested a further opportunity to read the manuscript while on her 1798–1799 visit to Godmersham. Austen says, presumably jokingly, she 'does not wonder' at her sister's 'wanting to read <u>first impressions</u> again, so seldom you have gone through it, & that so long ago' (8–9 January 1799). By 11 June 1799, of course, Martha has been suspected of memorising the original to publish it for herself almost 13 years before the revised version goes to press. In this, Austen demonstrates her understanding of both the reading and publishing processes. In 24 January 1813 Austen talks about the 'readers or retainers of Books' in their Chawton circle. On 29 Jan 1813 in a long letter to Cassandra, Austen describes her 'own darling Child *Pride and Prejudice*' as 'lopt & cropt', and with a second volume apparently shorter than that of *Sense and Sensibility* because there is 'a larger proportion of Narrative'. It has been calculated that *Pride and Prejudice* is shorter overall by 25 pages than *Sense and Sensibility* and that Volume 2, containing more 'Narrative', is in fact 39 pages shorter (Le Faye 2011, p. 420). The volume breaks are significant in the novels overall and both author and publisher would have been alert to this for the purposes of borrowing and 'retaining' by clients of the circulating library.

In 29 January 1813 Elizabeth Bennet is singled out as being 'as delightful a creature as ever appeared in print' but on 4 February Austen reins in her delight for Cassandra's amusement by claiming the novel too 'light & bright & sparkling'. An essay incorporated into it might satisfy the 'starched notions' of her sister as a literary critic who has participated in manuscript readings of the novel in progress. A printing blunder on suppers brings 'Mrs Bennet's old Meryton habits' into the letter as if she were an acquaintance like their Chawton neighbour Miss Benn who has been hearing the novel read aloud. Cassandra is visiting their brother James at Steventon and Mrs. Austen is failing to live up to Austen's realisation of the characters. Austen reflects also on the Chawton Cottage hours that are more unfashionable and economical in candles than those at Godmersham. In 24 May 1813, Austen is more inconsistent in the embodiment of her *Pride and Prejudice* characters. She seeks Elizabeth and her sister Jane on a visit to a London gallery amidst the 'dirt & confusion' of 10 Henrietta Street. She also worries that she is a 'wild Beast' then stays aloof and even disingenuous when an offstage letter from Fanny demands a fictional letter in the style of Miss Darcy: 'I cannot pretend to answer it. Even had I more time, I should not feel at all sure of the sort of Letter that Miss D. would write'.

Away from Fanny's notice, Cassandra is already aware of a new composition in progress. Austen confidently compares a real evening with its fictional counterpart when she numbers the guests around Mrs. Grant's *Mansfield Park* table (24 January 1813) and in 29 January 1813 asks about hedgerows in Northamptonshire where her new novel will be set. In 3–6 July 1813, Austen tells Frank that she has received £140 for *Sense and Sensibility* and so 'written myself into £250.–which only makes me long for more'. This demonstrates the value of more distant, less frequent correspondents who receive overview information that might otherwise have been difficult to recover along with the tone in which this success is expressed. The letter is to Frank as captain of the *Elephant*, and Austen adds in a postscript upside down at the top of the first page to save Frank the cost of postage in the Baltic: 'I have something in hand which I hope on the credit of P&P will sell well tho' not half so entertaining'. Frank's parallel career is a matter of both pride and competitive news-spreading juxtaposed with a parallel women's culture. Austen wants to mention the *Elephant* in her novel and has already done so expecting his approval. This is an instance where the postscript becomes a pre-script to the actual letter. This apparently mechanical operation in the text is clear in the manuscript version whereas in a printed edition such a section is usually, perhaps necessarily, a postscript even if its location is noted. There is an illustration of this effect in 11 June 1799 that mostly concerns shopping and visiting in Bath where Austen reacts to a letter from Cassandra and thus appears to prioritise her 'quarrel' with their friends the Bigg sisters (Figure 1.4). For Frank, the ships in the letters are discussed in a tone similar to that with which Austen brings her fictional characters into her life but on closer examination this is, of course, a reversal of her usual practice in that the real ships are to be made fictional. In a later scrap of a letter to Frank (21 March 1814) Austen describes her novels as 'in the world' like children being born but another letter related to the novel has childbearing ramifications in real life. In 2 September 1814 Austen is pleased in a postscript that Martha's friends the Deans-Dundases have praised *Mansfield Park*

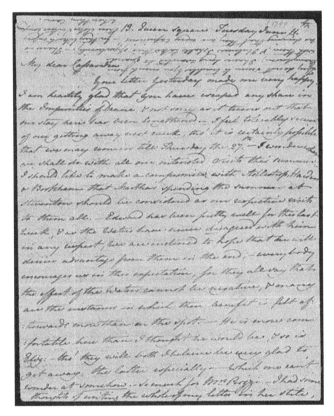

Figure 1.4 Austen to Cassandra Austen, 11 June 1799; detail of inverted postscript at head of letter. National Library of Australia.

but for the modern reader this information now immediately rebounds against our knowledge of the imminent death of Fanny Palmer Austen, wife of Charles, whose initially safe delivery of a child is included in the same postscript.

In a longer letter to Frank as captain of the *Elephant*, Austen refers to 'the 3^{d}' of her novels and thanks Frank and his wife Mary for their support in concealing her identity as author of the other two (25 September 1813). With Henry more effusive and confiding to others she adds that it is 'scarcely the Shadow of a secret now . . . I shall rather try to make all the Money than all the Mystery I can of it'. It may be, however, that the characterisation of Mary Crawford, who has been identified with his wife Eliza, was a warning to Henry to beware the perils of having a sister as an author. Austen later makes great play in her letters at the publication stage of *Mansfield Park* of having Henry read the novel on a coach journey via Cobham, alluding to the practices of dyers 'dipping their own Souls in scarlet sin' (2–3 March 1814). She claims to Cassandra that Henry 'understands' all the characters although this is with particular reference to Lady Bertram and Mrs. Norris. In the next letter (5–8 March) she describes Henry in real time 'this moment' guessing if Henry Crawford is to 'be reformed or would forget Fanny in a fortnight'. She reports him significantly as finding the last half of the last volume 'extremely interesting' (9 March).

It is now difficult to discern whether the fictional letters that reveal Mary Crawford's character in this part of the text have struck any chord with him as Cassandra might have been expecting. The sisters would have remembered Eliza's original quest to be a countess through her first marriage and her manipulation of her two cousins James and Henry during their own theatricals at Steventon over Christmas 1787–1788 (Honan 1987, pp. 50–52; Tomalin 1997, pp. 55–58). Mary Crawford's objections to marrying a clergyman, echoing Eliza's similar sentiments, are already well-known in the earlier parts of *Mansfield Park*. Henry Austen, of course, although intended for ordination like James, took on the more dashing profession of soldier and then army-based banker before his marriage to Eliza. '[H]is approbation has not lessened', Austen claimed in 9 March adjacent to a flurry of remarks about going to Covent Garden, failing to go to the Palmers in Keppel Street, lowering the bosom of a gauze gown with long sleeves, and having insufficient 'funds' to pay candle and tea suppliers (Brecknell and Twining respectively) on her mother's behalf. There may be a sense of nervous anticipation over Henry's reaction here but in fact the letters written from London often betray busyness and occupation caused by the need to impose control over the touristic opportunities of a visit in light of the sisters' limitations of pocket. Candles and tea were significant purchases verging on necessities for a genteel existence, and the alteration of existing gowns was an ongoing concern in the quest to achieve respectability. Publishing a daringly unpredictable novel experimenting with social norms and constructed out of the lives of her own brothers was reinforced for Cassandra in the context of the daily round of their dependent spinsters' lives.

When the first edition of *Mansfield Park* is sold out, Austen describes herself as 'very greedy' in a squeezed paragraph that heads the fourth address-panel page of one of the advice letters to Fanny (18–20 November 1814). Austen emphasises that she does not include any particulars of her commission to Henry for a second edition 'as you are much above caring about money' but can at least comprehend '[t]he pleasures of Vanity' arising from praise of the novel. Cassandra would understand both. Henry's serious illness pushed Austen more to the forefront of the publication of her next novel *Emma* and in 17–18 October 1815, she describes publisher John Murray as 'a rogue'. He has offered £450 for *Emma* to include the copyright of *Mansfield Park* and *Sense and Sensibility* although Austen has already thought of publishing for herself. She tells Cassandra that this apparent business communication is 'an amusing Letter. You shall see it' which we now cannot. Henry Jackson, Henry's future father-in-law from 9 Sloane Terrace who was married to Sarah Papillon seems to have been part of a 'pleasant visit' and, although 'fond of eating', does not like his Chawton in-laws, the Reverend John Papillon and his sister Elizabeth. In the background Henry is 'calomeling' as part of his self-treatment for what would become a very serious illness and, with Austen alarmed at his decline, Cassandra was apparently brought to London by James (Clery 2017, pp. 253–254).

Austen was there until 16 December proofreading *Emma* after nursing Henry and becoming aware of his business problems. She tells Cassandra that Henry has written to Edward and has read out this letter to her; although 'part of it must have amused him I am sure; – one part alas! cannot be very amusing to anybody' (24 November 1815). With the Alton bank branch on the verge of bankruptcy, Henry even has to absent himself from his head office (2 December 1815) making this an extraordinary juxtaposition of what Austen calls her 'affairs' (24 November) with the male world of business. She is nurse, manager of her 'Dirty Linen', published author, and literary celebrity invited to Carlton House. Henry the entrepreneur skulks in the provinces or receives medicine as 'a little aperient' from the much-praised physician Mr Haden who provokes Austen's interest by preferring *Mansfield Park* to *Pride and Prejudice* (26 November 1815). The subject of linen and that parcel costing 2/10 takes up almost as much of 26 November 1815 as any allusion to the novel whose fictional arrowroot reminds Austen of arrowroot for Anna. The whole is a juggling act to save money in the face of novel profits and pending bankruptcy in the usual context of the sisters' necessary economies. At the last Austen expresses delight at the sight of a letter from Charles and wants to send him all her copies of *Emma* including those destined for the Prince Regent and the Countess of Morley. Her professional concerns regain sway but are once more contextualised and complicated by the roles of men.

The letters in which the publication of *Emma* is embedded represent Austen as both author and correspondent. On receiving her advance copy of the novel,

Frances, Countess of Morley entered into the spirit of the Austen sisters' embodiment of fictional characters when she wrote on 27 December 1815, 'I have been most anxiously waiting for an introduction to Emma' (Le Faye 2011, p. 322). It is as if the group of women has been socialising at an assembly, and the tone of other letters suggests that the Countess herself described people in her social circle in terms of characters in Austen's other novels (Jarvis 1986). Although she seems eventually to have preferred *Mansfield Park* and *Pride and Prejudice* (Jarvis 1986, p. 11), Frances Morley may have met Austen as part of Henry's London acquaintance and so received the honour of an early copy of *Emma* on a personal basis, as referenced in 26 November. In December 1815, her note continues, 'I am already become intimate in the Woodhouse family, & feel that they will not amuse & interest me less than the Bennetts, Bertrams, Norriss & all their admirable predecessors'.

This brief exchange survives and serves to provide a commentary on Austen's authorship and the archive. Austen's reply in a note of three sentences was drafted and the draft retained by Cassandra to bequeath to Charles. This draft was given by J.P. Morgan to Cambridge University Library and has been clearly stamped by them '18 DE 1925' (Modert 1990, F-392) as if to re-date it with this library mark of their ownership. The note of 31 December 1815 actually sent was bequeathed by Alberta Burke to the Pierpont Morgan Library and contains slightly fewer dashes then the draft although the substance of the text is identical. Austen's reply acknowledges Lady Morley's note in its own terms by echoing her concerns about Emma's 'reception in the World'. The suggestion of Austen's 'state of doubt' as to this reception initially appears to reinforce the politeness of her response but her real doubt is set within the two dashes she has characteristically retained from her original draft. The Countess is being admitted to the sisterhood of letters discussed in Chapter 4 when Austen writes that the 'approbation' of her Ladyship has encouraged her 'to beleive that I have not yet – as almost every Writer of Fancy does sooner or later – overwritten myself'. The last five words of this sentence, along with the close, run over onto the reverse of the paper as if by design at least to reach a turn of the page but also to put that concern of exhausting her market out of first sight. For all its formality, this note is both personal and confiding.

Another surviving but now untraceable note accompanied a copy of *Emma* to a very different recipient in Catherine Ann Prowting, a Chawton neighbour and sister of Mrs. Ann-Mary Clement. The Clements and Prowtings often feature in Austen's letters from Chawton and it is likely that the sisters and Captain Clement of the Royal Navy were the people described in Austen's 1817 'last' letter to Frances Tilson (Le Faye 2011, p. 467) although their names were omitted in Henry's 'Biographical Notice' that is the only surviving version of this letter. Austen's 24 January 1813 letter reports to Cassandra that the impoverished Chawton spinster Miss Benn has dined with the Clements and the early 1816 note to Catherine offers the 'volumes' of *Emma* as a memorial to their 'poor friend' and reading companion who was buried on 3 January that year. There is a sense of shared spinsterhood – 'these volumes would have been at her service' – and Austen acknowledges both their 'habit of reading together' and their enjoyment of '<u>Works of the same hand'</u>. Catherine is being recognised in the circle of those appreciating Austen's self-deprecation. In 28–29 May 1817 to Tilson, Austen describes the sisters despite their inadequate petticoats, as 'all good humour and obligingness' and in 1816 tells Catherine 'I shall make no other apology for offering you the perusal of [these volumes], only begging that, if not immediately disposed for such light reading, you would keep them as long as you like, as they are not wanted at home'. The literary value of this unwitting survival no longer in manuscript copy is that Miss Benn was a living example of the life Mr Knightley projects in *Emma* for Miss Bates although her 'talking aunt' (*E*, p. 214) characteristics owe more to the 'foolishly minute' Miss Milles (26 October 1813) and Mrs. Digweed 'full of wonder & gratitude' (29 January 1813). In 1818 the unnamed Clements trio in the postscript to Henry's 'Notice' provide a prescript to Austen's two unpublished novels when Henry presents them as subjects of Austen's epistolary style and, hopefully, wearers of more fashionable 'longer petticoats'. It is a correspondence unwittingly continued within the novels that follow in this first edition. Henry Tilney proves himself a master of muslin in *Northanger Abbey* and Captain Wentworth in *Persuasion* likens his first command the *Asp* to 'an old pelisse' handed down by economising female acquaintances.

The countess and the spinster were acknowledged by Austen as readers in the context of a shared and recognisable women's culture. During the same period, in the aftermath of the dedication of *Emma* to the Prince Regent, Austen was engaged in another very different correspondence. No description of her visit to Carlton House survives, perhaps because Cassandra was with Austen in London tending to Henry, but the ongoing correspondence with the Prince's librarian does. Austen was willing to reason with the reverend as a published author but James Stanier Clarke has no place within any sisterhood.

In 11 December 1815, Austen wrote to Clarke of *Emma*: 'I am very strongly haunted by the idea that to those Readers who have preferred P&P. it will appear inferior in Wit, & to those who have preferred MP. very inferior in good Sense'. Austen has been trying to make a polite response to his requests for a novel based on his own experience and concludes, for now, 'I think I may boast myself to be, with all possible Vanity, the most unlearned, & uninformed Female who ever dared to be an Authoress'. In this boasted vanity of unlearnedness, Clarke has been honoured with a response worthy of a regular correspondent but on 21 December he proves he has misread the letter when he presses his point, offering books of sermons and the use of his 'Cell' at 37 Golden Square (Le Faye 2011, p. 321). He has actually, however, only read a few pages of *Emma* and when he commends the novel again in March 1816, he proposes that Austen's next 'Volumes' should be 'any Historical Romance illustrative of the History of the august house of Cobourg' (Le Faye 2011, p. 325). She is to dedicate her work to Prince Leopold of Saxe-Cobourg who is coincidentally Clarke's new employer and about to marry the Prince Regent's daughter.

The first two paragraphs of Austen's reply to this letter, ominously dated 1 April 1816, are textbook, letter-manual fare even though Austen might reasonably have been feeling like Mr Bennet enduring the correspondence of a Mr Collins. Austen acknowledges in her third and final paragraph the 'Profit or Popularity' of such a 'Romance' but vows to continue with her own 'pictures of domestic Life in Country Villages'. Her 11 December 1815 letter has pointed out her lack of reading and education in the classics, and in April she becomes more serious in her refusal, insisting, 'I could no more write a Romance than an Epic Poem'. Austen fears that writing a romance even to save her life would make her laugh and so result in being hanged 'if it were indispensable for me to keep it up & never relax into laughing at myself or other people'. Cassandra would remember their school-day claims of dying of laughter transferred to Lydia Bennet; Clarke has already shown himself to be impervious. Seriousness returns after this brief glimpse of her less considered but more characteristic response and Austen insists on her 'own style' and her 'own Way' even if she may never succeed again. The 1 April letter, now owned by the Jane Austen's House Museum, survives only as a draft that may never have been sent (Sutherland 2018, p. 117) although *Family Record* treats it as if it were (Le Faye 2004, pp. 227–228). The draft could have been a response for family reading and consumption only; particularly as Clarke's suggestions find their way into her 'Plan of a Novel' which has descended through Charles Austen's family but is now separated from the letter in New York in the Pierpoint Morgan. The 11 December 1815 letter was signed 'Your obligd & faith Hum. Servt. JA'. On 1 April, however, Austen closes 'Your very much obliged & very sincere friend' and signs herself with an almost masculine 'J. Austen'. The use of the word 'sincere' and her formal signature are testament to her seriousness in this tersely firm attempt to deter her unwanted correspondent with this plain-speaking defence against Clarke's proposal. Clarke may never have received it and her true reply may indeed be 'Plan of a Novel' but Cassandra retained the draft in her archive. It appeared in both the *Memoir* and *Life and Letters* before benefiting Charles Austen's granddaughters when it was sold on in the 1920s.

On the same 1 April, Austen was in professional mode for her reply to John Murray that was a letter of two very distinct halves. Austen initially thanks Murray for sending her Scott's anonymous *Quarterly Review* article. She appears hurt by the omission of *Mansfield Park* from the review and this is reiterated by her description of herself in the third person: 'The Authoress of *Emma* has no reason I think to complain of her treatment in it'. She is icily disappointed that the binding of her latest novel seems to have been prioritised over the text since she tells Murray about the Prince Regent's thanks for his 'handsome copy' of *Emma*: 'Whatever he may think of my share of the Work, Yours seems to have been quite right'. The second paragraph of this letter indicates, however, the stark realities of Henry's business collapse that Austen terms this 'late sad Event in Henrietta S^t'. In practical terms letters must in future be sent to Chawton and parcels by Collier's Southampton Coach. She has lost the convenience of transmission through the banking network and will have to pay for subsequent communications but must not lose touch with the future profits of her work, however humbling the admission. It is a letter about her lived experience of authorship and the fragility of her hold over her life.

With Cassandra at home during the last nine months of that life, epistolary sources of authorship revert to nieces and nephew, and in 14 March 1817 Austen tells Caroline, 'I have just rec^d nearly twenty pounds myself on the 2^d edition of S&S which gives me this fine flow of Literary Ardour'. This is obliquely a message for Caroline's brother James Edward who is applying for an Oxford scholarship in philology (*Report* 1852, p. 111) available under the terms of his relationship with the Craven family through his mother but unavailable through gender to either Austen or Caroline. Austen has her profit and Caroline is at the same time 'bearing Criticism' of a story being read by her aunt. Austen suggests that as 'sisters in letters' they can all manage without the patronage of an Oxford college since it is not through 'the Craven exhibition' but through his novel that James Edward 'will find his true fame & his true wealth'. Meanwhile, in 20–21 February 1817 to Fanny, Austen elides praise of *Emma* with women's sociable support of male endeavour: 'I have contributed the marking to Uncle H.'s shirts, & now they are a complete memorial of the tender regard of many.' Henry is now curate at Chawton under John Papillon and about to become Austen's memorialist. To his shirts Austen has added a kind of signature in Henry's name although ominously she has not made a major contribution because of her progressing illness. In the ongoing women's counter culture, this is reminiscent of the juxtaposition of Cassandra as a comic writer with Austen's neat sewing for Charles back in 1 September 1796.

Fanny is also told in 13 March 1817 of a 'something ready for Publication . . . about the length of Catherine' and 10 days later, in 23–25 March, Austen admits to her niece that Henry knows this. She offers Fanny the information to give her niece a sense of control while scolding her for teasing Mr Wildman by withholding knowledge of her (Austen's) authorship. In the revised last chapter of this new novel *Persuasion*, Anne Elliot will take her gender-based stance against Captain Harville in Wentworth's hearing and their conversation echoes Austen's phrasing in the letter to Fanny. Anne tells Harville hers is not a very enviable privilege, 'you need not covet it' (*P*, p. 256) and in her letter Austen tells Fanny of her novel called 'The Elliots', 'You will not like it, so you need not be impatient'. Austen has already described herself on the cover page of 23–25 March as being made 'sick & wicked' by 'pictures of perfection' and a single sentence immediately following at the top of the second page of the letter adds, 'You may <u>perhaps</u> like the Heroine, as she is almost too good for me'. Austen then launches into a description of her symptoms and apparent recovery or remission, creating a curious sense that writing Anne Elliot has cured her of the sickness that makes her 'black & white & every wrong colour'. Only five weeks later she drafts her informal but binding will (Le Faye 2011, p. 355). Austen can confide the existence of a new novel in her last letter to Fanny but as an aunt she uses authorship to postpone the sad inevitability of her death.

Letter survival has weighted our understanding and appreciation of Austen's life to the years of her publication and aunthood, with half the number of extant letters overall dating from the last four and a half years of her 41-year life. In using the letters as life evidence it should be noted that the pattern of the Austen sisters' lives must have dictated not just the writing of the letters but their later preservation. Cassandra lived the rest of her life at Chawton and the letters written to her were then inherited in the form in which she had been keeping them for 35 years. The preservation pattern of these letters might have been dictated by a need to suppress certain information as suspected by family and biographers since. Surely, however, the removal from Steventon had already limited the preservation of material from earlier years for reasons of storage capacity. There is evidence that the letters dating back to 1796 were kept in the sequences shown in Figure 1.2. At her death in 1845, Cassandra left 11 to their brother Charles and four to their niece Caroline. The 79 letters bequeathed to Fanny were discovered by Lord Brabourne (1884a, pp. x–xi) tied up in yearly divisions. In 1884, the letters that were once reminders of family business and substitutes for presence were about to be recopied with revised agendas that would translate them from mementoes into collectibles.

This story of the letters is part of Austen's story. The history of dispersal and re-collection has also contributed to the life of the author, and the next chapter explores the impact of the letters' immediate afterlife in early biographical works by the family. The new audiences of the *Memoir*, *Letters*, and *Life and Letters* were taught to read not like Cassandra but as consumers and owners of Victorian family history.

2

Austen's Letters in Family 'Lives'

Cassandra's real-time interpretation and decoding of her sister's letters has been succeeded by family misrepresentation and misreading. This began from very first publication in Henry Austen's 'Biographical Notice' of 1818. Henry quoted here from Austen's 'bit of ivory' reference in a letter where she deprecated her own work in the context of a nephew's missing chapters. Over time, progress into the Victorian era reinforced the family's distortion of Austen's approach to authorship. This chapter examines the evolution of the family narrative from the letters. It revisits interpretations of the letters as biographical representations of 'dear Aunt Jane' in the century after her death to include theories of archival suppression and survival. The chapter explores family collaborations within this project and the response of reviewers to their publications. It then examines the afterlife and transmission of selected texts into collectables when sold outside the family.

Henry Austen acted as a negotiator with publishers and provided accommodation in London when Austen was correcting the proofs of her four published novels. He was, therefore, uniquely placed close to his sister's public career. In his 1818 'Biographical Notice' to the posthumous publication of *Northanger Abbey* and *Persuasion*, Henry nonetheless founded the Austen industry of the family record, reiterating that there was nothing to know about his sister's authorship. Writing was not a profession since '[n]either the hope of fame nor profit mixed with her early motives' and Austen 'became an authoress entirely from taste and inclination' (Austen 1818, p. xii). Henry indulged his argument further by including letters as part of Austen's allegedly unlaboured composition. 'The style of her familiar correspondence was in all respects the same as that of her novels', he claimed. This declaration raised expectations about the content and style of the letters, swept up in the same argument of unrevised perfection: 'Everything came finished from her pen [and] . . . It is not hazarding too much to say that she never dispatched a note or letter unworthy of publication' (p. xvi).

The Life of the Author: Jane Austen, First Edition. Catherine Delafield.
© 2023 John Wiley & Sons Ltd. Published 2023 by John Wiley & Sons Ltd.

In a postscript, itself dated a week later than Henry's main text, samples from two letters were added as an afterthought to the 'Notice' to reinforce the argument, and discrepancies in the family narrative become visible in the editing. In the 'Notice', and again in the 1833 'Memoir' to a new edition of the novels in Bentley's Standard series, a letter ostensibly on authorship is quoted in which Austen is an aunt mounting a 'playful defence' to the charge of having raided a young relation's manuscripts:

> What should I do, my dearest E. with your manly, vigorous sketches, so full of life and spirit? How could I possibly join them on to a little bit of ivory, two inches wide, on which I work with a brush so fine as to produce little effect after much labour?
>
> *(Austen 1818, p. xvii)*

In the original volume, Henry's comment on 'finish' and Austen's on 'ivory' were laid side by side, verso and recto. The actual letter of 16 December 1816 has been carefully revised by Henry but can now be read and reread with an appreciation of other undercurrents at play. The letter in Henry's postscript to his 'Notice' impersonates one of Austen's own pre-script postscripts to her letters in life. In its 1818 context, the 1816 letter prefaced a novel satirising the reader of the novel of sensibility, and yet the author's representation of herself was distorted to set the family agenda.

The reader in the twenty-first century now knows that 16 December 1816 was Austen's last birthday and that the letter of this date was written to congratulate her nephew Edward on becoming esquire, and leaving Winchester for Oxford. This Edward was the James Edward Austen-Leigh who would become his aunt's first biographer more than 50 years later. Austen teased him in the tone of those novels of sensibility being mocked in *Northanger Abbey*, the novel that the 'ivory' extract will retrospectively preface:

> Now you may own how miserable you were there; . . . – your Crimes & your Miseries – how often you went up by the Mail to London & threw away Fifty Guineas at a Tavern, & how often you were on the point of hanging yourself – restrained only . . . by the want of a Tree within some miles of the City.

This was a letter written by the author of the three volumes of juvenile manuscript works that will be bequeathed in 1845 with the letters: not the author who has recently completed *Persuasion* but rather the one who is about to begin *Sanditon*. In 16 December 1816, Austen comments on the health and spirits of her two brothers, Charles the widowed naval officer and Henry the army man turned banker turned curate who were then visiting at Chawton probably in response to Austen's illness: 'they are each of them so agreeable in their different way, & harmonize so well, that their visit is thorough Enjoyment'. Perhaps the suggestion that Edward's father James was less agreeable was just left hanging. The comment on the 'bit of ivory' comes after Austen has suggested that Henry's 'superior Sermons' might be introduced into her and Edward's novels. Even Henry might have been discomfited by such a comment since at the time he had only recently been ordained and appointed as curate at Chawton, and his earlier bankruptcy in March 1816 has resulted in substantial family financial losses.

In December 1816, two and a half chapters of Edward's novel have gone missing and Austen has heard this from Edward's mother Mary Lloyd Austen whose relationship with Austen was also uneasy. Edward's aunt expressed her relief in the letter that she (Austen) cannot be accused of the theft of these 'two strong twigs & a half towards a Nest of my own'. What she then actually wrote is that even if she were guilty of the theft these chapters could not be useful to her:

> What should I do with your strong, manly, spirited Sketches, full of Variety & Glow? – How could I possibly join them on to the little bit (two inches wide) of Ivory on which I work with so fine a Brush, as produces little effect after much labour?

It is not known whether Edward himself made amendments in excerpting the letter for Henry or whether there was a further revision at the typesetting stage. If Henry has amended the remark for the 'Notice', he has done it in clear co-location with his own claim for the perfection of an original letter worthy of publication from his sister's pen. Given, however, the paucity of original information overall, there is some perversity in his beginning already the process of tidying up 'dear Aunt Jane'. 'Spirit' must be transplanted into the letter because 'glow' is not manly enough. Vigour must be introduced on the same principle and the grammar of the spontaneous conversational letter must be tidied up so that the 'little bit of ivory' is not pried apart by brackets (Austen 1818, p. xvii).

The other letter added in Henry's postscript was probably written to a female London acquaintance, Frances Tilson wife of Henry's former business partner James. Access to Austen's other letters reveals that Frances was often described in her repeated child-bearing as a 'poor Woman!' (1–2 October 1808; 24 May and 16 September 1813; 18 October 1815). Austen's 1817 letter will be adjusted over time although Henry clearly chose it for its tribute to Cassandra as an 'indefatigable nurse' and its reference to 'the anxious affection of all my beloved family' (1818, p. xxvi). The original is now untraceable so no other comparison can be made except to note that, when the letter reappeared in the 'Memoir' of 1833, Henry removed the 1818 reference to 'rather longer petticoats'. Without his earlier aberration, several more lines of an Austen letter could otherwise have been lost since 1818 is the only version of the 27–28 May 1817 letter now available. In 1833, the extract was also adjusted to conclude that Austen noted her own resignation to 'the appointment of God, however secondary causes may have operated' (1833, p. xxvi). The 'petticoat' allusion struck from the record in 1833 is, however, reinforced by Austen's writing to Cassandra in 9 March 1814, some time after Mrs Gardiner's similar advice to the Bennets, 'Mrs Tilson had long sleeves too, & she assured me that they are worn in the evening by many. I was glad to hear this'.

When Henry announced the '[s]hort and easy . . . task of the mere biographer' (1818, p. v) in the 'Notice', he was implicitly transferring that 'mere' reference to the actual life of his sister at the beginning of a long series of devaluations of her existence. In his postscript to the 'Notice', he 'submitted' the letter extracts 'to the public without apology' believing them 'more truly descriptive . . . than anything the pen of a biographer can produce' (p. xvii). Henry was raising the prospect of Austen telling her own story without fully unpacking what this might mean for the Austen family and certainly without fully accepting that there was a story to be told.

The unintentional value of the 'Notice' extends to its signposting of the biographical process. In spite of his efforts to align the authorial and domestic Austen, Henry failed to suppress Austen's own commentary on life writing that becomes visible in the novel that followed in 1818. In *Northanger Abbey* the relocation of the Gothic in contemporary society with its 'neighbourhood of voluntary spies' (1818, p. 186; *NA*, p. 203), its roads and newspapers, provides a critique on the potential misalignment of literary and life-writing categories. When Catherine Morland travels unaccompanied from the Abbey to Fullerton after her peremptory ejection by General Tilney she is apparently a failed heroine returning without the requisite triumphant phaetons full of noble relations and unaccompanied by servants in a chaise and four. The appearance of her carriage is an important event for the Morland family rather as the logistics of travel feature in the letters and in the Juvenilia. She arrives by 'mere' post-chaise and yet:

> Whatever may be the distress of Catherine's mind as she thus advanced towards the Parsonage, and whatever the humiliation of her biographer in relating it, she was preparing enjoyment of no every-day nature for those to whom she went; – first in the appearance of her carriage – and, secondly, herself.
>
> *(1818, p. 279; NA, p. 241)*

The author of Catherine's life could be sharing a heroine's glory but instead her biographer finds herself firmly and ironically invested in her subject's 'humiliation'. The tone of this life-writing reference seems to have been lost on the Austen family beginning with Henry in his negotiation of the evidence for Austen's 'mere' life. The failed heroine of the novel has made a good friend in Eleanor Tilney who offers to be a correspondent. Catherine has successfully negotiated the dangers of the transport network and will achieve the reward of marriage to the hero. Austen was recognising that biography is not a neutral medium and suggesting that biographers may have something to lose when they present the life of a heroine.

Henry's 'Notice' also prefaced Austen's concerns as an author that *Northanger Abbey* was 13 years out of date. She directly addressed the 'public' in an 'Advertisement' (1818, pp. xxiii–xxiv; *NA*, p. 1) that eventually bridged the text between her 'petticoat' letter quoted by Henry and the opening lines of the novel. *Northanger Abbey* dismembers the literary categories of the Gothic and the novel of sensibility leaving them delicately balanced as a critique of society. There is humour in the transfer of these categories into real life but also a brutal reminder of the parallel readings of that society. The advertisement was an open letter from an engaged author who had sought publication and not from the homely Aunt Jane about to be created for public consumption. In the novel, a letter from London rereads revolution through the lens of the Gothic novel (*NA*, pp. 113–114). For the family archiving project, however, Jane Austen's letters were viewed through a lens that was resolutely Victorian.

It has been suggested that any archive is surrounded by 'contingencies of value' in its organisation and context and that archival practice may misread the record (Gerson 2001, p. 7; p. 14). The 1870 *Memoir* of Austen, her *Letters* (Brabourne 1884a, 1884b) and *Life and Letters* (Austen-Leigh and Austen-Leigh 1913) shared a commonality of agenda in wanting to prove through her own letters that Jane Austen had never intended to be an author and expected no recognition of her professional approach to novel writing. It was agreed that she had been an author but that this was purely an impulse from nature and absolutely grounded in the domesticity of women's duty. These biographical publications set out to misread the letters and failed to understand the counter-cultural impulse behind them. Austen and Cassandra wrote their letters about what they could control. They gave life to their lives from the information that they held and circulated. The tone and inherent critique within the letters was at times hilariously misconstrued by the family record published up until the modern edition. Chapman (1932) then struggled to find the appropriate frame of reference for the texts he had carefully recovered.

The transposition of a 'Dearest E'. to reinforce familial ownership in the 'Notice' steers perilously close to a 'Mr E'. although looking further forward Austen-Leigh actually was 'Mr E' in the restored original wording in the *Memoir* (Austen-Leigh 1870, p. 155). In fact, the letter closes with an exaggeratedly familial 'Adieu, Aimable' after compliments about some pickled cucumbers supplied by James Austen. The further evolution of the life in letters can also be traced here when a new adjustment was made to tune with the new times. In publishing the letter written to him in the closing months of Austen's life, Austen's biographer excluded the allusion made to her projected marriage with John Papillon, rector of Chawton that was a regular family joke. The suggestion had apparently originated with Edward Austen's adoptive mother Catherine Knight (9 December 1808) but was not suitable for James Edward's 1870 audience. Also unsuitable was the incomplete watercolour of Austen painted in 1810 by her sister Cassandra. As the cover of this biography demonstrates, the original had to be finished and engraved to add a more Victorian cast to the image of the author (Kirkham 1983b, p. 29). It is an image that has achieved the widest possible circulation and currency on the British £10 note.

The *Memoir* was a project pursued by the children of Austen's eldest brother James. Caroline, the youngest of the three, wrote to her brother James Edward, 'I am very glad my dear Edward that you have applied yourself to the settlement of this vexed question between the Austens and the Public' (Le Faye 2004, p. 276), a 'Public' that Austen had herself addressed in the 'Advertisement' prefacing *Northanger Abbey*. Despite her involvement as a correspondent, Caroline believed that it would be a 'difficult task to dig up the materials, so carefully have they been buried out of our sight by the past generation' (p. 276). Without knowing about the bequest to Fanny Knight now Lady Knatchbull, half-sister Anna pointed out: 'Letters may have been preserved, & this is more probable as Aunt Jane's talent for letter writing was so much valued & thought so delightful amongst her own family circle' (p. 276). Caroline, however, thought any letters would not be 'acceptable to the public'; they 'detailed chiefly home and family events . . . so that to strangers they could be no transcript of her mind' (p. 276). If their aim was to make people know 'Aunt Jane' better, letters were not the means. Caroline did, however, suggest some comment should be made on Cadell's rejection of 'First Impressions' 'especially as we have so few incidents to produce' (Sutherland 2002, p. 185). The copy of George Austen's letter dated 1 November 1797 had been found in a sale of the publisher Cadell's papers in November 1840 (*C*, p. 659) by Tom (T.E.P.) Lefroy, nephew of Austen's dance partner Tom (9–10 January 1796; Sutherland 2002, p. 185) and husband of Anna's daughter Anna Jemima. This Jemima in turn features in the *Memoir* as a trade or proxy for a copy of *Emma* when Austen sends the novel in lieu of herself to meet the new baby in a scrap of a letter dated December 1815/January 1816.

In 1869, Caroline was critical of the Reverend George Austen's approach 'from an unknown' (Sutherland 2002, p. 185). There was knowledgeable talk among the siblings of 'Evelyn' and of "Kitty's Bower" (p. 186), two manuscript works that formed Volume the Third of the Juvenilia in James Edward's possession. Caroline had also inherited 'The Watsons', and Anna, perhaps in recognition of her attempted novel writing, both *Sanditon* and the cancelled chapter of *Persuasion*.

'Catharine or the Bower' views the letter from a number of angles and predates Austen's surviving letters by three years. In the unfinished novella, Mrs Perceval, Kitty's aunt considers '[a] correspondence between Girls productive of no good, and as the frequent origin of imprudence and Error by the effect of pernicious advice and bad example' (*J*, p. 262). She has lived for 50 years without a correspondent. Kitty's visitor Camilla exemplifies Mrs Perceval's view when she receives from her friend Augusta a 'long account of the new Regency walking dress' and Kitty marvels, 'She *must* write well . . . to make a long Letter upon a Bonnet and Pelisse' (p. 263). Camilla, a precursor of Isabella Thorpe, 'less governed by Propriety', also insists that a 'Correspondent' would have made Mrs Perceval 'quite a different Creature' (p. 263). Letters from friends are 'the greatest delight of my Life', Camilla explains, 'and you cannot think how much their Letters have formed my taste as Mama says, for I hear from them generally every week' (p. 263). The Austen-Leigh siblings were certainly concerned that it was this 'taste' for and frequency of letter writing that might prove untrustworthy even without the unknown material that had passed to Fanny.

It was James Edward who coined the term 'family record' that would be a subtitle (and from 1989 the main title) of the *Life and Letters* in 1913. A correspondent himself, he could be included within the biographical text of the *Memoir* as 'I, the youngest of the mourners' (Austen-Leigh 1871, p. 1) and 'living witness . . . of this excellence' (p. 3). He reiterated the sense of the family being all in all to Austen because '[h]er own family were so much, and the rest of the world so little' (p. 11). Kathryn Sutherland has pointed out in her modern edition that Austen-Leigh structured his account through Austen's Hampshire homes (2002, p. xli). He had some contact with the Kent family but the literary remains all seemed to be Hampshire-based and even when it was decided to publish *Lady Susan* in the second edition of the *Memoir* (1871) this was made possible because a copy was in their possession even though the original had devolved to Fanny with the letters. The comparison with Frances Burney that had originated in print with Henry and was often mentioned by reviewers emerged in the *Memoir* too but Austen-Leigh loftily claimed that 'native good taste . . . saved her [Austen] from the snare into which a sister novelist had fallen of imitating the grandiloquent style of Johnson' (Austen-Leigh 1871, p. 84). Most importantly in support of the non-professional argument, 'Jane Austen lived in entire seclusion from the literary world neither by correspondence nor by personal intercourse was she known to any contemporary authors' (p. 108) which was broadly speaking true.

In the *Memoir*, Austen-Leigh used extracts from the letters within his reach, 24 in 1870 and 36 by the second edition: twelve to Cassandra, eight to Anna, three to himself, three to James Stanier Clarke, four to the publisher Murray, and one each to Caroline, Martha Lloyd, Charles Austen, Alethea Bigg, and the Countess of Morley plus the composite to Frances Tilson. This created a record out of balance with the final evidence of the modern collected edition. A further 79 surviving letters to Cassandra and five to Fanny were unknown to him. In addition, Austen-Leigh saw the letters as his to manipulate in order to maintain his reverently constructed 'dear Aunt Jane' persona. He provided, for instance, very brief extracts from four of the letters to Anna discussed in Chapter 4 (1870, pp. 119–122; 1871, pp. 91–92) missing out the first. From these four, Austen-Leigh included only the 'wandering story' on which Austen and Cassandra disagree (1871, p. 91), the arrangement of 'Three or four families in a country village' (p. 91), the use of the slang expression 'vortex of dissipation' (p. 91) and the compliment to aunts jokingly made from London after Anna's wedding (p. 92). As Kathryn Sutherland observes, it is a 'partial and unconfiding life' (2005a, p. 80). The 'bit of ivory' and the '3 or 4 Families' advice to Anna (9–18 September 1814) were grafted onto the nest-building imagery suggested by Austen herself. The letters 'may be said to resemble the nest which some little bird builds of the materials nearest at hand, of the twigs and mosses supplied by the tree in which it is placed; curiously constructed out of the simplest matters' (Austen-Leigh 1871, p. 57).

The *Memoir* was received with interest and both editions were reviewed. Anne Thackeray Ritchie had already included Austen's life in her critique of 'Heroines and their Grandmothers', asking if authoresses have become more miserable since 'Miss Austen's heroines came tripping into the room, bright-eyed, rosy cheeked, arch and good-humoured' (1865, p. 630). Ritchie had praised Austen's 'placid days' (p. 631), acknowledging that the author's own life was 'more sad and more pathetic' but still peppering her argument with 'delicate sympathy', 'charming' and 'playful wisdom', and 'kindly humour' (p. 640). As a result Ritchie was primed, at least publicly, to read Austen-Leigh's 'little memoir' in a certain light and she duly reviewed it as 'one more glimpse of an old friend come back with a last greeting' (Ritchie 1871, p. 159). Ritchie quoted extensively from 'The Watsons' but 'would scarcely recognise *Lady Susan*'s parentage if it were not so well authenticated' (p. 162). She happily absorbed Austen-Leigh's pious sentiments and once again recycled the nest image: 'she built her nest, did this good woman, happily weaving it out of shreds, and ends, and scraps of daily duty, patiently put together' (pp. 172–173). Ritchie repeated the bulk of this review for the Austen chapters of her later *Book of Sibyls* (1883) including also Anna Letitia Barbauld, Maria Edgeworth, and Amelia Opie and without correcting the reference to 'Captain Benfield' for Benwick (1871, p. 166; 1883, p. 210) when she likened Anne Elliot to Austen 'speaking for the last time' (1883, p. 211). Ritchie found the alleged arch good humour of Austen and her heroines difficult to reconcile with the life evidence. She wanted the novels to be letters to 'the Public' because they were more considered and made safe by an agreement to publish. Other reviewers were more persistent, however.

Reviewing the first edition of the *Memoir*, Margaret Oliphant detected a remorseless truth (Oliphant 1870, p. 296) in Austen's 'subtle power, keenness, finesse and self-restraint' (p. 294). Her comment that Austen-Leigh casts 'a passing gleam of light upon the fine vein of feminine cynicism which pervades his aunt's mind' (p. 294) suggests that Austen can and will emerge from her victimhood, remaking Austen-Leigh's own tentative and defensive comment that 'a vein of humour continually gleams through the whole' (Austen-Leigh 1870, p. 79). Julia Kavanagh had already suggested in her *English Women of Letters* that Austen is 'cold' (Kavanagh 1863, p. 235) and Oliphant observed that 'it is scarcely to be expected that books so calm and cold and keen, and making so little claim upon their sympathy, would ever be popular' with the public (Oliphant 1870, p. 304). Her conclusion, however, was to express a preference for Miss Mitford: 'Miss Austen was by much the greater artist, but the sweetness of the atmosphere about her humble contemporary was far above anything possible to the great novelist' (p. 313). Although able to detach Austen from her domestic imprisonment, Oliphant could not reward her with open praise from within the complex construction of women's authorship in the later nineteenth century.

Other reviewers fed into concerns – especially the comparison with Burney – that would later animate Lord Brabourne when he presented his larger cache of letters. H.F. Chorley commented on Austen's 'home simplicity' (Chorley 1870, p. 197) and compared the domestic *Memoir* with Burney's *Diary* that he termed 'little more than a hymn in her own praise, sung 'at the request of friends' (p. 217). Shakespeare scholar Richard Simpson also regarded Austen as non-Burney like and described her building her plots and characters by the accumulation of delicate touches (Simpson 1870, pp. 136–137), sitting apart on her rocky tower and exercising the 'critical over the poetical and imaginative faculties' (p. 133). By contrast with the family, Simpson recognised that 'what she wrote was worked up by incessant labour into its perfect form' (p. 140) and that 'the action is such as is necessary to display the characters, not such as is invented for the purpose of mystifying and surprising the reader' (p. 141). His final act, however, was to controvert the whole tone of his critique. He concluded by subscribing to the 'dear Aunt Jane' myth promoted by the apparent eye witnesses. He agreed with the family that, despite the further evidence of the letters, 'her powers were a secret to herself' (p. 150).

The letters were an ongoing focus of contention for a new generation of Austens as the family's debate with 'the Public' continued. Anna's daughter Fanny Caroline Lefroy started the conversation in *Temple Bar* by responding to a review ('Jane Austen' 1882) of Bentley's 1882 six-volume Steventon edition of the novels. Fanny insisted that, unlike Burney, Austen 'never knew she was a lion', and the rest of the family was blamed for allowing the 'blank' of Austen's life to do injury to her fame (Lefroy 1883, p. 270). Fanny Caroline was herself the author of some morally instructive novels and believed that Cassandra thought the destruction of letters 'a sacred duty' (p. 271). Through those missing, Fanny sweepingly declared, 'we might have been enriched also by the posthumous companionship with a heart of such rare sweetness and strength that it would have exalted our standard, not only of the capacity of feeling in feminine nature, but in all humanity' (p. 278). This was once again to ignore the ongoing discussion of washing expenses, trashy novels, and any reference to Mrs Austen's health. Fanny claimed that Austen's graver thoughts were kept out of her novels (p. 279), that contrary to all evidence, the sisters had no love of millinery (p. 281), and that Austen and Cassandra's exclusiveness – which sounds like the 'family selfishness' later described by Sarah Tytler (1880, p. 18) – was like that of 'husband and wife' (p. 282).

The year 1882 would prove even more significant for the family archive. When the *Memoir* was reprinted for this 1882 Bentley edition, the facsimile of a letter to Anna was promoted to the frontispiece. It read: 'If your uncle were at home he would send his best love but I will not impose any bare, fictitious remembrances on you' (p. xii; 29 November 1814). The text was a conveniently signed and well-spaced single page for publication but was also slightly missing its mark as a reinforcement of Austen's affection for Anna. In addition, the idea of 'fictitious remembrances' as a prelude to allegedly factual letters seems an unusual choice although the facsimile had already appeared opposite page 41 of the second edition. Anna herself had died in September 1872 followed by James Edward in November 1874 and Caroline in November 1880, further dispersing other material. Deirdre Le Faye notes that Fanny Caroline passed original Austen papers to Austen-Leigh's publisher son Cholmeley who was involved with the original publication of the *Memoir* (*C*, p. 693; pp. 686–687) and also that Cholmeley was paid 50 guineas by publisher Bentley for copyright in November 1882 (p. 696). This was a matter of weeks before the death of Fanny Knatchbull on 25 December when Lord Brabourne inherited a further 84 letters unread for more than 25 years.

These letters had been in Fanny's possession since Cassandra's death 37 years before. Around 2 August 1856, Fanny had added a memorandum initially leaving them to her daughter Louisa, who predeceased her in 1874: 'I shall also prefer your having Aunt Jane's letters which however you must not shew indiscriminately & may destroy any you think right' (Wilson 1990a, p. 175). With Fanny uncommunicative in her old age, the Knatchbulls had denied the existence of the letters during enquiries for the *Memoir*. Fanny had, of course, written to her sister Marianne on 23 August 1869 that Austen and Cassandra as women had lacked 'refinement' and were only fit for 'good Society' through the kindness of Mrs Knight and Kent family connections (Le Faye 2004, pp. 279–280). Fanny announced to Marianne that this sentiment had taken over her letter writing: 'I felt it at my <u>pen's end</u>, and it chose to come along & speak the truth' (p. 280). The letter betrays that Austen was viewed as unrefined in part because of her pursuit of 'Pewter' as she called it in her letter to Fanny on 30 November 1814, appropriating a male term used by Fanny's brother Edward Knight II.

The additional manuscripts rediscovered in 1882 and read again by Brabourne in February 1884 (*C*, p. 696) took on a dual role as both memorials and investments. This duality of memento and 'Pewter' in the archive becomes even more apparent because Lord Brabourne also inherited from Fanny the letters of his father's uncle Joseph Banks that appeared more valuable in scientific and monetary terms than those of his great aunt. There is a record in February 1884 of Brabourne's offer to sell papers, including a journal of Banks's Newfoundland voyage, to the British Museum for £250 (Dawson 1958, p. xvi). Some papers were sold to the Australian government for £375 in 1884 and the remainder for £200 at an auction in 1886 (p. xvii) when the first group of five Austen letters was also sold as discussed below. Having signed a contract with Bentley to publish Austen's letters, Brabourne was visited by Cholmeley Austen-Leigh and went himself to Chawton in May 1884 to see Montagu Knight the owner of Chawton Manor and grandson of Edward Knight (Wilson 1990a, p. 176). This was Brabourne's first ever Hampshire visit presumably as a consequence of the estrangement ongoing between the families since 1826 over the marriage of Edward Knight II, Brabourne's uncle, to Mary Dorothea Knatchbull, Brabourne's half-sister. Montagu was a son of Edward II's second marriage to Adela Portal, ensuring that this 1884 visit was not a disloyal act to Brabourne's father who was also father to Mary Dorothea.

Despite the unavoidable fact that Austen was born in Hampshire, Brabourne's resulting *Letters* began in Kent, where Austen visited but never lived. Brabourne felt the need to confront the activity of the 'non-Kentish Austens' (1884a, p. 24) and averred: 'It is much to be regretted that the 'Memoir' should have been published without the additional light which many of these letters throw upon the 'Life', though of course no blame attaches to Mr Austen-Leigh in the matter' (p. xi). Having been too young to attend Austen's funeral as Austen-Leigh did, Brabourne could not resist the opening jibe that Fanny, his mother, was the favourite niece (p. 1). He echoed his mother's view about Kent contacts and 'the relationships which accrued to Jane Austen through the marriage of her brother' (p. 23) and glossed over the fact that his uncle Edward Knight II, Austen's nephew was 'married twice' (p. 25). With a sense of false modesty, he claimed that he would 'attempt no "Memoir"' but nonetheless present the 'confidential outpourings of Jane Austen's soul' (p. xii). He ominously promised to 'give the letters as they were written, with such comments as I think may add to their interest' but observed their inability to tell their own story since 'they form no continuous narrative and record no stirring events' (p. xiv). When he expressed fears of mistaking 'real meaning' (p. 124), he seemed half to understand that he was not a qualified reader of the texts in his keeping. He manoeuvred around the 'vein of fun, or of originality, if the phrase be better' by insisting that most of the letters were written in 'the purest spirit of playful nonsense' (p. 23) with a wary acceptance that he might have missed improper references.

Brabourne suggested that the *Memoir* 'affords' him assistance but that his is not a 'regular biography' (1884a, p. 43). These are 'biographical letters' that 'go forth to the world with such additional information as I am able to impart with respect to the people and things of whom and of which they treat' (p. 2). His aim was rather turgidly to 'fill up and complete' the *Memoir* (p. 4) while reinforcing that 'the chief beauty of Jane Austen's life really consisted in it being uneventful', a 'home life' as the 'light and blessing of a home circle' (p. 5). In this the *Memoir* and *Letters* seemed to agree.

Brabourne also cohered with the *Memoir* in wishing to dismiss any Burney comparison (1884a, pp. 62–73) and he tackled bluntly the perceptive insights of Sarah Tytler whose *Jane Austen and her Works* relied on the *Memoir* (p. 81). Tytler's biographical chapters had expressed concern about the letters' lack of continuity so that 'they fall vaguely and flatly on the reader' (Tytler 1880, p. 18) although this was partly to do with the lack of framing and often perfunctory discussion in the *Memoir*. Tytler decided that the later letters addressed to Anna were more lively possibly because of their discussion of novel writing. Austen's noble nature was found to be present again in meeting 'her last enemy' (p. 39), 'meet reward of Jane Austen's faithful performance of the home duties which no literary career, however arduous and distinguished, absolved her' (p. 41). Tytler was here wrestling with the 'parallel currents' in the lives of women authors defined in Elizabeth Gaskell's *Life of Charlotte Brontë* (1857). There were concerns about Austen's intolerance and 'spirit of exclusiveness' (Tytler 1880, p. 15) as well as the suggestion that her neighbours must have noticed the 'mingled instruction and diversion' she derived from their lives (p. 18). Tytler also, however, contradicted the family by insisting that 'the tales and the life are calculated to reflect light on each other' (p. vii). Most potently Tytler not only deplored Burney's 'transparent literary vanity' but described Austen as 'the clear-sighted girl with the sharp pen' (p. 16).

Having dismissed Burney and Brontë with Tytler, and side-stepped George Eliot (1884a, p. 73), Brabourne bemoaned the 'letterless years' (1884b, p. 82) and spent time bringing heated drawing rooms up to date (pp. 78–79). Despite the density of his earlier descriptions, he could not find out how Margaret Beckford was a cousin and settled grumpily for being 'not disposed to stop and inquire' (p. 80). His Aunt Marianne, Fanny's younger sister and inheritor of the housekeeping duties at Godmersham, has told Brabourne there were 'all sorts of secrets together, while we were only children' (p. 118), promoting Fanny to the status of confidante to Austen and Cassandra. During a trip to London for theatres and shopping, he is grateful for the aid of his mother's pocket book through which he is 'happy to be able to narrate the fact' that Austen and Fanny previously went to church at St Paul's Covent Garden (p. 219) and also that a basket of provisions was supplied from Godmersham to Hans Place on 15 November 1815 (p. 245). These pocket-books indicate that there should be 30 letters from Austen to Fanny but only five survive and Brabourne fretted that 'my mother was in the habit of keeping the letters of so many of her correspondents through life, that it is difficult to imagine how these came to be destroyed' (p. 247). With the Tilson letter in the public domain, he was quick to claim that Austen 'only ceased the correspondence when health and strength began rapidly to fail' (p. 249). He concluded with the two let-ters written by Cassandra to Fanny in July 1817 to which he had exclusive access. He did this with a grand gesture to impose his exclusivity on the reader and on the Austen-Leighs: 'They are indeed sad letters, but they form the proper conclusion to the series which I give the world' (p. 331).

Within his bombastic exposition, Lord Brabourne did not find time to interpret the concerns of women: 'Jane Austen's letters . . . leave us to find out all these things for ourselves' (1884b, pp. 71–72). At the same time, Brabourne devolved responsibility back to the texts. He claimed that 'the even tenor of her own life affords no materials from which a romantic story could be woven' but will 'once again refer to the letters to tell their own tale' (1884a, p. 55). The letters were thus contrarily unthreatening and informative, overly confiding and uneventful, and contextualised as family history. In fact, Brabourne was continuing the family pro-ject inaugurated by Henry's 'Notice'. Henry had provided letters as an apparently innocent frame for life writing in fiction but now the letters would overspill their frame and challenge the gentry culture of Brabourne's commentary.

Reviewing Brabourne's edition, the novelist Mary Augusta Ward was outraged that the letters should subvert her concept of the author with 'half-edited matter along with incongruous and boring "family pedigrees"': 'By this publication of a newly-discovered collection of Miss Austen's letters, Miss Austen's great-nephew has done as ill a turn as it is in anybody's power to do to the author of "Pride and Prejudice"' (Ward 1884, p. 84). Ward blamed Brabourne for a lack of 'sprightli-ness' in the 'ponderous effort of the introductory chapters with their endless strings of names and wandering criticism of the novels' (p. 85). She condemned the editor of the letters for failing to provide any sense of 'the workshop which preceded the novels' (p. 86). More generally, Ward denounced the fashion for 'prodigal' works of biography in the form of documents (p. 84) deciding that the first dozen Austen letters fill up a gap in the *Memoir* but have 'slight claim to belong to literature' (p. 87). She therefore named Austen-Leigh Austen's 'first biographer' (p. 84). The letters themselves were given no critical attention as life evidence with Ward suggesting that Austen was not a letter-writer because she was outside the world of ideas (p. 87). There was no apparent perception of the role played by the letters in Austen's actual life, and in addition her letters were deemed 'below rather than above the average in interest, point and charm' (p. 88). After the epistolary Austen reaches the age of 31 this is 'the mere ordinary chit-chat of the ordinary gentlewoman with no claims whatever to publication or remembrance beyond the family circle . . . neither amusing nor sufficiently instructive to make it worth publication' (p. 87). Ward praised Austen's 'power of choice and discrimination' (p. 89) and highlighted 'self-restraint' as her 'determining quality' (p. 91) but decided that the letters could just as well have been published as an addendum to the *Memoir*. This degree of collaboration was not possible, however, for the first century of Austen's afterlife.

Elsewhere, a bibliography in Goldwin Smith's biography of Austen complimented Lord Brabourne's 'genial industry' (Smith 1890, p. 12) from within a male coterie of county historians. Thomas Kebbel in *Fortnightly Review* felt the weight of Lord Brabourne's judgement and was indebted for his explanation of the jokes and allusions (Knebel 1885, p. 262). George Barnett Smith, biographer of Shelley and Gladstone had found the *Memoir* 'very entertaining' (1885, p. 27) and his review of *Letters* highlighted Austen's 'retired lot' by comparison with Burney and even Charlotte Brontë (p. 32). He agreed with Thomas Macaulay (1843, pp. 560–561) and Simpson (1870, p. 136) in pronouncing her 'able to touch the hand of Shakespeare' (Smith 1885, p. 45). Smith decided that the letters provide little of value 'from a literary point of view' and 'add very little knowledge of a personal character' (p. 38). Having spent half of his review on the *Memoir*, he then took it upon himself to speak on Austen's behalf, concluding that 'if Jane Austen were now living she would probably be extremely angry at their publication' (p. 38). 'Letters of Jane Austen' in the *Saturday Review* agreed they were 'mere gossip – written conversation of a quality it is pretty safe to say Jane Austen would have been the very last to think worthy of print' (1884, p. 637). This reviewer, however, at least pointed out that Austen was unlikely to be writing her autobiography in letters to Cassandra and suggested like Ward that re-editing the *Memoir* to include the letters would have been more palatable.

After this wealth – or disappointment – of new material, the second decade of the twentieth century brought some intergenerational collaboration but this still owed much of its tone to the biographical foundations established by James Edward and Lord Brabourne, most of which seem to have little to do with any actual reading of the letters. Merely having the letters was proof of ownership of the image of the homely domestic biddable aunt. Brabourne died in 1893 and the remaining letters were sold off but his text was now in the public domain. In 1911 James Edward's son William Austen-Leigh and Edward Knight's grandson Montagu Knight wrote a historical account of Chawton Manor with a sense that they could revitalise some of the memories already created. Cassandra was 'clever and sensible, a real power in the family' (Knight 1911, p. 161) and Henry had 'almost exasperating buoyancy and sanguineness of temperament and high animal spirits which no misfortunes could depress and no failures damp' (pp. 163–164). Jane's 'deferential affection' for Cassandra, although not as husband and wife, was noted but it was observed that family members (nephew and nieces) from a different generation would not have been 'recipients of her most intimate confidences' (p. 164). In terms of the letters the 'imperfection of the record' was bemoaned again since Cassandra's belief in the 'sacredness of this correspondence' was such that 'she destroyed all the letters in which special emotion had been shown, and felt sure she had left only what no one would care to publish' (p. 164). Although this was another allusion to the perceived value of Brabourne's edition, William Austen-Leigh at least was already working on the amalgamation of the *Memoir* and *Letters* because his collaboration with his nephew Richard Arthur, son of Cholmeley, was published in 1913 under the definitive title *Jane Austen: Life and Letters: A Family Record*.

In this new century, the Austen-Leighs endeavoured to contain the letters by calling them 'mémoires pour servir' but they nonetheless presented the texts as documents of the life rather than just as memorial objects. They continued the line that 'Cassandra purposely destroyed many of the letters likely to prove the most interesting, from a distaste for publicity' (Austen Leigh 1913, p. v). The *Memoir* had added to 'the stock of information available for her biographers' (p. v) but the Austen-Leighs downplayed the importance of the letters at the same time as they echoed the Chawton Manor publication: 'The *Memoir* must always remain the one first-hand account of her, resting on the authority of a nephew who knew her intimately [father and grandfather of the authors] and that of his two sisters' (p. vi). The *Life* was to provide 'greater distance' while simultaneously claiming a further generational gap from James's children, the 'three eyewitnesses' (p. 404) who were too young to know about Austen's earlier years (p. vii). The Austen-Leighs claimed to offer not 'a piece of literary criticism' but new facts and a fresh light on the 'narrative' (p. viii). They could not, however, resist invoking Anne Elliot 'loving longest' (p. vii) in allusion to the one romance recollected and retold by 'unimpeachable authority', Cassandra (p. 83).

In *Life and Letters*, Lord Brabourne was afforded a footnote (Austen-Leighs 1913, p. 84) but the Hampshire Austens received fuller acknowledgement. These family members were descendants of the other Austen brothers namely James Edward's daughter Mary Augusta, J.G. Nicholson 'their kinsman of the half-blood' descended from the Reverend George Austen's half-brother William-Hampson Walter, father of Phylly, Jane granddaughter of Charles, Margaret Bellas great-granddaughter of James (p. viii), and John Hubback and Captain Ernest Leigh Austen grandsons of Frank (p. ix). There was reference to the Hubbacks' *Sailor Brothers* (Hubbacks 1906) that had restored five letters written to Frank to the reconstructed letter chronology and to Constance Hill's *Jane Austen: Her Homes and Friends* (1902). Hill literally took a copy of *Letters* tucked under her arm (Hill 1902, p. 10) as a guidebook for the literary pilgrimage that produced *Homes and Friends*. Hill's sister's illustrations inserted Constance into the text as a bystander, almost another niece, at Austen's memorial tablet in Winchester (p. 263). Through the progress of their publication in the late nineteenth century, the letters were already escaping the family record to become a reference tool for literary tourism and an extension of the person of the novelist.

Echoing Hill, the authors of the *Life* announced rather quaintly that '[t]he extant letters of Jane herself begin in 1796 and will accompany us through the rest of the story' (Austen-Leigh 1913, p. 81). The Austen-Leighs prepared the reading public with a warning not to 'try to extract more out of the letters than they will yield' (p. 81) at the same time as they noted the 'freemasonry' of lost meaning (p. 82). Cassandra was again implicated in the withholding of information and the sisters' epistolary style had to be excused despite authorial provenance being proclaimed by the inclusion of the letters as evidence. The authority of scholar A.C. Bradley, to 'take the letters as they are', was invoked, along with an acknowledgement of their author's 'inveterate playfulness' (p. 83). This was presumably an explanation for any jokes about 'the simple regimen of separate rooms' (20–21 February 1817) or experiments with haricot mutton and ox-cheek (17–18 November 1798). The Austen-Leighs insisted that Austen was 'secure of her correspondent' (p. 83) despite the fact that these private letters were now on public view and would have meaning wrested from them under twentieth-century, albeit Edwardian, eyes. An additional 10 letters were now available and the Austen-Leighs repeated the happy analogy pursued in the *Memoir* that 'the same hand which painted so exquisitely with the pen could work as delicately with the needle' (p. 70). William Austen-Leigh was also conscious of his responsibilities to the Kent Austens now resident at Chawton Manor who were generously reintroduced in the *Life* at the death of Elizabeth Austen. Montagu's grandfather Edward '[i]n the midst of his grief . . . wished to bind his mother and sisters more closely to himself' (p. 215) by offering them Chawton Cottage as a home. The Austen-Leighs in 1913 expressed their gratitude by describing Edward's daughter Fanny as 'admirably adapted' (p. 211) to be companion, mistress, and adviser compared with their nearer connection Anna who was 'more brilliant both in looks and in intelligence, but also more mercurial and excitable' (p. 241). It is noteworthy that Anna remained 'mercurial' when the revised *Life* became *Family Record* in 1989 but Fanny became 'staid and prosaic' (p. 170).

In the original *Life*, the Austen-Leighs also had to negotiate their way around a fictional letter-writer in the form of *Lady Susan*, a bombshell planted for the family by James Edward himself. After the success of his first edition, Austen-Leigh was persuaded to publish extant manuscripts in the second edition of his biography including an epistolary novel alongside the factual letters. Lady Susan demonstrates a vicious but exemplary grasp of the letter as a weapon in the social and less than civil war of matrimonial gain. The voices of the epistolary novella were juxtaposed in this new edition with the letter extracts that Austen-Leigh had already shared and the whole steered dangerously close to the tone that the *Memoir* sought to underplay. In 1913, the Austen-Leighs sought to contextualise the novella while also placing greater reliance on the letter as a life-writing vehicle. They suggested that Austen 'wrote because she must and with very little prevision of the path which her genius was afterwards to mark out for her' (pp. 52–53). They went on to call *Lady Susan* a 'study' (p. 80) adding that the 'purity of her imagination and the delicacy of her taste should have prevented her from repeating such an experiment' (p. 81). The presentation of Austen's letters in largely unabridged form in the *Life* suggests that this style of writing was far from suppressed in private and in this way the fictional Lady Susan is a letter disruptor from within biography. Other disruption becomes apparent when the *Life* chooses to mask biographical chronology. In October 1798 Cassandra is left behind for a Godmersham visit after a section of third-person description and so 'we find ourselves in the company of the letters once more' (p. 109) with no suggestion that the narrative will be altered by a reliance on these separations and fragmentations of the life. Through the letters we 'accompany the author to London' (p. 244) and the biographers decide that they 'had better let her speak for herself' (p. 258). Attempting to ally the life and the fiction, the actual letters are deemed to provide the parallel experience of leaving the reader 'always in the confidence of the heroine' of *Pride and Prejudice* (p. 264). The account provided cannot finally, however, shake off the confidences supplied by the letter-writing Lady Susan.

Family treatment of the letters as publications is complicated by this still ongoing correspondence between fact and fiction, and by the letters' revaluation and re-collection for the marketplace. The collation and sequencing of the letters that may have informed original preservation and retention practices was dissipated by the sale or donation of the manuscripts in the late nineteenth and early twentieth centuries. The rediscovery of original manuscripts has continued into the twenty-first century. Two manuscript letters sold by Brabourne were found in the private Honresfield Library in 2021 during the writing of this biography. These were placed in the Jane Austen's House Museum collection on 16 December 2021, the anniversary of Austen's birthday.

In the earliest stages of the dispersal, Lord Brabourne sold five letters on 14 April 1886 in his final sale of Banks material but only one out of the further five offered on 7 June 1889 (Wilson 1990a, p. 178). On 11 May 1891, Brabourne sold his topographical books but was disappointed with the performance of 10 Austen letters and in June 1893, after his death, the remaining 68 letters bequeathed by Cassandra were sold (p. 178). The five surviving letters to Fanny were not sold but remain in the Kent Archives office in an inadvertent parallel with the five 1814 letters to Anna that are in St John's College Library in Oxford. Even the letters given a family value have thus been reclassified either as Kent artefacts or as tributes to the Leigh family and their male descendants. Anna's father and her uncle Henry, founder of the letter conundrum, both attended St John's College as 'Founder's Kin', beneficiaries of their mother's family's right to an education. Austen and Cassandra only benefited indirectly from this kinship when they were visited by college fellow James, who came to see them in Oxford during the earlier part of their ill-fated attendance at Mrs Crawley's school in 1783 (Le Faye 2004, pp. 47–48). Other groupings of letters have taken other routes into a range of collections. The letters inherited by Charles Austen were sold in the 1920s by his granddaughters around the time of Chapman's research for his edition and a sequence of four of these from 1813 are now held by the Jane Austen's House Museum Trust (Sutherland 2018, pp. 54–87). The letter of 21–23 April 1805 from Bath to Ibthorpe in which Austen mentions 'our intended Partnership with Martha' was briefly owned by the composer Jerome Kern but is now at Princeton alongside 27–28 December 1808 in which Austen talks with her fingers (Le Faye 2011, p. 395; p. 406).

This redistribution and onward transmission into collections can be broadly illustrated by tracing the destinies of a selection of the extant manuscripts. Many were valued as autographs in the nineteenth century and this divorced them from their original context as substitutes for presence. Their role as mementoes was also dissipated over the course of time as their archival life-writing role was apparently exhausted by the Austen-Leighs and Brabourne. The ongoing fate of the letters gives a representative overview of the future disposition of materials beyond Austen's original process of writing to the moment within her own life. Such an overview also brings into question the new value system applied to the letter as a collectable artefact divorced from its life-writing context.

The Banks sale of 1886 tested the market at the time. This section takes the opportunity to reread these texts in parallel with the evolving market valuation and suggests how the dispersal might have related to any family valuation of the original material. Among the first five Austen letters sold, 28 December 1798 announced that 'Frank is made' a commander and that Charles is moving to a frigate. The physical appearance of the letter separated male and female concerns in a stark representation of their differing life expectations. Frank and Charles are effectively on the cover of the letter; Austen and Cassandra are on the reverse although still overtly claiming pride in the naval officers' achievements. This was an extravagantly spaced letter using only two sides of the four and with only 16 lines per page. It was also sent out of sequence assuming that Cassandra would be happy to pay for this good news despite the fact that Austen's previous letter has been sent only two days earlier on 26 December. For the sale nearly 90 years later, the letter may have seemed more readable and also representative of understandable masculine achievement. As a communication, the letter was 'to be dedicated entirely to good news' and on the reverse, very different topics were aired to balance the success of the brothers. In Cassandra's case, Austen thinks this should be an opportunity to apply for 'washing and letter expences' presumably while her father was feeling flushed with Frank's success. Bank account evidence demonstrates that Cassandra's application was paid by a draft of just under £13 on 23 February 1799 (*C*, p. 221) and Austen hopes already that this will be the excuse for a new muslin gown. The future transmission of the letter itself illustrates the stark contrast of authorship and ownership. Cassandra as recipient would have paid an extra 2d or 3d in postage for which she was dependent on her father. By 1932 the letter was owned by Oliver R. Barrett of Chicago and was sold by his heirs in 1998 for £22,500 (Le Faye 2011, p. 379).

Three other letters in the sale were written from Bath, two as a tourist with brother Edward and his wife (17 May 1799; 11 June 1799) and one as a resident after the journey consequent on the removal from Steventon (5–6 May 1801). The 1799 examples were sold separately from intermediate (2 June) and succeeding (19 June) letters and there seems to have been no sense of keeping such a rare and informative sequence together for archival purposes; the sale thus dissipating Cassandra's preservation methods originally retained for Brabourne's edition. The contents of 17 May have become more notable for Austen's apparent malice towards her neighbours although her turns of phrase reflect that exuberance of the Juvenilia apparently suppressed in her published works. Austen tells Cassandra about meeting a Dr. Hall, '& Dr Hall in such very deep mourning that either his Mother, his Wife, or himself must be dead'. This letter was catalogued in the autograph collection of Frederick Locker-Lampson by 1895 and was bequeathed to the Houghton Library at Harvard by 1960. The 11 June 1799 letter followed a slightly different path after being bought by the archivist Edward Petherick who was perhaps directly involved because of interest in the Banks papers. Petherick presented the letter to the National Library of Australia in 1911 (Le Faye 2011, p. 382). In it Austen offered to write in the style of Mrs Piozzi's letters (see Figure 1.4) and accused Martha Lloyd of planning to publish 'First Impressions' from memory.

In 5–6 May 1801, Austen continued trying to make the best of the loss of her home and stability. It seems likely that her immediate reaction to the Bath move has been edited out by Cassandra but there are five previous surviving letters from January 1801, all in the Pierpont Morgan Library, that preserve some details of the sacrifices involved in moving from country to city, family home to rented lodgings. The discussion of food prices, which are higher in the city, and of fashion, which is more accessible, still suggests a dichotomy or division of opinion. In May, Austen and her mother were at 1 Paragon Buildings as guests of the Leigh-Perrots, an often divisive couple in terms of the family's dependency for both living and future legacies. Control, however, can be asserted even in the Leigh-Perrot household. Austen is comfortably established in her 'own room up two pair of stairs' although perhaps the message for Cassandra is that she is a little too close to the servants' quarters for actual comfort. Before selling the letter, Brabourne had shown himself to be oblivious to its counter-cultural messages, insisting that '[h]er home was wherever her own people were' (1884a, p. 229). Despite the evidence of the letters, Brabourne transferred his masculine and patriarchal sense of place to Austen: 'whether at Steventon, Bath or elsewhere, her cheerful temperament was even and unvaried, and assured her own happiness as well as that of those with whom she lived' (p. 229).

The 5–6 May 1801 letter was presented to the Fitzwilliam Museum Library in Cambridge in 1917. In terms of archival geography, Cambridge is also bound in with the publication of *Emma*. Austen's 1 April 1816 letter to John Murray about the Prince Regent's 'handsome' copy and the 'sad Event in Henrietta S[t]' has been in King's College Cambridge Library since 1990 having passed through an autograph collection. As discussed in Chapter 1, Austen's draft of her letter to the Countess of Morley is also in Cambridge University Library along with the Countess's own note to her.

At the 1886 sale, Brabourne's publisher Bentley himself bought the fifth letter (14 June 1814) suggesting Austen's more cosmopolitan life as an author of three published novels. In the letter, arrangements were being made to visit the Cookes in Great Bookham. The Cookes have 'claims', Austen explained to Cassandra and it is possible that Austen could have investigated Box Hill as an *Emma* location while in the Bookham area. In the letter itself, however, the 'sensible Novel' *Mansfield Park* was reportedly admired by Austen's godfather, Samuel Cooke and this allusion may have been a driver for the purchase. The letter was bought by Bentley for £6.18s., sold again for £130 in 1938, and bequeathed to the Pierpont Morgan Library by Austen collector Alberta Burke. The 54 letters in this New York library represent the greatest concentration of Austen letters, originally donated by J.P. Morgan in 1920. Burke supplied six other letters: the note to Charles Haden and the actual note to the Countess of Morley; the "gap" letter from Lyme Regis (14 September 1804), the one letter to Anne Sharp (22 May 1817), 16 February 1813 to Martha Lloyd seeking 'Justice in Epistolary Matters', and 17–18 October 1815 to Cassandra in the midst of Henry's illness. Courtesy of Burke, the library also holds one of those two letters sent by Cassandra after Austen's death and prized by Brabourne in 1884, the other having been purchased by Jane Austen's House Museum for £30,000 in 2015.

When researcher/pilgrim Constance Hill was pictured in the scene in Winchester Cathedral she was viewing a new brass plaque installed by James Edward Austen-Leigh in 1872 as an extension and commemoration of the *Memoir*. According to the plaque, Austen was 'known to many by her writings, endeared to her family by the varied charms of her character, and ennobled by Christian faith and Piety'. Her nephew sought to draw Austen back into the family from the clutches of her public but was surely aware that 'varied charms' had an ambiguous ring. He quoted doggedly from Proverbs: 'She openeth her mouth with wisdom and in her tongue is the law of kindness'. In his own piety, he was hoping to disguise a truth already visible, and made visible by him, that kindness was not the habitual style of her tongue. Austen uses humour in her exploration of her society but her comedy is sometimes brutal. The letters could similarly pay ostensible respect to the serious requirements of duty but for public consumption were often only just bordering on civility. Sarah Tytler's understanding of this duality gleaned from James Edward's *Memoir* was the source of Brabourne's Kentish panic in the *Letters*.

In 1922, James Edward's daughter Mary Augusta was over 80 when she entered the family business with a further riposte to 'the Public'. Brabourne's letters had all dispersed in the posthumous sale of June 1893 and the granddaughters of Charles Austen were about to seek outlets for the material inherited from their aunt, Cassandra's goddaughter Cassy Esten. In the period after the *Life* and before Chapman's 1932 edition, Mary Augusta described the letters as 'a peculiarly restricted selection', and not 'a specimen of her general correspondence' (Austen-Leigh 1922, p. 7) despite their supply of facts for the biographer. The past generation was blamed for its discrimination in destruction since Cassandra only spared letters 'in the full belief that they contained nothing sufficiently interesting to induce any future generation to give them to the world' (p. 7). Mary Augusta reproduced almost all of her Aunt Caroline's 'Reminiscences' that include the account of Cassandra's 1843 bonfire (p. 145).There continued, however, to be no recognition that there are potentially hundreds of missing letters to Austen's brothers of which only nine survive. Eight are to Frank, including two announcing George Austen's death, one the poem from 26 July 1809 and two mere scraps: the signature only of 17 February 1813 and a slightly more informative postscript of 21 March 1814. If Austen's letter-writing pattern were maintained through life, it still seems unlikely however that further letters would yield the moralistic tone that Mary Augusta was seeking. 'How vain then', she nonetheless mourned, 'must be any attempt to extract from this unvalued remainder of that wine of the spirit with which all the spontaneous and uncensored works of Jane Austen's imaginative soul are richly filled' (p. 49).

Owners, buyers, collectors, and bequests feature in the re-collection and re-creation of any letter series. The evidence of 'First Impressions' circulating in manuscript, possibly epistolary, form was present in 11 June 1799 now in Australia and this letter in turn looks back to a first surviving reference in Austen's hand to the manuscript that will become *Pride and Prejudice*. In 8–9 January 1799, the place of the still unrevised novel being performed in the Austens' life is intriguingly juxtaposed with the recycling and disposal of an old petticoat: 'I have long secretly wished it might be done, but had not courage to make the request'. Austen was equally lacking the courage to 'look back into' Cassandra's previous letters for other information about Kent neighbour Maria Montresor, and this seems a percipient if accidental reference to the activity of the family and future researchers looking into epistolary accumulation since.

Mary Augusta had, of course, absorbed the family myth without recognising the resulting dichotomy. A century on, the novels must still appear to be unlaboured despite all the evidence that Austen herself was a rigorous censor of her own work. The surviving letters are deemed 'entirely unworthy specimens of her correspondence in general' (Austen-Leigh 1922, p. 49) and yet a domestic life should produce only familiar letters. Mary Augusta hinted that the letters were no longer spontaneous and that their contents had been censored, and yet any suggestion that the letters were being written with a view to publication would have exposed Austen to the accusations aimed at Burney. For Cassandra, however, the letters were not an 'unvalued remainder' but a highly valued reminder, and through Cassandra the letters become life evidence preserved by an editorial figure with a purpose.

3

Cassandra and Correspondence

One of Lord Brabourne's more perceptive statements in his edition of *Letters* was his description of Cassandra as 'the other self of Jane' (1884b, p. 331). He was drawing on a letter to Fanny in which Cassandra wrote in July 1817 'it is as if I had lost a part of myself' (Le Faye 2011, p. 360). As an alternate self, Cassandra also lives on as 'Tnua Ardnassac' in the backwards letter to Cassy Esten (8 January 1817). Cassandra emerges as an alternate aunt played off as domestic and authorial critic. She is recognisably interleaved with Austen in the letters and aligned with her as one of 'we the formidables' (3 November 1813). Letters will also reveal that Austen has not always been completely honest. Although Cassandra tells her niece in the 20 July 1817 letter, 'I had not a thought concealed from her', Fanny knows, as Brabourne will in 1884, that this is not strictly reciprocal. The discussion of Fanny's suitor Mr Plumptre was kept from Cassandra with notes circulating in parcels of music to keep the secret (18–20 November 1814). After Austen's death, mourning letters recorded both the creation of portable memorial objects and the fulfilment of sisterly obligation. On 29 July 1817 Cassandra requests Fanny's preference for Austen's hair in a brooch or ring and maintains, 'You can need no assurance, my dearest Fanny, that every request of your beloved aunt will be sacred with me' (Le Faye 2011, p. 364). How then to interpret 24–26 December 1798 in which Cassandra as a memorialist would read again Austen's injunction to 'Seize upon the Scissors'?

Cassandra of the letters is Austen backwards, mirrored, cloned, and mingled. It is perhaps fitting that family records hold only two images of her, both silhouettes (Figure 3.1). In any biography of her sister, Cassandra as archivist and correspondent becomes an absent presence. This chapter addresses Austen's letters as 'a joint endeavour in which meaning is the product of collaboration' (Bossis 1986, p. 68). The sisters' skills are also made adjacent when juxtaposed in 'The History of England' giving a glimpse of sisterly projects and the future economies and contrivance of their own controllable world of dress and housekeeping. Despite the

The Life of the Author: Jane Austen, First Edition. Catherine Delafield.
© 2023 John Wiley & Sons Ltd. Published 2023 by John Wiley & Sons Ltd.

Figure 3.1   Silhouette of a young Cassandra Austen c. 1809 by John Meiers. Private Collection.

Annes, Janes, and Fannys in Austen's novels no one is named Cassandra (except the 'beautifull' in the Juvenilia) but she is both everywhere and nowhere in the letters. On 30 January 1809, addressing Martha Lloyd's plans for being in town with her friend Mrs Dundas, Austen comments 'I need not dilate on the subject' which is a statement true of much of their correspondence. Cassandra knew; and in reading like Cassandra we should also consider how Cassandra wrote. The chapter investigates the stance of commentators on Cassandra and rereads letters for their shared and covert meaning. It considers the roles of Hester Lynch Piozzi and Thomas Gisborne in the coding of the letters and the role of sisters in the novels before assessing Cassandra's role as family scribe. The final section uses some of Cassandra's own words to construct her further life and to consider the influence of Austen on her elder sister's letters.

For newly licensed readers wanting to hear Austen's voice, the Austen of the letters has been hidden in plain sight by Cassandra. The letters should be read, however, with a clear perception of their audience and their point of composition. Not only were the letters extremely localised at Godmersham, in London, and at Chawton, but 60% (by number) of the letters were addressed to Cassandra in a location removed from Austen's. Cassandra's retention and valuation of the letters as objects is on a parallel with her preservation of more portable memorial artefacts such as the two mourning rings she later bequeathed to their niece Cassy: one set with the hair of Austen and the other with that of their two sisters-in-law Fanny Palmer and Mary Gibson. These were worn daily (*C*, p. 664). The letters were also created to make the absent present but were daily and accumulating reminders of Austen's life as it was lived.

The rings were ongoing reminders of death but Austen was very much alive when she wished her elder sister a happy twenty-third birthday in the first extant letter dated 1796. After this Cassandra collaborated, received, repatriated, stored, and lived with the letters for more than 40 years up to the time of her own death in March 1845. The path to their survival marks the preserved letters as reminders of an anniversary, birthday or Christmas, recalling a special message or particular sequence of absence. It is essential to consider where Cassandra was and why she kept at the time and then preserved for future reading the letters in her care. Cassandra is recipient and reader, re-reader, guardian, curator, and collector, and this chapter of the life of the author addresses the (un)written letters and (un)written lives of Austen's first editor and family memorialist.

It is notable that many of the titles and roles applied to Cassandra, and the accusations levelled at her by subsequent commentators, relate specifically to her absence as a correspondent. She is a shadowy 'participant in a dialogue who never replies' (Rees 1976, p. 124), a 'veiled' (Jenkins 1938, p. 154) or 'subsuming presence' (Shields 2001, p. 5) and a 'darkling seen shape' seeking divine justice (Tomalin 1997, p. 197). In the *Memoir*, Austen-Leigh embellished the response of actual visitors to Chawton Cottage after Austen's death, claiming that 'the chief light was quenched and the loss of it had cast a shade over the spirits of the survivors' (1871, p. 87). Reviewing the *Memoir* Anne Thackeray Ritchie identified Cassandra as 'more critical, more beautiful, more reserved' (1871, p. 168), wanting her to be some amalgam of Jane and Elizabeth Bennet. For Carol Shields, Cassandra has played a part in creating the 'intractable silences' that 'throw long shadows on [Austen's] apparent chattiness' (Shields 2001, p. 5) and Mary Poovey blames Cassandra for creating 'incompleteness and opacity' by blocking access to Austen's attitudes (Poovey 1984, p. 173). Thus, over time, Cassandra has become that shade to Jane's light. Critics seem to want her to embody, if vaguely, the classical associations of her name adopted through intermarriage with the family of Chandos. As shown in Chapter 1, Cassandra was named after her own mother born Leigh who was named after her great aunt Cassandra Willoughby, second wife to the Duke of Chandos. Cassandra, translated from the Greek, is 'one who excels over men' but the mythical Cassandra was punished by being given the gift of prophecy that would never be believed. With the benefit of Chapman's 1932 edition of the letters, Elizabeth Jenkins describes Cassandra as another mysterious prophetess, a 'sibyl' (1938, p. 154), and Ritchie, of course, included Austen herself in her *Book of Sibyls* (Ritchie 1883).

For Claire Tomalin, Cassandra is condemned as a 'virgin widow' (1997, p. 197) with the suggestion inherent that she indulged this role and eschewed marriage in the future. In Austen's letters there are only two references to Cassandra's unfulfilled engagement although interest from the £1,000 legacy of her fiancé Tom Fowle contributed to the household's income throughout her life. In 1 September 1796 Cassandra is commended as a 'comic writer' and is told that their brother Edward's sister-in-law supposes her to be making her wedding clothes. In 15–16 September 1796 also from Rowling, Austen refers to two local acquaintances: 'I took the opportunity of assuring Mr J[ohn] T[oke] that neither he nor his Father need longer keep themselves single for You'. There is also a surviving letter from Mrs Austen welcoming Mary Lloyd as her daughter-in-law and referring to Cassandra's future in Shropshire as wife to Tom Fowle (30 November 1796; *AP*, p. 228). In addition there are letters preserved from Cassandra's visits to Kintbury to her potential in-laws: two in January 1796 as a fiancée and two in May 1801 as part of a farewell to the area. After the death of Mrs Austen in 1827 and 30 years after Tom's death, Cassandra asks in a letter to cousin Phylly that future letters be addressed to '<u>Mrs</u> C.E. Austen' (p. 277). Although this title was a courtesy extended to her as an older woman, she was at last able to exert herself as a householder. Perhaps after the losses of Tom and of Austen, she had effectively been widowed for a third time.

In her life of Austen as a professional author, Jan Fergus offers an elective form of match between the sisters although this might not signal equality. She reflects Fanny Caroline Lefroy in regarding Austen and Cassandra as 'married in mind' (1991, p. 70), and has more recently described the sisters as a 'community of two' (Fergus 2005b p. 28). They had at least this shared occupation (Spencer 2005, p. 190) but Carol Shields regards Cassandra as 'infantilising' her sister (Shields 2001, p. 116), a more pejorative form of Terry Castle's suggestion that Cassandra was Austen's real mother (Castle 1995, p. 6). The *Life* adopted Brabourne's image of Cassandra as Austen's 'other self' (Austen-Leigh and Austen-Leigh 1913, p. 235) claiming that the sisters never disagreed. The authors, one a godson of Cassandra's, quote a letter from James Austen to James Edward at the time of Austen's death when there is the least hope of restoration: 'Your Grandmama has suffered much but her affliction can be nothing to Cassandra' (p. 392). Park Honan conversely concludes that Austen 'used and flattered [Cassandra], learned from her and pried into her mind and nearly monopolized her heart' (1987, p. 402). He reads this from the 20 July 1817 letter to Fanny first published by Brabourne where Cassandra suggests 'my affection for her made me sometimes unjust to & negligent of others' (Le Faye 2011, p. 360). This is, however, a letter written at a particularly emotional moment to a very specific correspondent. Cassandra has a duty not to be 'over-powered' and so to provide Fanny with the gift of this letter. Noting the allusions to their mother's health, Carol Houlihan Flynn observes rather that 'Cassandra presides over the letter as its most adroit reader, providing the hidden knowledge that is not allowed into the text' (1997, p. 108). This is in itself a healthier reading although it may not have helped the early interpreters whose word was allowed to rule the marketplace for Austen's life and so rob Cassandra of her significance as a correspondent. They wanted to remember her as a censor and destroyer, the dark avenging side of the classical figure.

Modern editor Deirdre Le Faye believes that Cassandra's 'censorship was car-ried out in the cause of diplomacy' to make the letters 'non-controversial' (2004, p. 270) although there is some evidence that the association with Frances Burney could have motivated her editing in 1843 (Delafield 2020, pp. 116–120). The revised *Family Record* suggests, for instance, that criticism of brother James in particular was censored by Cassandra (Le Faye 2004, p. 160) but 8–9 February 1807 nonetheless survives in which James's 'Chat seems all forced', 'his Opinions . . . copied from his Wife's' and his time spent banging doors or ringing for a glass of water. Regarding Burney's 'epistolary voice', Julia Epstein reads like Cassandra the 'split narrative persona, at once self-effacing and self-congratulatory' (1986, p. 164). Cassandra understood but Lord Brabourne wanted to impose the patriarchal habit of exposed personality within letters. The *Life* continued this male reading by using the term 'freemasonry' (Austen-Leigh and Austen-Leigh 1913, p. 82) to categorise lost meaning without trying to understand the sisters' code of fashion and movables. Tomalin may suggest that Austen 'struggled to concern herself with fashion and dress design' (1997, p. 112) but discussions on dress and the associated contriving of resources was surely code for their inability to afford what was even needful for polite society; shared economy, was behind the discussion rather than indifference. More recently it has been suggested that fashion acts as a part of language and closeness (Tavela 2017).

For Chapman, however, Cassandra 'was not an evocative correspondent' (1948, p. 215). He wants to blame her not just for letter destruction but for her influence over the content of the letters in real time. Some letters from Cassandra herself survive in archives and family publications as discussed below but for the time period of Austen's life we have to read Cassandra as an alternate within her sis-ter's letters. Even single letters should be reread for the intensity of their messag-ing and the meaning to be derived from the content and appearance of Austen's composition. Shared meaning between the sisters was also enhanced by the sharing of epistolary space with other correspondents both real and imagined.

Over Christmas 1798, 24–26 December is a well-populated example of all things epistolary with news of Frank's commission, reflections on family illnesses, and discussion of the economies of fashion. Confirmation of the anticipated naval promotion should be quicker through the military post than for civilian letters. There has been a 'thin' but not 'unpleasant' ball at which Austen's black cap has been admired. Their quarterly allowance of five guineas is due and so Austen thinks that Cassandra at Godmersham should be uniting with her sister in considering a new gown. Austen meanwhile threatens to turn her own 'coarse spot' into a petticoat. Mrs Austen's health and supposed illnesses are run into the fashion discussion:

> My Mother's spirits are not affected by her complication of disorders; on the contrary they are altogether as good as ever; nor are you to suppose these maladies are often thought of. – She has at times a tendency towards another which always releives her, & that is, a gouty swelling & sensation about the ancles. – I cannot determine what to do about my new Gown; I wish such things were to be bought ready made.

Mrs Austen enjoys her 'disorders' and Cassandra is invited to 'suppose' they are a frequent topic of conversation for a woman who will survive for another 30 years. Austen tries to write 'as closely as possible' to repay her sister's efforts in a letter received on the second day of the three-day composition period, apparently Christmas Day. News of Martha Lloyd and of the various people who are to dine at the rectory is passed on. Messages about a hen house are sent to Edward 'for I know no one more deserving of happiness without alloy' although this is written in the context of hypochondriac tendencies equal to his mother's that Cassandra might have had to suppress on reading in the Godmersham family. During this absence the sisters have been apart for Austen's birthday and will also be for Cassandra's. The letter is extraordinarily densely written but Austen still concludes, before stuffing in a weather update below the address panel, 'You deserve a longer letter than this; but it is my unhappy fate seldom to treat people so well as they deserve'. There is complex attention to the fate of the brothers, both pride and self-belittling over Frank's commission and an edge of resentment about Edward's illness in entitlement. Even though her exhortation here to 'Seize upon the Scissors' seems to refer to a potential news clipping about Frank's promotion, it could be read as a request to edit that Cassandra carried out for the rest of her life.

Cassandra's long absences create this palimpsest of information and opinions but while fulfilling her epistolary duty Austen is often wishing for her sister to return and make herself present. In 25 January 1801 Austen threatens to withhold letters because of the extended period of their separation: 'Neither my affection for you nor for letter-writing can stand out against a Kentish visit. For a three months' absence I can be a very loving relation and a very excellent correspondent, but beyond that I degenerate into negligence and indifference'. Cassandra has been away since at least 25 October 1800 and has missed the announcement of the Bath removal plan. This is the last extant letter from Steventon (25 January) as Austen is at Manydown by 11 February writing to Cassandra who is in London and finally on her way home. In the later 1808–1809 absence Austen writes, 'Take care of your precious self, do not work too hard, remember that Aunt Cassandras are quite as scarce as Miss Beverleys' (24 January 1809). This was an allusion to the heroine of Burney's *Cecilia* (1782) and a coded reference to Book 5 Chapter 5 of that novel where Mortimer Delvile exclaims: 'How could a thousand Lady Honorias recompense the world for the loss of one Miss Beverley?' (Duncan-Jones 1995). Cassandra has been at Godmersham for over four months helping the family to readjust after the death of Elizabeth Austen and leaving Austen in charge of housekeeping in Southampton including the 'contest' with the splashing 'Storecloset' that flows more freely than ideas for the 'composition' of a letter. This may be another appeal for Cassandra's return but it is driven this time by anticipation of the projected house in Chawton already under discussion.

Occasionally the sisters share their epistolary space with other correspondents as part of family communication and they also use that space to share the experience of reading other texts like *Cecilia*. This sharing impacts both the future survival of a letter and the complexity of meaning within the text. In 19 June 1799, Austen alerts Cassandra to the inclusion of 'letters' from Edward's children Fanny and Edward, aged six and five respectively. Their dictated insertions are shakily signed by them in capitals on the fourth leaf, leaving Austen to announce the all-important details of her return journey at right angles under the address panel. The inclusion of these infant communications must have directed Cassandra to the preservation and onward transmission of this letter to the adult Fanny. The letters from Austen's 1813 visit to Godmersham fulfil the commissions and duties of travel. *En route* to Kent, 15–16 September 1813 is dated '½ past 8' the morning after Austen's arrival in London and paints a picture of the letter-writing process in shared space. No time will be wasted after their journey with Austen writing promptly to convey the news that 'Weather & roads excellent' and 'Martha's Letter is gone to the Post'. From Henry's diminished quarters over the bank in Henrietta Street, 'Here I am, my dearest Cassandra, seated in the Breakfast room, Dining, sitting room, beginning with all my might'. Austen promises 'nothing but short Sentences. There shall be two full stops in every Line' with Edward in the scene of sociable communal writing 'seated by me beginning a Letter, which looks natural'. Henry's new home in Henrietta Street is 'like Sloane Street moved here' and Henry too, despite his widowerhood, is unchanged in owning Austen's authorship against her wishes. Austen seems slightly pleased that, after a trip to Matlock, Henry is 'paying a little for past pleasure' and in 16 September his stomach 'is rather deranged'. Despite all the shopping, this is a more textually relaxed letter, written 'after dinner' for sending 'By favour' of Mr Grey. The next letter of the trip sent from Godmersham (23–24 September) is much more closely written because paid for and crossed with an almost decorative hanging postscript on page 2. Austen also attempts to manage the flow of information on her visit. In 11 October 1813 she has planned a full journal letter counting up her lines and running onto four sides but she begins: 'You will have Edward's letter tomorrow. He tells me that he did not send you any news to interfere with mine, but I do not think there is much for anybody to send at present'.

This same letter is 'interrupted' by Fanny who adds her lines in at the salutation but other more shadowy collaborators in life and in literature shed further light on the sisters' life and understanding of each other. Austen's 9 December 1808 responds to Cassandra's 'joint & agreable composition' with Mr Deedes, Edward's brother-in-law who has 'great merit as a Writer'. This letter goes on to incorporate a further correspondent whose published letters commend not only the openness of the letter as a familiar communication but also the compactness represented by the text, its organisation, and contents. For Austen and Cassandra, the open and known editor Hester Lynch Piozzi becomes part of a closed system of meaning.

The sisters have been corresponding on the subject of the Chawton house offered by Edward. The 9 December letter 'opens' with an upside-down pre-script postscript between the address and the opening line. This is a closely written document composed on one day and Austen asks Cassandra at Godmersham to 'Distribute the affec^te Love of a Heart not so tired as the right hand belonging to it'. Co-writer William Deedes, husband of Elizabeth Austen's sister Sophia is eventual father to 19 children and in 1808 already has 13 of them. Austen will later comment on his sleeping arrangements to Fanny (20–21 February 1817) but in 1808 gives an assessment of his letter writing:

> he does ample justice to his subject, & without being diffuse, is clear & correct – & tho' I do not mean to compare his Epistolary powers with yours, or to give him the same portion of my Gratitude, he certainly has a very pleasing way of winding up a whole, & speeding Truth into the World.

Deedes has been drawn into the letter-writing coterie but at the same time there is a subtle reflection on 'speeding' children into the world. This is continued with a reference to another favoured correspondent, Piozzi, who shares the letters in a different way.

Piozzi acts as a connection with Samuel Johnson, that important source of eighteenth-century letter-writing manuals whose 'Notions' rather than facts are utilised in Austen's 8–9 February 1807. In her preface to *Letters to and from the Late Samuel Johnson* Piozzi has defined the value of the familiar letter where 'none but domestic and familiar events can be expected' in 'private correspondence' (1788, p. ii), thereby removing the disappointment felt by those reading it with different eyes. In her *Letters*, Piozzi allowed herself to be part of Johnson's correspondence in a way that Cassandra now is not. She provided the Austen sisters with the ground rules of their exchanges in her appraisal of 'familiar chat spread upon paper for the advantage or entertainment of a distant friend' (p. iv). In 11 June 1799 from Bath Austen had written: 'So much for Mrs Piozzi. – I had some thoughts of writing the whole of my letter in her stile, but I beleive I shall not' moving quickly on to the discussion of Cassandra's hair-dressing 'Sprig'. In 9 December 1808, Austen quotes almost exactly from 'my dear Mrs Piozzi' on 'flight & fancy & nonsense', comparing her brewer husband Mr Thrale's casks with the Austens' spruce beer. In her edition, Piozzi reasoned that a journey abroad was impossible: 'Well! now all this is nonsense, and fancy, and flight, you know for my master has his great casks to mind, and I have my little children' (1788, p. 270). This suggests a well-known shared even masonic understanding of the allusion interwoven with the usual concern about homemade beverages. Cassandra has Edward's 'little children' to care for and cannot be spared but it is William Deedes who speeds more children into the world while Austen is confined with the spruce beer in Southampton.

Another published work recommended by Cassandra was part of the shared code. Thomas Gisborne's *An Enquiry into the Duties of the Female Sex* (1797) provided a commentary on women's lives that also fed into the novels and in 30 August 1805 Austen is reading the book on her sister's recommendation. The reluctant Austen was doing so at Goodnestone when the sisters alternated between there and Godmersham after their father's death and before an autumn stay in Worthing where Fanny notes waiting for Cassandra to come out of the warm baths on 20 September (*C*, p. 319). In 1805 the homeless unmarried Austen would have read at Cassandra's urging that Gisborne regarded women as being 'bound together by a looser texture' and 'cast in a smaller mould' but enabled, by God, to 'fascinate' (1797, p. 20). Men are geared for political economy, government, and defence, and women for refreshment, delight, benevolence, and sympathy (p. 21), gearing up in fact to be Victorian Angels in the House. Austen, already author of 'First Impressions', would have been relieved to find that it was now 'universally acknowledged, that the intellectual powers of women are not restricted to the arts of the housekeeper and sempstress' (p. 19). The discussion between Miss Bingley and Mr Darcy in the later incarnation of her rejected novel (*P&P*, p. 43) treats ironically Gisborne's acceptance that 'Genius, taste and learning itself have appeared in the number of female endowments and accomplishments' (1797, p. 19). For him, however, learning is a leisure activity to encourage women's 'placid cheerfulness' (p. 80). 'Conscientious vigilance to avoid an improper choice of amusements' is 'a duty of great importance' for 'time spent amiss can never be recalled' (p. 140). Like Fanny Price after him, Gisborne actively discourages private theatricals as 'injurious to female performers' (p. 174), tending to 'exalt attainments better not possessed' and introducing 'unrestrained familiarity' (p. 175). He also passes judgement on women as letter writers and so incidentally emphasises the dichotomy of letters as life writing for authors: 'Those letters only are good, which contain the natural effusions of the heart, expressed in unaffected language. Tinsel and glitter, and laboured phrases, dismiss the friend and introduce the authoress' (p. 112). Austen was surely amused to find that letters must tread a narrow path between glitter and inanity. Gisborne claims that 'women of improved understanding' should avoid 'vanity' by writing 'with simplicity and employ[ing] their pens in a more rational way than retailing the shapes of head-dresses and gowns' (p. 113). In her 18–20 April 1811 letter the newly published 'authoress' will be gleefully occupied shopping in Covent Garden and New Bond Street. In her letters, when Austen offers to write short sentences (15–16 September 1813) they are often her most compact in terms of meaning.

Gisborne's reasoning on the life of spinsters would have been read by the sisters with special force. Unsurprisingly, marriage is for Gisborne a 'state of subordination' (1797, p. 223) for women but at the same time unmarried women 'are persons cut off from a state of life usually regarded as most desirable' (p. 408); 'certain peculiarities of deportment, certain faults of disposition are proverbially frequent in women who have long remained single' (p. 409). When reading the *Enquiry* in 1805, Austen was 29 and so entering 'the years of danger' identified by Elizabeth Elliot in the first chapter of *Persuasion* (p. 38); Cassandra was already 32. Gisborne, however, offers the sisters a life-line when he decrees that women can remain single in three specific circumstances: if their chosen lover dies, if they only receive offers from objectionable men or if they are caring for a parent (1797, pp. 408–409). The Austen sisters qualify to be spinsters on all three counts. Tom Fowle died in 1797 and Mary Lloyd Austen witnessed in 1840 that Cassandra wore mourning as if she were his widow (*C*, p. 660). Mary was also witness to Austen's withdrawal in December 1802 from her engagement to the unsuitable Harris Bigg-Wither when the sisters returned from Manydown and demanded that James take them back to Bath (Austen-Leigh and Austen-Leigh 1913, pp. 92–93). The sisters subsequently joined forces with Martha Lloyd to help with the care of Mrs Austen to whom they were jointly devoted for 23 years.

This endorsement of their spinsterhood would, however, be tempered by Gisborne's astute observation on dependence as an alternative to marriage. He observes that unmarried women are 'compelled by a scanty income to depend on the protection, and bear the humours, of supercilious relations' (1797, p. 410). The Austen sisters were reliant both on their brothers' 'protection' and on the whims and 'humours' of Mrs Leigh-Perrot. As a product of family, the small world in which both this text and its readers circulated is highlighted by the relationship between Gisborne and Austen's sermon-publishing cousin Edward Cooper, writer of those 'Letters of cruel comfort' (15–16 October 1808). In 1802 Gisborne acted as godfather to Cooper's third son Henry and as a result Henry Cooper was curate, after Gisborne (1758–1846) and his son James (1792–1872), at Barton under Needwood in Staffordshire from 1838 to his death in 1876. In the 1871 census, widower Henry Gisborne Cooper is living with his elder and unmarried sisters Cassandra and Jane under his 'protection' in the Barton vicarage.

The pattern of Austen's correspondence is indicative of Cassandra's life and this can be read also in terms of gaps and silences. The 1797 gap in the letters is believed to be related to the death of Cassandra's fiancé, and there is then a gap of 16 months between 19 June 1799 and 25 October 1800. In the period after the Bath move there is only one letter to Cassandra between 27 May 1801 and 8 April 1805. It may mean that the sisters were together through these four years other than for the extra stay in Lyme in September 1804 but this does beg the question of why Cassandra was not required at Godmersham as usual for the births of Edward's children: Marianne (born 15 September 1801), Charles (born 11 March 1803), and Louisa, Austen's goddaughter (born 13 November 1804). Letters from this period could have been difficult to preserve when life was more transient before the move to Southampton. There is another 16-month gap between 30 August 1805 and 7 January 1807 when the Austen women would have been finalising their arrangements in the wake of George Austen's death with the likelihood that travel plans were on hold until finances were understood. In 7–9 January 1807 Austen is urged to pass on a message from their mother in order to be 'explicit' about her wealth which has increased by £30 in a year and puts her in a 'comfortable state' once she has written an undefined response to Mrs Leigh-Perrot. The gaps can be filled to an extent by the letters of their brothers discussed below. The later gaps (26 July 1809 to 18 April 1811 and 6 June 1811 to 24 January 1813), when there are only eight letters in three and a half years, cover the period of publishing two novels and beginning two more. Austen was busy as an author in her life but biographers and critics have been frustrated by her lack of any reflection on the actions of her professional career. Cassandra as conspirator did not need to be told and authorship was otherwise not for discussion in documents to be read aloud, leaving lacunae in the extant letters. These continue to be full of encoded 'important nothings' (15 June 1808) about their brothers' children with only occasional if heartfelt references to the novels as Austen's children and their characters as her friends.

In terms of the preserved correspondence there was a journalising element to Austen's familiar letters designed to keep in touch and to make use of the paper in front of her. The sequencing of the extant letters to Cassandra suggests the pattern of their composition in relation to the sisters' movements. There are letters written from the road such as that from Cork Street (23 August 1796) and from Dartford (24 October 1798). When the absences are long, waiting for transport to link up, the letters flow on like conversation with reports updated and dates overlapping across the letters of the two sisters. We can hear Cassandra's letters arriving for comment and expansion as the timing of each letter locates them. Lord Brabourne's habit of eliding the dates made the original collected edition seem even more disconnected and wandering than necessary. There are in fact seven significant longer sequences. In 1796 there are five letters from London and Rowling and in 1798–1799 ten letters to Godmersham. The 1799 Bath visit produced three letters. In 1800–1801 eleven letters to Godmersham include the telltale gap in December after the relocation to Bath was announced. The four letters written in May 1801 after the removal were received while Cassandra herself was on the move between friends. After three early 1807 letters and four June 1808 letters from Godmersham, twelve letters to Godmersham in 1808–1809 cover Cassandra's extended stay stabilising Edward's household after the death of his wife. Nine letters for 1813 were from Austen's last visit to Godmersham after which there are only twelve letters to Cassandra in total. This effectively reverses the overall balance of correspondence over Austen's life since nearly 90% of the letters to Cassandra were written before the publication of *Mansfield Park*. For the majority of the letters Austen was therefore an unpublished author and Cassandra was a participant in manuscript reading and circulation. Reading and discussion took place as a function of Cassandra's presence; the letters are the product of her absence.

The single Austen letters and others from 1817 were souvenirs and last or end-of-life letters. It is not Cassandra who preserved the reference to longer petticoats (28 or 29 May 1817) or the request for an orange wine 'Receipt' (24 January 1817) because she was actually there with Austen. The last letter Cassandra received was a veiled plea for her return from Cheltenham (8–9 September 1816). The modern edition of the letters includes Austen's will as if it were a letter to Cassandra but this is more appropriately an outward facing document giving Cassandra executive power over other letters. The will punctures this very last 10-month gap, however, until Cassandra's own letters preserved by Fanny provide her heartfelt account of Austen's death.

The women's wealth recalled in the will is a particular backdrop to the letters that does not need to be made explicit to Cassandra although the accounting process can be uncovered from scraps as discussed in Chapter 7. The role of income and its impact on their living and spending forms an interesting overlap between the letters and novels courtesy of the evidence from family letters that partially fill the gap of 1805–1807. Henry Austen writes to Frank in Portsmouth on 27 January 1805 about the death of their father George: 'I prefer silence to imperfect praise' (*AP*, p. 233). He dubs the women left on a reduced income 'our dear trio' who can be trusted to accept God's will in their 'long habitual resignation to the decrees of Heaven' (p. 233). Henry also refers in this letter to his own 'precarious income' and so concludes that furnished lodgings are for the best. By 28 January 1805 James has offered £50 a year to the household and Frank has been persuaded to reduce to £50 his 'noble offer' of £100. Charles's letter offering an imprudent contribution to match is to be burned. Henry is exuberant about the resulting income of £450 a year: 'With the fondest exultation of maternal tenderness the Excellent Parent has exclaimed that never were Children so good as hers' (p. 234). Mrs Austen and Cassandra have income of £210 but Austen alone is unable to contribute. There is, however, a suggestion that the wealthiest of the brothers has been slower in coming forward: 'If Edward does the least he ought, he will certainly insist on her receiving £100 from him' (p. 234). Henry tells Frank that his mother

> will be very comfortable, & as a smaller establishment will be as agreeable to them, as it cannot but be feasible, I really think that My Mother & sisters will be the full as rich as ever. They will not only suffer no personal deprivation, but will be able to pay occasional visits of health and pleasure to their friends.
>
> *(p. 235)*

Although the impression created by this portion of preserved correspondence may be misleading, Henry and his brothers could perhaps have found themselves immortalised in a similar financial discussion that takes place between Fanny and John Dashwood in the opening chapters of *Sense and Sensibility*. In Chapter 2 of Austen's first published novel Fanny Dashwood reasons with her husband:

> Altogether, they will have five hundred a-year amongst them, and what on earth can four women want for more than that? – They will live so cheap! Their housekeeping will be nothing at all. They will have no carriage, no horses, and hardly any servants; they will keep no company, and can have no expences of any kind! Only conceive how comfortable they will be!
>
> *(S&S, p. 14)*

Here in print is the Austen women's £450 a year, 'smaller establishment' and 'comfortable' life of dependence on Gisborne's 'scanty income'. In this novel there is also a dissection of the differences between 'wealth' and 'competence' (*S&S*, pp. 105–106) and discussions of the relative value of livings (p. 320; p. 418). James Austen holds seven livings (Le Faye 2011, p. 486) and in 1805 it is only four years since he has hurried the 'trio' out of Steventon Rectory. He writes to Frank a few days after Henry on 30 January 1805 that Mrs Austen is 'always composed and at times cheerful' and will spend her summers in the country and her winters in 'comfortable Lodgings in Bath' (*AP*, p. 236). This dependence has future consequences because Henry's bankruptcy in 1816 and James's death in 1819 will reduce the trio's income still more in the future although they include Martha Lloyd in the household and live rent-free at Chawton from July 1809. Before this, however, the women who have already been reduced to the dampness of Green Park Buildings in 1805 will find themselves in despised Trim Street (3–5 January 1801) by April 1806.

Prompted by these resemblances, it is inevitable that we want to read sisters in the novels for sisters in life. When Austen's fictional sisters are together they are differentiated in ways that are tantalising for the reader of Austen's actual letters. In *Pride and Prejudice*, Elizabeth rereads her sister Jane's letters at Hunsford identifying 'a want of . . . cheerfulness' and an 'uneasiness' unnoticed on 'first perusal' (p. 210). Letters are kept to be reread and reinterpreted. In her own letters, Austen tires of social niceties and can be critical of her brother's family. In *Sense and Sensibility*, Marianne refuses to compliment Lady Middleton to the Steele sisters and 'was silent; it was impossible for her to say what she did not feel, however, trivial the occasion; and upon Elinor therefore the whole task of telling lies when politeness required it always fell' (p. 141). Just when we think that we can recognise the Austen sisters here, Elinor seems to speak as Austen might when she tells Lucy Steele, 'I confess that while I am at Barton Park, I never think of tame and quiet children with any abhorrence' (p. 141). Elinor must once more adopt the 'post of civility' (p. 182) on the journey to London and only later does Marianne consent to 'practise the civilities, the lesser duties of life, with gentleness and forbearance' (p. 393). In taking her farewell of Mr Collins in *Pride and Prejudice*, Elizabeth vies with Elinor in trying to 'unite civility and truth in a few short sentences' (p. 239).

The roles and duties of women are under scrutiny even though the sisters in life cannot apparently escape them. In *Sense and Sensibility*, Anne Steele studies Marianne's appearance and is 'not without hopes of finding out before they parted, how much her washing cost per week, and how much she had every year to spend upon herself' (p. 282), seeming to position the topics circulating between Austen and Cassandra as comic relief despite their daily seriousness. The Steeles and Dashwoods, Bennets and Bingleys and later the Wards and Bertrams, Elliots and Musgroves are part of the exploration of sisterhood originally stifled in Austen's unfinished novel *The Watsons* that remained in manuscript and in Cassandra's possession until she left it to spinster niece Caroline. Elizabeth Watson tells her sister Emma that she could happily remain single with 'a little company, and a pleasant ball now and then . . . but my father cannot provide for us, and it is very bad to grow old and be poor and laughed at' (*LM*, p. 82). Austen and Cassandra's real lives illustrate her argument, and Austen knew this without Gisborne's revelation of dependence on 'supercilious relations' because *The Watsons* was already abandoned by the end of 1804 (Le Faye 2004, p. 144).

Cassandra is to be found as patron and family scribe in other forms within Austen's earlier work and in her letters. In 11–12 October 1813, Austen revisits the 'Heroine' as a concept dissected in *Northanger Abbey* when she admires 'the Sagacity & Taste of Charlotte Williams' who has 'large dark eyes' that 'always judge well'. Cassandra would have been reminded of a much earlier manuscript work in which Cassandra was herself complimented as the subject and 'Heroine' of one of the Juvenilia. Austen proposes to 'compliment' Charlotte her, by naming a Heroine after her'. The heroine of the fragment later called *Sanditon* will be named Charlotte Heywood making this a compliment postponed to the year of Austen's death beyond *Emma* and *Persuasion* with Emma perhaps too flawed and Anne Elliot too perfect to be named after real women.

In Volume the First of Austen's Juvenilia 'The beautifull Cassandra . . . dedicated by permission to Miss Austen' was 'a novel in twelve Chapters' and only fifteen sentences. This piece was plainly mocking the volume of words in the novels the sisters shared and making extravagant claims for the girls' ability to act outside social norms. The fictional Cassandra, daughter of a milliner, steals a bonnet commissioned by a countess and fails to pay for six ices. It is unclear why Cassandra is described as a 'Phoenix' (*J*, p. 53) in the dedication although the allusion adds to the mystery of her classical associations. She had perhaps recovered from an illness or from a romantic disappointment. The full dedication reads like a letter equally exaggerated in tone, praising patron Cassandra for her refined taste, noble sentiments, innumerable virtues, and majestic form. The polish of her manners and rationality of her conversation add to her perfections reflecting their negative opposites described in *Pride and Prejudice*. After their meeting at Pemberley in the novel, Miss Bingley can find only Elizabeth Bennet's teeth 'tolerable' in her angry list of the failings in her rival's appearance (p. 299). 'The beautifull Cassandra' may also be aimed at the Hancocks, aunt and cousin to the Austen sisters. George Austen's sister Philadelphia was apprenticed to be a milliner before taking her chance on the Indian marriage market and elements of that experience will later feature in the unfinished 'Catharine; or the Bower', originally written by 1793 and also dedicated to Cassandra. Philadelphia's daughter, cousin Eliza had expected to become a countess in 1781 in return for her dowry. The Comte de Feuillide's title was a dubious one (Le Faye 2002, p. 51) but he was nonetheless guillotined in February 1794 (p. 121).

Cassandra was thus both a heroine and patron of juvenile works. For 'The History of England' completed by early 1793, the sisters were direct and visible collaborators. 'The History' predates the first surviving letter (9–10 January 1796) and Christine Alexander suggests the piece was 'a covert representation of the Austen family scene' (2014, p. xxvii) demonstrating their 'close creative bond' (p. xxiv). As a joint enterprise it represents also the letters as we now come to read them: creatively bonded. The medallion portraits of 'The History' resemble not just Austen family members but the insertion of Cassandra herself into the plot of Austen's correspondence. In the letters, the sisters share a separate but similar outlook on characters in a shorthand representation of their social world. This is an approach learned through the practice of 'The History' and in life they will jointly read the appearance of their letters and of the processes that create them. In Cassandra's solo performance in her 20 July 1817 letter to Fanny, of course, Austen is elevated beyond a mere painter to become 'the gilder of every pleasure' (Le Faye 2011, p. 360).

Cassandra's contribution as an illustrator is elided with her role as family scribe. She has been described as a scribe for 'general domestic news' (Le Faye 1986a, p. 6) and there is evidence from letters around the death of Elizabeth Austen that letter writing was allocated around family members. Austen's letter to Philadelphia Walter on the death of her father in 1798, for instance, suggests that Cassandra should have been the one writing, and it may be that this was the elder sister's duty or that Cassandra was designated as communicator with this arm of the family. The elision of painter and scribe is demonstrated in a poem from the letter gap of 1809–1811.The Austen women moved to Chawton Cottage on 7 July 1809 and Austen's 26 July 1809 poem at the birth of Frank's son Francis William suggests that Cassandra was responsible for writing this news. Writing from Chawton to China, Austen laughs at her 'affected' poem: 'As for ourselves, we're very well; / As unaffected prose will tell. – / Cassandra's pen will paint our state, / The many comforts that await/ Our Chawton home, how much we find/ Already in it, to our mind'. This allusion to Cassandra's painting skills is an improvement from Austen's original draft of the poem left to Charles by Cassandra where the line reads 'Cassandra's pen will *give* our state' (my italics). In real time Charles and his wife are expected at Chawton Manor in the last few lines and Cassandra's painterly and archiving skills have kept both versions of the poem in play for the record. After this 1809 poetic notice of Austen's life in which Cassandra is appointed observer and housekeeper, there is a long but creative gap. The poem represents the only written document extant between Austen's 1809 letter to Crosby demanding the publication of 'Susan' and her 1811 visit to Sloane Street to proofread *Sense and Sensibility* (18–20, 25, 30 April London to Godmersham). It is also assumed that this is the period when Cassandra drew her sketch of Austen now in the National Portrait Gallery, seeing, creating, and preserving another chain of correspondence between the medallions of 'The History of England' and the author of *Pride and Prejudice*.

Two letters written by Cassandra as family scribe in 1811 and 1812 survive from Austen's life time. There is no record of any commiseration to their cousin on the death of Mrs Walter in March 1811 at the age of 95 but Cassandra wrote to Philadelphia Walter on 18 August 1811 to congratulate her on her marriage. In the same period, records in Fanny Knight's pocketbook suggest that 'Aunt C' wrote twice a week to Godmersham sometimes via Fanny's brothers on their passage to and from school in Winchester (*C*, pp. 408–411). Charles Austen, his wife and daughters have been visiting Chawton Cottage along with Eliza de Feullide. Phylly, at the age of 50, has finally married Dr Whitaker on the death of her mother, and Cassandra 'cannot give you a better wish than that you may be as happy as you deserve and that as a Wife you may meet the reward you so well earned as a Daughter' (*AP*, p. 248). The graver tone is reminiscent of Austen writing to their cousin back in 1798 but its formality is wonderfully debunked by: 'I am determined you shall be happy whether you will or no' (p. 248). This addition hints at sisterly collaboration in the style of letter-writing manuals and of the novel in progress. Letter XX of *The British Letter-Writer* recommends that a 'young lady' should write to a friend: 'Though from your last I had Reason to think you approached the indissoluble Bond, I could not apprehend the Change would have been so sudden . . . However, as I have no Doubt of your Happiness, I sincerely rejoice in the Event' (1760, p. 60). Phylly was one of seven children. She was born when her mother was in her mid-forties and her eldest brother Weaver, who died without issue, was 14. Her sister Sally died suddenly when Phylly was nine and two brothers died in the West Indies, predeceasing their own father as did another boy who died young. Phylly's immediately elder brother James was rector in Market Rasen and fathered 18 children, eight of whom survived to be the subject of future letters. The first reference to Phylly's husband George Whitaker is as 'a Beau' in a letter from Eliza de Feuillide (22 September 1797; Le Faye 2002, p. 148) so he has proved a very faithful suitor when they marry 14 years later. After their 23 years of marriage, he outlives Phylly by a further 12 years.

The evidence of surviving letters is that Cassandra and Phylly were irregular correspondents in the same way as Mrs Austen and Phylly's mother were before them (*AP*, pp. 24–31) but the letters preserved by niece Anna Philadelphia and great-grand-nephew John Charles Nicholson help to fill out the picture of Cassandra's life. There is some sense of her letter-writing style albeit to one specific alternative correspondent. On 20 March 1812 in the second letter Cassandra reflects her own life as conveyor of little news: 'I have been in your debt more than two months for a very kind letter, I have not written before because I have had nothing to communicate and perhaps the same reason ought to keep me silent longer' (p. 250). In Letter IX of *The British Letter-Writer* Miss Seymour writes: 'I am a thousand Years in writing to my dear Miss Drury but my extreme Inconsequence, and the little I can say worthy her Perusal, is an unanswerable Apology' (1760, p. 30). Unable to leave Mrs Austen who is now over 70 Cassandra reports 'little company to increase our cheerfulness' but 'no illness to diminish it and I am old enough to find considerable comfort in the quiet and warmth of a small fireside circle' (*AP*, p. 251). She can add news of 'absent branches of our family' because she keeps memorandums of previous letters, presumably as family scribe, since Mrs Austen now struggles to see and hold a pen and Cassandra sends 'our united love' (p. 253), united also with that of her sister.

In the letter, Cassandra responds to news of potential marriages amongst Philadelphia's nieces and nephews and apparently refers to Edward's children in the context of James Walter: 'Your Brother does seem fortunate in his children, but so it will generally be in a large family where discreet and good Parents live to breed them up' (*AP*, p. 252). Cassandra seems to be concerned that the death of Elizabeth in 1808 has left the Knight children prey to extravagance from 'so indulgent a Father and so liberal a stile of living', leaving them 'unfit' for 'the rubs they must meet' (p. 252). These 11 children are now aged between 4 and 19. Fanny will not marry Sir Edward Knatchbull, father of Lord Brabourne, for another eight years; George is about to join his eldest brother Edward at St John's College Oxford and Charles, future rector of Chawton, is still to follow his elder brothers to school at Winchester College. Other than the unspecified 'love' there is notably no reference to Austen at all in the letter. This was a letterless year apart from 29 November 1812 to Martha announcing the sale of *Pride and Prejudice*, but the revised *Family Record* (Le Faye 2004, p. 190) suggests that Austen was at home. Cassandra respects Austen's wishes and has 'nothing to communicate' in either of her Phylly letters about the progress of *Sense and Sensibility*'s publication or the revision and composition of *Pride and Prejudice* and *Mansfield Park* taking place in the 'small fireside circle'.

No further Phylly correspondence survives for the period up to Mrs Austen's death in 1827. After the commemorative brooch sent to Fanny (Le Faye 2011, p. 364) and a bodkin sent to Anne Sharp both in 1817 (p. 362), other memorial objects and letters are in circulation that help to track Cassandra in her life after Austen's death. According to a letter from Mrs Austen to Mary Lloyd Austen, Edward is on an extended visit to the Manor when he takes Cassandra to Steventon to meet Henry's new wife (*AP*, p. 267). On 11 April 1820 Henry, temporary rector of Steventon until his nephew William is ordained, marries Eleanor Jackson, and Cassandra presents her with Austen's turquoise ring. This ring is now in the Jane Austen's House Museum having been purchased by donations for over £150,000 in 2013. Eleanor returned it to niece Caroline in 1863 and her accompanying note still survives but the ring's heritage value is once again a long way from the Austen sisters' way of life. In 1822 Cassandra surfaces in a postscript to a Mrs Austen letter. She owes Mary Lloyd Austen £1.2.6. that could have been sent through James Edward who has recently visited: 'I really never thought either of the Table Cloths or my debt owing during his short stay' (p. 270). It is possible that Mary, once treasured as a nurse in Austen's last hours, has overstepped her authority in supplying linen that is unsuitable or expensive. From the available evidence, Mrs Austen values her daughter-in-law more than her daughters do and this regard has been augmented by James's death in December 1819. The loss of her eldest son has robbed her, however, of more of the income built up for the original 'trio' in 1805 and in a letter of 4 January 1820 Mrs Austen is grateful for an annuity from her sister-in-law Mrs Leigh-Perrot which in turn enables her to support Mary further (pp. 264–265). In the main letter to Mary of 24 March 1822, Mrs Austen has 'waited in hope I might have something worth writing about' and occupies herself with patchwork and creeping around the garden where she has previously been so active (p. 268). On 24 November 1822 Henry writes to Charles from his new parsonage in Farnham mentioning that Cassandra is looking old (*C*, p. 620) although when Edward dines at the cottage the following 19 April both she and Mrs Austen are well (p. 620). While Mrs Austen creeps around the cottage for the next few years, her grandson Cholmeley, youngest son of Frank, dies on 11 January 1824 aged six months and Charles's son George dies in the summer aged two. On 18 August 1825 Charles's baby daughter Jane also dies and he writes to Cassandra (p. 628). On 13 May 1826, the elopement of Edward Knight II and Mary Dorothea Knatchbull to Gretna Green takes place and a letter from Caroline to Anna (21 May 1826) indicates that Cassandra was then visiting Mrs Leigh-Perrot at Scarlets but left earlier than planned to receive the 'fugitives' (p. 630). They were married again at Steventon by permanent rector William Knight and settled at Chawton Manor.

Cassandra is in her own words again when she writes to Phylly on 14 February 1827 that Mrs Austen has at last been 'removed from a state of severe endurance' (*AP*, p. 274). Cassandra has prayed for her mother's release but cannot resist adding an Austenesque aside that 87 is 'a great age for a person who had been ailing for the greatest part of her life!' (p. 274). Cassandra now plans to be 'less at home' and four weeks after the death is writing from brother Frank's current home in Gosport mentioning also 'brother Henry' and 'brother Knight' (p. 276). There is a marked difference in her view of the children of the brothers. Cassandra apologises for 'blunders' in her letter caused by the scene of composition:

> in which half a dozen nephews and nieces are repeating their different lessons of Geography, Arithmetic &c. and tho' I must approve of the manner in which their Father employs their mornings, I cannot but acknowledge that a school room is not the most favorable field for letter writing, at least not to such a crazy head as mine.
>
> *(p. 276)*

Craziness is an unusual association with Cassandra based on the retrospective comments of her nieces and nephews but 'merciless sister' Austen would have been happy to promote this trait in the 'finest comic writer' with whom she corresponded in 1801 and 1796. Cassandra does not comment on the infant deaths but explains, 'The family circles of my brothers are now too large for me to enter into a particular description of them' (*AP*, p. 276). She tells Phylly she has not been to Godmersham for eight years since 1819 but Edward writes to Mrs Leigh-Perrot that a Kent visit in the summer of 1827 is improving her health (*C*, p. 633) presumably away from responsibility for Mrs Austen. Mrs Leigh-Perrot in turn informs James Edward that Cassandra has been ill in the winter of 1830 (p. 640). In February 1831 Mary Lloyd Austen stays at the cottage and there are visits to and from other family (pp. 642–643) before Cassandra is contacted by John Murray in May about a new edition of her sister's novels (p. 643).

In a letter to Phylly of 20 January 1832, Cassandra confirms her many visits including one to Godmersham between June and November 1831 and a fortnight in November/December 1831 at the new Steventon Rectory (*AP*, p. 284). Edward now has 22 grandchildren and the only events to report are 'a regular addition to their respective nurseries' (p. 284). Henry 'resides on his little piece of preferment between six & seven miles from me & is a very good neighbour' with an 'indefatigable' and excellent wife although he always needs more income (p. 284). Henry was 'preferred' for a new living in April 1824 as Perpetual Curate of Bentley near Farnham. This letter suggests there has been no communication between the cousins since 1828 as is made clear when Cassandra wryly updates Phylly on Frank: 'In the year '28 he married first his eldest daughter and then himself' (p. 285). The loss of his eldest daughter in marriage would perhaps have encouraged Frank in the pragmatic choice of Martha as his second wife, by now 63 years old but competent and convenient as manager of a household of her own. Frank's first wife Mary had died in 1823 and the marriage of 21-year-old Mary Jane would have left only 13-year-old Cassandra Eliza to manage a household with four other children under 10 at home. As a result Chawton Cottage has had 'no constant inmate' (p. 284) widowing Cassandra again although she is visited by brothers, nephews, and nieces. Cassandra is now in her sixtieth year and Philadelphia over 70 so conventional epistolary excuses come into play. Like Lucy Steele reminded by her paper 'to conclude' (*S&S*, p. 315), Cassandra closes, 'I will not tire either your eyes or my own by crossing my writing' (*AP*, p. 285). Unmentioned to Phylly, Cassandra has already replied on 20 May 1831 to Murray about a new edition of Austen's novels (*C*, p. 643) but a sale of copyright by Henry results in a new publisher as witnessed by a further letter from Henry to Richard Bentley in July 1832 (*AP*, p. 286). Henry describes himself as 'joint proprietor' of Austen's work with Cassandra and proposes further 'biographical relics' for the edition. Cassandra remains invisible but Lucy Steele will soon be reissued in Bentley's Standard edition of 1833 where Henry's revised 'Memoir' of Austen – with revised letters – will appear as a preface to *Sense and Sensibility*.

Cassandra's 6 February 1833 is a reply to a letter from Phylly that has followed her to Anglesey, Charles's home near Gosport. She is thankful for her blessings in response to an appeal for sympathy and unencumbered 'with vain wishes for what is unattainable' (*AP*, p. 287). Such sentiments have a formality that should not sit in judgement over Cassandra and her 'crazy head' as there is ample evidence to suggest that she was also wise enough to know her audience. Cassandra reports that she will 'miss the cheerfulness of a large family, but home always ought to have its comforts, & it certainly has for me' (p. 288). She commends her 'amusement from needlework. I am likewise a great worker & have varieties of knitting & worsted work in hand' and the garden (p. 289) inherited from her mother. Edward Knight II, former 'fugitive', is nearby at Chawton Manor with four children and, until 1838, first wife Mary Dorothea Knatchbull. The record of memorandums is no longer enough to keep track of the family: 'My possessions in great-nephews & nieces are so extensive that I have done keeping an exact account of them' (p. 288). In fact they totalled 86 children, 46 of them grandchildren of Edward. Cassandra repeats the news of Henry with his 'very small benefice about six miles from Chawton' where he 'is happy in an excellent wife & moderate wishes' (p. 288). This suggests that her brother's life experience has caused his wishes to be reined in but also has the tone of a rehearsed reply constructed to balance Austen's 'Oh! what a Henry' of 23 June 1814. The 1833 comment respects her audience but in fact it barely sounds like Henry at all.

With Martha, now Lady Austen, in residence, Cassandra probably finds Frank's Portsdown Lodge home even more amenable and she visits in May 1834 (*C*, p. 649). Phylly dies in July that year but a further epistolary trail can be followed in the letters preserved by Anna Lefroy who occupied a series of rented homes during her widowhood. The preserved documents contain family news and summaries of events that must have been factors in their survival even though Anna was part of the conspiracy to avoid understanding Cassandra's own retention of Austen's letters during the lead-in to the *Memoir*. Six letters now in Princeton University Library and others in the Austen-Leigh archive illustrate Cassandra's visiting pattern. The letters provide evidence of the death of Martha Lloyd who was Anna's aunt twice over as her mother's sister and her uncle's wife (5 February 1843; Le Faye 2001, p. 554), the final inheritance of the Leigh-Perrots' home Scarlets (3 April 1838; p. 549) and the lingering death of Fanny's eldest daughter (29 January 1845; p. 560). In February 1835 Cassandra donated £100 to the building of a new church at Chawton at the instigation of her nephew Edward Knight II (Austen-Leigh and Knight 1911, p. 60). A letter from Mrs Leigh-Perrot to James Edward reveals that Cassandra has lost her teeth and does not visit because Mrs Leigh-Perrot would now be too deaf to communicate with her (29 August 1835; *C*, p. 652). When her aunt died on 13 November 1836 at the age of 92, Cassandra was, however, dutifully present at Scarlets. She has already benefited from a £5,000 legacy paid out in 1833 to avoid death duties (p. 647) and will leave the substantial sum of £16,000 in her own will (Clery 2017, p. 320).

By 1 June 1837 Cassandra has once more returned to Chawton from a month in Portsmouth with Frank and Martha, and is staying at the Manor waiting for paint to dry at the cottage. She urges Anna to come for a visit: 'There are so many little matters I should enjoy talking over with you that are not worth writing about' (Le Faye 2001, p. 546). After being in Westham for this letter, 3 April 1838 finds Anna in Basingstoke for a visit from Edward who returns a sovereign Cassandra owes her niece along with the letter. There has been at least one previous letter about the death of Mary Dorothea Knight at Chawton Manor (*C*, p. 657). Cassandra is 'living here so quietly' (Le Faye 2001, p. 549) but plans two months in Kent. She has not gone to Scarlets despite the potential 'novelty' now that Mrs Leigh-Perrot has died and passed her property to James Edward. Cassandra is perhaps revisiting her old style when she tells Anna that 'the most remarkable circumstance which has occurr'd in our annals' is a visit from Sir Edward Knatchbull following the recent death of his daughter: 'He spent one whole Sunday here a fortnight ago, & I need scarcely say that we were not sorry when Monday came' (p. 550). In 1838 Cassandra has been sorting linen at Chawton Rectory for nephew Charles Knight and providing him with a kitten (Hurst 2010, p. 111). She then tends to him when he has gout (p. 112). Once more there is a hint of the Austen tone in 26 August 1842 to Anna when Cassandra reports James Edward's officiating at the wedding of Frank's daughter Catherine: 'Your Brother read the Service most impressively, & I thought every body seemed to feel it – I am sure some did' (Le Faye 2001, p. 552). There is a double meaning here. Anna's half-brother has been suffering with a voice complaint for eight months but Cassandra is also succinctly suggesting that some of those present were not 'feeling' the seriousness of the service and apparently expecting Anna to know who that would be. A letter survives to James Edward's wife Emma in which Cassandra declines to travel to Scarlets to be William Austen-Leigh's godmother in person (*C*, p. 664) but in the *Life* she is reported to have been there with five-year-old Mary Augusta Austen-Leigh the witness to 'a pale dark-eyed old lady with a high arched nose and a kind smile, dressed in a long cloak and a large drawn bonnet, both made of black satin' (Austen-Leigh and Austen-Leigh 1913, p. 402). Charles Knight reports a visit in April 1843 (Hurst 2010, p. 113) but the christening was in July (*C*, p. 664).

There are hints of Cassandra's manuscript priorities in the latest letters. Her 1 February 1844 letter from Mersham Hatch on a week's visit from Godmersham to see Fanny acknowledges the *Foreign and Colonial Review* reference to Austen copied and sent by Anna. In an article reviewing four American novels, the reviewer described Austen as 'the greatest of all female novelists' once more in the familiar company of Burney and Edgeworth. They praised her 'absence of affectation' and 'power of investing the common-place with interest' (American works of fiction 1843, p. 459). Although no reference survives, it seems likely that Anna and Cassandra would also have known about the continuing alliance with Burney from Macaulay's review of Burney's *Diary and Letters* that year. Austen was described as approaching Shakespeare in her characterisation (Macaulay 1843, p. 561). In the letter to Anna, Cassandra proposes, Austen-like, to 'let nature take its course & write first about myself' (Le Faye 2001, p. 556). She describes a visit to Sandgates to see the Deedes although her former co-writer William has been dead for nearly 10 years. In 25 January 1801 Austen proclaimed in an imaginary conversation with cousin Edward Cooper that 'for the present we greatly prefer the sea to all our relations'. In 1844, Cassandra's comment 'I have always pleasure in seeing the Sea' (Le Faye 2001, p. 557) suggests another reason for the retention of the Lyme letter of 1804. These letters rest in the packets Cassandra has already made up, in the wake of Martha's death and perhaps with Burney's *Diary* in mind, to be distributed in accordance with her will, and supplemented by her testamentary letter to Charles.

By 29 January 1845 Cassandra is not feeling 'equal to much in the visiting way' and when she proposes 'taking leave' of Frank who is about to take up a new three-year posting, she is perhaps already thinking they will be together for the last time: 'I must get what enjoyment I can from this business, tho' it may perchance be only imaginary for their going must be attended by real, substantial evils to me!' (Le Faye 2001, p. 560). She has a stroke and dies in Portsmouth on 22 March aged 72. Frank cannot be spared from his new duties so it falls to Henry and then to Charles and Caroline to attend to her. Charles Knight conducts the funeral service at Chawton and in his diary summary for 1845 notes the 'very great loss to us all, & to all in the parish, for whom she had been doing good & living among them almost interruptedly for 35 years' (Hurst 2010, p. 115). He has already bought black-edged envelopes (p. 114) in anticipation but notes himself the other recent 'losses . . . amongst our relations' (p. 115). His brother Henry has died in 1843 and his sister Cassandra Jane in 1842. Eight of the nieces and nephews predeceased Cassandra as well as Elizabeth Austen (1808), Martha and Mary Lloyd (both 1843) and their husband's first wives, Mary (1823) and Anne (1795), Eliza (1813) and Fanny (1814) first wives of Henry and Charles, and brothers James (1819) and George (1838). Brother Henry will die in 1850 and Edward and Charles in 1852; Admiral Frank lives until 1865 surviving his younger sister Jane by nearly half a century.

In 8 January 1799 Austen urges her sister to read her own letters over 'five times in future' to understand how entertaining they are to her as the recipient. The implication is that Austen gains five times the value of Cassandra as a correspondent. Despite their invisibility, Cassandra's letters are valued by her sister as part of the visible collaboration between correspondents and the marks of that value have been preserved. By 23–24 September 1813 from Godmersham Austen is thanking her sister 'five hundred & forty times' for her 'exquisite piece of Workmanship' delivered with the post at breakfast. Other 'very inferior works of art' are not read with the same 'high glee' as those from the painterly scribe. Cassandra's letter is 'rich in striking intelligence' and Austen's commentary creates the mirror-image or aunt-alternate role for Cassandra at the same time as teasing her about the relative importance of their concerns. At Godmersham in September 1813 and in spite of Gisborne's admonitions, headwear is under discussion. Fanny is 'out of conceit' with her new cap while Austen is satisfied with her old one; it is 'one of the sweet taxes of Youth to chuse in a hurry & make Bad bargains' while her aunts continue to contrive. At the same time Austen is also sharing the experience of illness with the Godmersham nursemaid Sackree and tells Cassandra 'I read all the scraps I could of your Letter to her'. Cassandra's letter bridges gaps within their culture and in their relative wealth. James Edward, his father's son, will later observe primly that Chawton Cottage was 'a comfortable and ladylike establishment, though the means which supported it were not large' (Austen-Leigh 1871, p. 81). Austen's own letter is closely written with an artistic postscript in the middle of page 2 and, unusually, crossed on page 1 so that the reference to Chawton's tea and white wine stores themselves become part of the overall economy in paper and postage. She says appropriately for Cassandra's particular understanding: 'my present Elegancies have not yet made me indifferent in such Matters'.

Cassandra may be categorised as a reflected Ardnassac or as a dark sybilline destroyer but the alleged editing of Austen's letters is finally a version of Cassandra's original informed reading. Cassandra has been a well-versed reader of the novels too and Austen even involves her sister as an author in the publication of *Pride and Prejudice* when she comments on the length of the novel's volumes but then praises Cassandra's charades: 'There is so much beauty in the Versification however, that the finding them out is but a secondary pleasure' (29 January 1813). In 2 December 1815 Austen writes from Hans Place about binding *Emma* for the Prince Regent and a 'flounce on your Chintz'. Prompted by Cassandra, Austen seems to be inflecting or adding a flounce to Thomas Gisborne's contempt for the single state when Emma declines marriage outright: 'It is poverty only which makes celibacy contemptible to a generous public . . . a single woman of good fortune is always respectable' (*E*, p. 91). And yet Cassandra Austen should perhaps not be regarded as single since she was eventually able to accrue wealth without marrying; she first had Austen and then Martha before becoming 'Mrs Austen' of Chawton.

With Austen, Cassandra performs 'the dance between absence and presence' (Milne 2010, p. 52) that is correspondence. In the letters Austen imagines Cassandra's journeys and corrects Cassandra's impression of her own journey; she recreates the sites of composition and familiar locations and situations whether at home or on her way. Austen's surviving letters and our readings of them are the result of this collaboration. The existence of the letters from which Cassandra cannot be effaced is a component of the epistolary dichotomy of authorship enjoyed by laughing 'wild beast' Austen in the 'solitary elegance' of Henry's barouche (24 May 1813).The next chapter examines other members of the extended sisterhood of the letters but it is for Cassandra's specific notice that Austen observes in this same letter: 'whatever I may write or you may imagine we know it will be something different'. Austen's letters and life have become a complex collaboration between what has been written by Austen and what can be known if we read and imagine like Cassandra.

4

The Sisterhood of the Letters

This chapter explores ways in which Austen was seeking and finding sisters through her life and through her fiction. Letters allowed women an opportunity to write and letters gave Austen her first taste of her fictional powers in her early manuscript writings. The chapter examines communities of women portrayed in the letters as well as their fictional counterparts. Sisters in the novels are both genetically and communally created as they were in Austen's life. The Dashwoods and Bennets evolve into the Ward sisters who become mothers and aunts in *Mansfield Park*. In *Emma* and *Persuasion*, alternative communities of women are set against family groups, and families are recreated and re-set in all the novels traced across Austen's writing career.

The term 'sisterhood' is borrowed from the novelist and critic Margaret Oliphant. In 1862, eight years before her comments on James Edward's *Memoir* in 'Miss Austen and Miss Mitford' (Oliphant 1870), Oliphant wrote a review entitled 'The Lives of Two Ladies' in which she subjected Lady Llanover's *Autobiography and Correspondence of Mary Granville, Mrs Delany* (1861–1862) to withering scorn. The other 'lady' was Austen's 'dear Mrs Piozzi' and the review also touched on 'sister author' Frances Burney, friend of Delany and target of Llanover's ire in her edition. Oliphant suggested that Llanover was almost guilty of becoming a fictional writer and so joining the 'sisterhood' of 'female authorship' (1862, p. 411). The confluence of women's letters as life writing and of women as authors in this article lends an appropriateness to Oliphant's term coined after the event.

In exploring how communities of women translated into fictional families, the chapter provides evidence of the creation of sisterhoods through interfamilial and geographic relationships cultivated through letters. Letters and their composition are part of the sisterhood itself learned from both manuals and the practice of writing. Letters provide a space in which to nurture the sisterly sharing of news, fashion, and economic contrivance. This is not a space for the discussion of novel composition except when Austen adopts the role of critical aunt; the letters to

Anna in 1814 offer a partial mirror held up both to the novels and to the life. The expansion of the reach of sisters takes place in a number of ways through marriage, extended cousinship, and friendship. Geography and George Austen also had a part to play since Austen's father introduced the Lloyds and the Fowles into his daughters' lives. Austen's life includes examples of new sisterly circles but sometimes little extant evidence so this chapter will focus on a network expanding from the letters. The chapter demonstrates the importance of female counterculture for Austen at the same time as indicating ways in which she was on its periphery as an aunt and as an author.

Austen's now one-sided conversations in letters provide evidence of women's communities created by the relationship with Cassandra explored in Chapter 3. If correspondents 'become co-authors of the narrative' (MacArthur 1990, p. 119), this is because they actually shape the letters dependent on both the relationship between recipients and the material conditions of writing and transmission. The women 'of' the letters include Cassandra, of course, as well as Catherine Knight, Miss Benn, Catherine Prowting, and Lady Morley who have been previously discussed in Chapter 1. Letters from Austen's cousin and sister-in-law Eliza de Feuillide survive but her role as a sister is made doubly shadowy because of an assumed parallel correspondence with Austen and Cassandra evidenced from Eliza's now one-sided correspondence with Phylly Walter. Having explored the Eliza connection, this present chapter considers the letter sisterhood with nieces Anna and Fanny and with sister-in-law Martha Lloyd for which evidence exists in the form of correspondence on Austen's side. The chapter also traces the Bigg sisters in the extant letters before using the evidence of sisterly communities to explore fictional sisters in the mature novels.

Eliza de Feuillide and Phylly Walter are cousins because Eliza's mother Philadelphia is half-sister to Phylly's father William. In 21–23 January 1799, Austen seems to discount the Walter family when she comments to Cassandra, 'Our first cousins seem all dropping off very fast' through death, marriage, and removal to a far county. In the letter, Austen counts Eliza as 'incorporated into the family' at her marriage to Henry a year before. Edward Cooper of the published sermons and son of Mrs Austen's sister Jane is about to go 'into Staffordshire' to take the living of Hamstall Ridware. His sister Jane, an early ally at school and recipient of the 'Collection of Letters' now in Volume the Second of the Juvenilia, has died in a carriage accident on the Isle of Wight in August 1798. Lord Brabourne observes rather grumpily 'it is somewhat straining a point to claim the relationship of 'cousin' for the second generation after the indisputable first cousinship' (1884a, p. 11) and accuses James Edward of 'making the most of it'. Marriage and cousinship has its part to play in the forming of communities, however, and Mrs Austen has always addressed Phylly's mother Mrs Walter as 'sister' despite their relationship being that of half in-laws (*AP*, pp. 24–32).

Cousin Eliza has attracted interest as inspiration for Austen's characters and for her love of the theatre. Like Miss Steele, she writes about 'Beaux' (4 August 1797; Le Faye 2002, p. 146), like Mrs Bennet, she recommends to Phylly that sea bathing 'will set you up for the whole winter' (22 September 1796, p. 124), and like Lady Bertram, she is fond of pugs (17 October 1796, pp. 126, 7 November 1796, p. 129, 4 August 1797, p. 144). Her description of her 'dissipated life' (19 September 1787, p. 79) and of herself as 'the greatest Rake imaginable' (9 April 1787, p. 76) along with her declaration 'that the most effectual mode of getting rid of a temptation is to give way to it' (22 September 1796, p. 123) have caused her to be likened to Austen's Lady Susan. Eliza relinquishes 'dear Liberty, and yet dearer flirtation' (13 December 1796, p. 132) when she remarries on 31 December 1797. In the first surviving letter after this second marriage, she insists that 'like a Wise man [Henry] has no will but mine' (16 February 1798, pp. 152–153) and adds, 'Perhaps I may never be Mistress of a Rectory' (p. 153), a reverse preference that has linked her with Mary Crawford. The main sequence of Eliza's surviving letters is not to her cousins Austen and Cassandra, daughters of her mother Philadelphia's brother but to Phylly, probably as her mother's goddaughter. A sequence of letters from Eliza's father writing back from India has also been preserved in which he wisely proposes some basic education in writing and arithmetic: 'her other Accomplishments will be ornaments to her, but these are absolutely necessary' (28 August 1771, p. 29). Tysoe Hancock was very concerned about finances and wrote his wife at the birth of the fifth Austen child Cassandra, 'I fear George [the Reverend George Austen] will find it easier to get a family than to provide for them' (9 August 1773, p. 34).

Eliza was clearly educated in the ways of the letter manual, telling Phylly 'my epistles can be by no means worth the postage' (16 May 1780; Le Faye 2002, p. 45) and protesting at her own 'long silence' (7 May 1784, p. 59). She is 'the worst Correspondent in the world' but 'if my friends would be contented to write without requiring Answers I should like to hear from them seven times pr. Week' (3 May 1797, p. 136). She provides journal descriptions of her 'racketing life' and 'naturally delicate' constitution (27 March 1782, p. 54), contrasting 'the hurry and dissipation' of the 'gay town' of Paris with 'the tranquillity of the country' (27 June 1780, p. 49). In 1797 from London, 'the very busy Life of this Metropolis' (3 May, p. 136) provides both news and the reason for being too busy to communicate it together with the report of Henry's 'considerable Share of Riches & Honours' better fitting him to be a soldier than a 'Parson' (p. 139).

In default of any letter from Austen, the epistolary novella 'Love and Freindship', completed on 13 June 1790 is 'inscribed' to Eliza in her character of 'La Comtesse De Feuillide' possibly following a visit to Steventon in 1789 (Le Faye 2002, p. 96). The 'novel in a series of Letters' is curiously prefaced with an epigram 'Deceived in Freindship and Betrayed in Love' that provides a source for the title and the piece opens with Isabel asking her friend Laura to recount 'the Misfortunes and Adventures' of her life to Isabel's daughter Marianne. Laura's parentage and origins range from Ireland to Wales, Scotland, Italy, Spain, and France (Letter 3rd; *J*, p. 104), a joke perhaps about Eliza's 'wandering spirit . . . so early accustomed to a vagabond Life' (7 May 1784; Le Faye 2002, p. 60) and her own description of herself as an 'outlandish cousin' (17 January 1786, p. 68). Laura recounts Isabel's warnings against 'the insipid Vanities and idle Dissipation of the Metropolis of England' (Letter 4th; *J*, p. 105). Her friend has seen the world after spending two years at school in London, a fortnight in Bath, and one night in Southampton. Laura as the only source of information is also forced like Eliza to recount her own 'Perfections' and accomplishments (Letter 3rd, p. 104) as well as her later raving and swooning (Letter the 13th, p. 130). When Laura meets her illegitimate half cousins Philander and Gustavus, they have spent a fortune of £900 in under two months having 'parcelled' the money into nine subheadings of expenditure, the last being an Eliza-like 'Silver Buckles' (Letter the 15th, p. 138). Laura has since retired from her adventures to 'a romantic Village in the Highlands of Scotland' where she laments the loss of her parents, husband and friend 'uninterrupted by unmeaning Visits' (p. 140).

References within Eliza's letters indicate that a correspondence between her and the Austen sisters did take place. Its tone might be expected to mirror that used in the letters to Phylly, retained by her and numbered in a sequence of 36 although some are now missing (Le Faye 2002, p. 175). Austen was only 14 when she wrote 'Love and Freindship' and the novella was also a parody of novels of sensibility later fine-tuned in *Northanger Abbey* but the vagabond life may be an exaggerated account of Eliza's, a gift in lieu of actual letters. At the same time there seems to be a desperate gaiety about Eliza's letters demonstrated by her attempts to classify herself in her vagabondage: to excuse her lack of structure and value her love of display and theatricality. In the 'outlandish cousin' letter she describes her expected child as a 'brat' (17 January 1786, p. 68) perhaps as a defence mechanism after suffering miscarriages and she keeps up the description of her epileptic son Hastings as 'my wonderful Brat' (11 February 1789, p. 94) while trying to find palliative treatment during his short life (1786–1801). It is also likely that Eliza died of breast cancer having nursed her mother through the disease and so she would have anticipated the sufferings of her own final illness. Latterly she seemed to be living the retired life of the fictional Laura. Despite having 'entirely left off trade' immediately after her marriage, she plans 'flirtation' with 'my Brother Officers' (16 February 1798, p. 154) but by 29 October 1799 she proposes 'shunning all society' and Phylly herself reports the Henry Austens' intention of 'retiring into Wales & resigning the world' (p. 159). Responding to a condolence letter on the death of Hastings, Eliza reminds Phylly, 'I am not given to visiting' (29 October 1801, p. 160). Eliza then visits Godmersham for a fortnight but she was probably only in Kent twice more, in 1809 (*C*, pp. 370–371) and 1811 (p. 411) although Henry was a frequent guest.

Eliza had no other children and died in 1813 aged 51. From the nine marriages of her siblings, Austen acquired 16 nieces and 17 nephews. Although five of these children died young, more than half of this generation of Austens lived to be over 70 years old with Marianne Knight and George Austen son of Frank living into their nineties. The eldest nieces Anna and Fanny were born into very different lives in 1793. Anna's father James was a pluralist clergyman fond of hunting who had given up his literary ambitions after marriage. Edward Austen Knight was at the head of two substantial estates bestowed by chance and generating both a large income and all the responsibility incumbent on a landowner with 11 children. Mrs Austen herself writes to Mrs Jane Leigh-Perrot that 'Mr Knight . . . is quite a man of business' as opposed to James, now deceased, with his 'Literary Taste and the power of Elegant Composition' (4 January 1820; *AP*, p. 265).

Austen's correspondence with Anna and Fanny is more plainly suspended in time than that with Cassandra; they are young women and nieces who will become widows after Austen's death: Anna in 1829 and Fanny in 1849. Austen was playing the part of an aunt at the same time as instituting them in the role they each had to play. In the absence of other evidence, and in the face of missing letters and the fragmentation of what remains, any reading of the letters written to them in the latter part of Austen's life – in fact over a period of only three years – needs to beware of taking sides. Despite Lord Brabourne's attempt to correct them, these 'neices' are part of the counterculture of Austen's letters even if Fanny and Anna did not assert themselves when Austen's life came to be told.

Of the 16 extant letters addressed to Anna, one is a spoof review of 1812, eight others are now scraps divided as souvenirs, and three are notes about logistics carried locally. There are five letters to Anna discussing the 'books' that she sends for Austen to review between July and November 1814. Anna was married in November 1814 and had her first child in October 1815. The letters about novel writing contrast sharply with contemporaneous advice being offered to Fanny about her suitor John Plumptre. In *Letters*, Lord Brabourne unites the two themes by observing that his mother's cousin would have had 'ample leisure for her story' because she was too poor to have 'the expensive and enormous trousseau now thought necessary' (1884b, p. 315). This piece of spite aligns Austen with Anna through authorship in a way probably not intended by Brabourne who specifically targeted *Letters* as a tribute to Fanny.

Anna of the 'fluent pen' and 'cropt' hair (24 January 1809) is an Anna 'with variations' (25 April 1811). In 25 September 1813 to Frank, Austen assumes that her brother has heard of Anna's engagement through his wife Mary: 'It came upon us without much preparation; – at the same time, there was <u>that</u> about her which kept us in constant preparation for something'. The reiteration of this news appears in the same letter as confirmation that a second edition of *Sense and Sensibility* has been recommended by the publisher Egerton. After the early death of her mother in 1795, Anna was often in the care of the Austens at Steventon and was sent to Godmersham in winter 1809–1810 in the aftermath of which she called off an unsuitable first engagement (Le Faye 2004, pp. 181–182). In 3 November 1813, Austen distinguishes between '[a]n Anna sent away & an Anna fetched' and it is in this letter that Austen judges it would be a good time for her new suitor Ben Lefroy to visit Mrs Austen at Chawton. This is because she and Cassandra 'the formidables are absent' separately at Godmersham and in London.

Austen's surviving letter to Anna of mid-July 1814 has been cut down and half of the existing text is written by Mrs Austen whose tired eyes are suffering although she has previously helped with making petticoats for the 'Bride expectant'. The fact that the letter was mostly by Mrs Austen probably explains its omission from the *Memoir* although the novel critique page was used in *Letters* (Brabourne 1884b, p. 304). Brabourne groups the letters to Anna supplied by one of her daughters presumed to be Fanny Caroline, and commends Austen's care in her detailed criticism of 'the young authoress' (p. 304). In the surviving manuscript of July 1814, there is a touching message before Austen fills up the fourth page. Mrs Austen will sit and think of Anna while eating the fruit from her gooseberry tree 'tho I can do that without the assistance of ripe gooseberries; indeed my dear Anna, there is noboddy I think of oftener, very few I love better'. The community of women is further strengthened by Anna's 'MS' being read aloud to Mrs Austen and Cassandra, and Austen treats Anna's characters as seriously as her own. She tells her: 'The Spirit does not droop at all'. Cecilia the character has been made fittingly older and the social niceties of introductions are corrected. Among 'verbal corrections' is an allusion to Lord Orville from Burney's *Evelina* but Austen kindly suggests that she need not be minded if Anna thinks differently about the use of the third person. The 'Book' itself is awaiting 'safe conveyance' while Austen is 'impatient for more'.

Austen was working on *Emma* in 1814–1815 and there is both a gap between letters and a longer time period of composition for 10–18 August 1814 to Anna. Austen has, however, kept notes of questions and ranges over a number of areas including the chosen title which has been changed from 'Enthusiasm' to 'Which is the Heroine?' The previous choice was so 'superior' but Austen is sure she will 'grow to like' the new one. Naming is a sensitive task but distances, etiquette, and practicalities are also elements of this feedback. Austen confirms no 'Blunders' in the presentation of Dawlish and, in passing, her own trip to the resort in 1802. The travelling practicalities of a two-day journey from Dawlish to Bath are thus more likely to be based on experience. The word 'blunder' itself occurs frequently in *Emma* and particularly in the double-dealing anagram game played by Frank Churchill. Austen has established that the title of 'Desborough' is not in use,

Cassandra approves 'St Julian', and Austen looks forward to the wonderfully named but mysterious 'Progillian'. Lady Helena's postscript is to be omitted as being too like 'P&P' so there must have been an epistolary element and in fact it is reported that Susan in the novel later writes to Cecilia (28 September 1814). It is suggested that fewer words are sometimes needed and the aunts do not agree about the change of scenes and groupings of characters. 'Your Aunt C. Does not like desultory novels', Austen tells Anna; 'I allow much more Latitude than she does' since 'Nature & Spirit cover many sins of a wandering story'. Austen herself sends the Dixons to Ireland but does not accompany them and the existence of this letter at the time of *Emma*'s composition could be read as her own tribute to the advice she offers.

This otherwise business-like letter has two postscripts that create a contrast between authorly comment and the life being lived. In the panel below the simple address to 'Miss Austen', 'Dorsetshire' has been altered for 'Devonshire' on geographical probability based on the location of Dawlish, home of Mr Griffin. Upside down, and overwriting 'Dear Anna' at the head of the letter begun over a week before despatch, is a message about 'bits of Irish' found in Austen's work bag, presumably linen left over from the making of items mentioned by Mrs Austen in her previous letter. In *Letters*, Brabourne omits both these postscripts which show clearly on the surviving text since they are further than ever from his chosen plotline than the main body of the letter. He does not want his narrative interrupted by the discovery that Anna was at least preparing a part of her trousseau, however humble.

The 9–18 September 1814 letter is written after Austen has been in London (as evidenced by 23–24 August 1814 to Cassandra and 2 September 1814 to Martha Lloyd in Bath) where Henry's new garden at 23 Hans Place is 'quite a Love' (23–24 August). There is more criticism on the latest three 'Books' than Austen thinks Anna will like. Etiquette and parenting are corrected but this is the letter where characters are found to be 'favourably arranged' in their 'Country village' more specifically reinforcing Austen's own disposition of characters in *Emma* which is, by design, the most geographically constrained of her novels. The evidence from her account of reading Anna's novel is that it is even more 'wandering' than her aunt's more variously located works. Indeed Austen seems emboldened to suggest that one scene is 'prosy & nothing to the purpose'. She calls for 'curtailment' and revision on the model of her own methods visible in the extant manuscripts; significantly, she suggests that writing more will make Anna 'equal to scratching out something of the past'. In real time, Austen retains this letter so as to return the package of 'Books' via William Digweed, tenant of Steventon Manor and as a result the main body of the letter has been written before the Chawton family receive news of the death of Charles Austen's wife Fanny in childbirth on board ship on 6 September. Although there is less of an attempt to crowd the page because of the free transit, page 3 concludes with a joke about 'Cargo' which is squeezed in so that the section above the address can be targeted at influencing Anna to visit her grandmother before she leaves the county on her marriage. There is the promise of handmade shoes and a request for a visit of 'more than a day' contrasting with Austen's insistence that Mrs Austen is not much worse for the 'Shock' of her daughter-in-law's sudden death. It will not be long before Austen describes Anna to Fanny as a 'Poor Animal' (23–25 March 1817) because of the frequency of her pregnancies. Anna survives, of course, but it is probably only her husband's death in 1829 when Anna is 36 that limits the number of children to the seven who reach adulthood, her sixth daughter being born in 1827.

The critique of Anna's novel continues, however, in 28 September 1814 when the manuscript's return is postponed because of a 'public reading' for Mrs Austen. There has, nonetheless, been a private exposition while the sisters are undressing in their own room. This is an indication of the sharing of manuscript readings which themselves have degrees of public and private value in the family context. Many of the opinions in the letter are prefaced by 'We' combining Austen and Cassandra, and Austen enters into the characters by observing that fiancé Ben's approbation must be "beyond everything", a shared allusion to a favourite expression of Alton neighbour Mrs Jane Digweed (23 June 1816). Mrs Digweed is shorthand within the sisterhood as evidenced earlier when Austen writes to Cassandra about the delivery of a parcel, 'Martha may guess how full of wonder & gratitude she was' (29 January 1813). Conversely, Austen's efforts to include Ben note that he will not understand the value of the name Progillian. The letter migrates into Anna's new domestic responsibilities with the recommendation to her marital home in Hendon of a housemaid formerly with the Frank Austens. Austen also links the suggestion to the Webb family who have recently moved from Chawton and this produces a characteristically acerbic and self-deprecating comment more appropriate to the Cassandra correspondence. Austen has seen the wagons for the move: 'I began to reproach myself for not having liked them better – but since the Waggons have disappeared, my Conscience has been closed again – & I am excessively glad they are gone.' The layout, with its closing reference to a fondness for Sherlock's Sermons, may have allowed Anna to edit these fourth-page remarks for family consumption in reading out loud.

The last letter to address the composition of the novel (30 November 1814) was written from London following a visit to Hendon from Hans Place. The corpus of surviving letters now yields two letters dated 30 November 1814, one each to Anna and Fanny. In Fanny's letter, Austen masks her latest advice about Plumptre with a first page about Anna's 'bed-room, & her Drawers & her Closet'. She makes a specific point about women's access and control since Fanny's father Edward will inevitably not be able to provide details of 'Paraphernalia of that sort'. Austen also deplores 24 guineas spent by Anna on a piano when towels will be wanted and remarks of a new purple pelisse 'it looked very well & I dare say she wanted it' but had bought it secretly: 'She is capable of that you know'. This sharp opinion is tempered by Austen's relief that Anna has the authority to invite her to stay overnight even though the newly married couple are living with Ben's elder brother Edward. The contemporaneous letter to Anna sits curiously beside these remarks in the modern collection.

In real time, there had been three other letters to Anna (22, 24, and 29 November) two of which are now fragments presumably divided as souvenirs. Anna's 30 November 1814 is missing its second leaf and is less closely written than 28 September suggesting Austen's intention to write less than she will to Fanny whose letter is more densely packed. Anna has perhaps thought her 'Books' not welcome reading and Austen returns to the pattern of suggestion and approbation along with the technique of including Ben. This introduces a ghoulish suggestion, that might have been less acceptable, about 'Neices' being 'seldom chosen but in compliment to some Aunt or other. I dare say Ben was in love with me once, & w^d never have thought of <u>You</u> if he had not supposed me dead of a Scarlet fever'. Hindsight has given even greater weight to this flippancy since in 1848 nephew William Knight's three daughters all under five will die of scarlet fever at Steventon Rectory (*C*, p. 670). When Lord Brabourne prints the part-letter of 1814 in 1884 he also uses the final paragraph of another letter to Anna now in scraps from early March 1815. In it, Miss Blachford's marriage has not been in the papers '[a]nd one may as well be single if the Wedding is not to be in print' (Brabourne 1884b, p. 323). This amalgamation dilutes the effect of the vaguely incestuous suggestion in the actual November text but introduces some of the hilarious illogicality of the Juvenilia.

Anna was physically close to the Austen sisters because of her closeness to Mrs Austen and her stays at Steventon. Her presence in the house as a young child will have made her part of their daily life and her rebellion would have been made evident in a household of adults. Her cousin nearest in age, Fanny Knight née Austen was associated with holidaying and affluence. Cassandra would have encountered her in the wider daily context of Godmersham but it was to Austen that Fanny turned for advice on John Plumptre. Fanny reported in her pocketbook that she had received a 'Lecture from Aunt C on <u>Astronomy</u>' (12 June 1811; *C*, p. 407) concerning another suitor, George Hatton, codenamed 'Jupiter'. Fanny's pocketbook entry for 22 November 1814 notes mysteriously 'At. Jane Austen full of advice *&c &c*' (p. 492) responding to Austen's 18 November letter that was followed up by the reply to Fanny on 30 November.

Fanny has been summed up, almost dismissed, as 'a prosaic, unadventurous girl, conscientiously devoted to her large family and to her peaceful Kentish home' (Le Faye 2002, p. 171). She was subsequently widowed for over 30 years and represented the 'epitome of the Victorian matron' (Wilson 1990b, p. 122). She herself left behind the 69 diaries or pocketbooks (p. 2) quoted first by Lord Brabourne but these provide very little introspective comment. An early Knight family governess, Dorothy Chapman preserved 150 letters written over 50 years and these were returned to the Knatchbulls in 1857 (Selwyn 2010, p. 79). According to Brabourne, the 'two natures' of Fanny and Austen 'singularly harmonised' and 'whilst on earth, contributed in a remarkable degree to the happiness of those among whom its lot was cast' (Brabourne 1884b, p. 345). Brabourne has been encouraged by Cassandra's second letter to Fanny after Austen's death in which she pronounces Fanny and Austen 'counterparts' (Le Faye 2011, p. 363). In her grief, Cassandra reinforces the sense of sisterhood when she writes to Fanny that her niece is 'doubly dear to me now for her dear sake whom we have lost' (p. 359).

The five extant Fanny letters are made up of the two linked by matrimonial advice (18–20 and 30 November 1814) and three also received close together in February and March 1817. Fanny's pocketbooks suggest that a further 25 letters were received (Wilson 1990b, p. 37). The 18–20 November letter demonstrates how seriously Austen takes her role as adviser simply by the extent of her text and by the fact she has allegedly chosen to evade Cassandra in order to read Fanny's previous letter at the first available opportunity. On the third page of this letter she commends the ruse of sending the letter via Edward but in a package of music so that 'Your Aunt C'. does not suspect anything. Austen does not think Fanny can be in love. She has only felt so because of the charm of Mr Plumptre as 'the <u>first</u> young Man who attached himself' to her. Austen uses the full extent of the inside pages of the letter to argue both sides of 'the question' concluding, of course, 'Anything is to be preferred or endured rather than marrying without Affection'. Conveniently shareable news follows including the information that letters from Anna 'have been very sensible & satisfactory, with no <u>parade</u> of happiness'. When page 4 is headed with the news that the first edition of *Mansfield Park* is sold out, Austen balances the income and vanity of authorship. Fanny is 'above caring about money' and so is not plagued 'with any particulars' but she can comprehend 'The pleasures of Vanity'. Another inverted pre-script postscript further disrupts the final tone, however. Fanny has visited Mr Plumptre's room to 'excite' her feelings and Austen exclaims, 'The dirty Shaving Rag was exquisite! – Such a circumstance ought to be in print. Much too good to be lost'. It is perhaps to be found 'in print' in *Emma* when Harriet Smith treasures the pencil end and plaster abandoned by Mr Elton (*E*, p. 366).

Fanny's 30 November 1814 letter opens with the shared information and open criticism of Anna's acquisitions in her temporary marital home. The continued discussion of 'a subject which comes in very naturally' begins on the first inside page so it will not be immediately visible. Here Austen raises concerns of Fanny's being 'fettered' even by what she calls a 'tacit engagement'. The back page of the letter revisits the debate over a second edition of *Mansfield Park* along with the juxtaposition between praise and 'Pewter' from the previous letter. Austen fears that any reply will not be fit even for discussion. In the same way as she has used the layout of the letter to categorise her topics, so Austen asks Fanny to 'write <u>something</u> that may do to be read or told' for even the outside of the letter will be marked as from her niece. Austen hopes to find Fanny's 'pleasant, little, flowing Scrawl on the Table' when she returns from accompanying the Miss Moores and when Austen dreads her own 'uphill work to be talking to those whom one knows so little', Fanny is returned to the womanly fold of female acquaintance management. Once again the letter layout is maximised with a brief recurrence below the address to the subject of Evangelicalism that is capable of being concealed since it refers once again to 'Mr J.P'.

The three letters to Fanny of 1817 concern 'the fluctuations of your Fancy' (20–21 February). Fanny is not serious about potential suitor James Wildman despite the influence of Chilham Castle and the letters are interspersed with clues about Austen's health. Austen is reminded by Anna's blooming innocence of the events of her 'girlish days'. The 13 March letter contains the well-known admonition in favour of matrimony that 'Single Women have a dreadful propensity for being poor' as well as the information that 'Miss Catherine' or *Northanger Abbey* 'is put upon the Shelve for the present' and the hint about *Persuasion* that continues in 23–25 March: only Fanny is to know that the 'Heroine . . . is almost too good'. Although Anna is in this letter a 'Poor Animal', the pregnancy must have been short-lived as no child was the result but the prospect of death and multiple childbirths hangs over any discussion of marriage in the five Fanny letters. In 20–21 February Fanny's Aunt Sophia has had her eighteenth child and will have one more the following year suggesting that 'the simple regimen of separate rooms' recommended by Austen in the letter was not adopted. Sophia Bridges was 19 in 1791 when she married Cassandra's co-writer William Deedes and she lived until 1844 although her sisters Fanny and Elizabeth were married in the same month as Sophia and died in 1805 and 1808 respectively. The triple event was marked by Austen's juvenile epistolary piece 'The Three Sisters' discussed in Chapter 5. In 13 March 1817 Fanny's friend Mrs Hammond née Mary Oxenden 'is growing old by confinements & nursing' with the suggestion that not being married is a form of contraception. Frank Austen's wife Mary who will die after the birth of her eleventh child in 1823 will be confined in April and 'is by no means remarkably large for her' with her seventh. In 23–25 March Austen is 'tired of so many Children' with Mrs Clement pregnant and Mrs Benn having a thirteenth. Elizabeth Benn lived to be 89 and Ann-Mary Clement sister of Catherine-Ann Prowting to be 71 although this child does not appear to have survived. Fanny herself postpones the process of 'Mothering' in the sense of giving birth by not marrying Sir Edward Knatchbull until she is 27 in 1820 and she subsequently lives to be one month shy of her ninetieth birthday. She does, however, become stepmother to six sometimes difficult children of her husband's first marriage and bears another nine children of whom three daughters and two sons die young. Her daughter Louisa predeceases her and one of her three other sons is Lord Brabourne the future editor of Austen's letters (Wilson 1990b, pp. 69–88). The description of her in Austen's letters as 'the Paragon of all that is Silly & Sensible, common-place & eccentric, Sad & Lively, Provoking & Interesting' (20–21 February 1817) is overshadowed by her later, now public, opinion of her aunts as unrefined but for their connections with the Kent family. The surviving evidence is weighted against her being silly, eccentric, and lively and it is now Austen who represents that side of their correspondence. Austen has only been allowed to speak to Fanny aged 24; Fanny aged 50 is the suffering matron in Cassandra's later letters to Anna (5 February 1843; Le Faye 2001, p. 555, 1 February 1844, p. 556).

In 7–9 October 1808 Austen commends the 15-year-old Fanny as 'almost another Sister' at the very point when her niece is about to assume her first mater-nal, although not 'Mothering' responsibilities, as eldest sister at Godmersham. The death of Elizabeth Austen also serves to make explicit another community-based sisterhood with Martha Lloyd, sister of sister-in-law Mary who is step-mother to Anna. From Southampton, 7–9 October announces 'that Martha comes today; yesterday brought us notice of it, & the Spruce Beer is brewed in conse-quence'. It is a letter of cakes and keyholes with messages to and from Martha who has arrived 'during' the letter. In the background Martha will hear from her sister Mary about the death of Fanny's mother, and Austen writes in her next to Cassandra, who is enduring the loss firsthand: 'With what true sympathy our feel-ings are shared by Martha, you need not be told; – she is the friend & Sister under every circumstance' (13 October 1808).

Martha is first encountered in Austen's letters in September 1796 although 'Frederic and Elfrida' written about 1787 is dedicated to her, possibly retrospec-tively as discussed below. The Austens and Lloyds provided mutual support for each other up to the deaths of the Reverend George Austen and Mrs Lloyd in 1805 after which Martha became a 'partner' in the Austen household (21–23 April 1805). She spent time away on her own family responsibilities but was based at Chawton until her late marriage to Frank in 1828. Cassandra is at Portsdown when Martha dies there in 1843 and she writes to Anna briefly but movingly of her sister-in-law as 'an affecte., a tried & faithful friend for at least half a cen-tury . . . we have been connected by so many interesting ties, that she must retain a prominent place in my thoughts during the short remainder of my Life' (5 February 1843; *AP*, pp. 554–555). These ties are those of family, friendship, and sisterhood shared among the three women, and Martha's death reminds Cassandra that she has been left to be their memorialist.

When the Lloyds make their first appearance in Austen's letters, Martha and her sister Mary are expected at Steventon from Ibthorpe (15–16 September 1796;

18 September 1796). The sisters have been entwined in the Austen family since an elder sister Eliza married one of the Steventon pupils. The Lloyds had lived at Deane, vicarage of the Reverend George Austen's other living, after moving from Enbourne at the death of their father Noyes Lloyd in 1789. They were about 16 miles away in 1796 and at Ibthorpe because the Deane vicarage had been occupied by James Austen since his first marriage in 1792. Unmentioned in September 1796 is Martha's attachment to the mysterious Mr W. but on 30 November 1796 Mrs Austen welcomes Mary Lloyd as her son's intended (second) wife and adds: 'Tell Martha, she too shall be my Daughter, she does me honour in the request – and Mr W shall be my Son if he pleases' (*AP*, p. 228). Sistership is thus doubly proposed; they are 'now all of one family' (p. 228). Mr W. remains unidentified and a disappointed 32 year-old Martha will remain unmarried for another 30 years. Two years after Mary's marriage to James, Austen passes news of Martha to Cassandra that she is 'in better looks & Spirits . . . & I flatter myself she will now be able to jest openly about M^r W'. (27–28 October 1798). By this time Martha is visiting her old home at Deane where Mary has just given birth to her son (James) Edward. In 24–26 December 1798 Austen anticipates that Lord Spencer will give happiness in the continued recovery from Mr W. and in a birthday letter to Cassandra recounts how she and Martha stayed awake talking until two in the morning after James Edward's christening. Rather than suggesting any potential rivalry, the declaration 'I love Martha better than ever' (8–9 January 1799) reinforces their shared presence through letters and is a gift to Cassandra to reassure her of Austen's contentment in her absence.

Partnering and community is signalled in many letters. Martha participates in them and is also represented as a correspondent through whom information can be traded. In June 1799, Martha is united with Cassandra in commissions for proxy shopping in Bath where 'the office is now closed' (19 June), and keeping Martha with them all summer is envisioned as being bartered for visits to blood family at Adlestrop, Harpsden, and Bookham (11 June). Martha is significantly present when Austen receives news of the Bath removal. The 12–13 November 1800 letter to Martha concerns the visit from which Austen will return for this shock announcement and she writes almost flirtatiously that they can meet 'to talk all this over, till we have tired ourselves with the very idea of my visit, before my visit begins'. To Cassandra, Austen then writes from Ibthorpe where she and Martha, 'such Desperate walkers' (30 November–1 December 1800), have been confined by the weather. In this letter, the three women are all re-entwined in a final paragraph where Martha 'has neither time to read nor I to write' after Martha's receipt of a letter from Cassandra. In accompanying Austen back to Steventon on this occasion, Martha inadvertently participates in Cassandra's diplomatically engineered gap. When the letters resume, Ibthorpe must be visited *en route* since Martha is presumably reading along, and in a postscript below the address panel of 3–5 January 1801: 'Martha desires her best Love & says a great many kind things about spending some time with you in March – and depending on a large return from us both in the Autumn'. This letter's content is intriguingly reprioritised in manuscript because bees occur in a prescript; as Martha was removed by James from Deane, so Austen, Cassandra, and the bees are being moved from Steventon.

Once in Bath, 'Martha triumphs' (5–6 May 1801) but this is unexplained and now cryptic in a way that reinforces their shared concerns. In the same letter, Austen's new dress will be gathered with fullness 'just like some of Marthas' and the fashion commentary continues in 21–22 May where Cassandra is urged to make a cloak of the same materials as a bonnet she has made for Martha at Kintbury, home of her sister Eliza. There is detailed knowledge of Martha's black silk spencer and comparison with Catherine Bigg's armhole trimming. Austen is trying to make the best of her situation in Bath and Martha must be invoked as part of the triumvirate with Cassandra. In a postscript Austen describes a visitor to Paragon as 'the most elegant looking woman I have seen since I left Martha' (21–22 May 1801). The outlying letter of 14 September 1804 from Lyme to Cassandra at Ibthorpe performs a tripartite sharing function, offering further jus- tification for its own survival. Austen is anxious for news of both Mrs Lloyd and Martha but there is then a postscript below the address panel: 'I hope Martha thinks you looking better than when she saw you in Bath. – Jenny has fasten'd up my hair to day in the same manner that she used to do up Miss Lloyd's, which makes us both [very] happy'. After Mrs Lloyd's death, three months after that of George Austen, there are letters offering family information and sympathy. In 8–11 April 1805 from Bath to Ibthorpe, Austen again reinforces the triumvirate and the gift of Cassandra's company: 'As a companion' who 'will be all that Martha can be supposed to want'. '[O]ur intended Partnership with Martha' that is no longer to be concealed appears in 21–23 April 1805 and Martha fulfils Mrs Austen's desire for a daughter in 30 August 1805 when Austen assumes with Cassandra that they can be 'sure of my mother and Martha being happy together' while the sisters pay visits prior to their installation in Southampton.

From this point, Martha is even more embedded in the dance between absence and presence that is correspondence and logistics. In 7–8 January 1807 from Southampton, Austen tells Cassandra 'You must have heard from Martha by this time' and by 8–9 February she has heard from Martha herself that she will be back from Steventon by the twenty-fourth: 'I shall be truely glad if she can keep to her day, but dare not depend on it'. In 21–22 February, 'When Martha comes she will supply me with matter'. The women plot to be together but ironically our knowl- edge of this is based on their being apart. They plan a 'snug fortnight' possibly to include the Bigg sisters (20–22 June 1808) and Martha's jokey 'attachment' to the married Dr. Mant 'however immoral, has a decorous air' (24 January 1809).

Martha is used also in Austen's appeal for Cassandra's return during the long 1808–1809 visit to Godmersham. In the body of 17–18 January 1809 Martha is to travel with the Fowle children to Kintbury: 'We shall not have a month of Martha after your return – & that month will be a very interrupted & broken one; – but we shall enjoy ourselves the more, when we <u>can</u> get a quiet half hour together'. In the dominating pre-script postscript, however, 'Martha . . . hopes to have the pleasure of seeing you when you return to Southampton. You are to understand this message, as being merely for the sake of a Message, to oblige me.'

Martha is firmly implicated in an ongoing debate on the frequency and length of familiar letters that formed part of women's counter-cultural response. In 2 June 1799, this network is shown to be dependent on men for present and future income to meet the very costs of maintaining a correspondence. Uncle James Leigh-Perrot has queried the number of letters sent and received but 'as long as we can keep the frequency of our correspondence from Martha's Uncle, we will not fear our own'. This is probably Uncle John Craven whose second wife makes demands on Martha (26–27 May 1801; 23 June 1814). When Austen writes from Godmersham to Southampton, a previous exchange prompts the excuse of long letters and an unfortunate fondness for receiving them reminiscent of Eliza de Feuillide: 'As to Martha. She had not the least chance in the World of hearing from me again, & I wonder at her impudence in proposing it' (30 June–1 July 1808). In 16 February 1813 Austen replies in one sitting to Martha's 'long letter' that deserves a second from Austen 'in an handsome manner before Cassandra's return; after which event, as I shall have the benefit of all your Letters to her, I claim nothing more'. There is explicit news of Anna, Mrs Austen, Miss Benn's eviction, the transfer of students to Winchester, Frank at Deal, and the continuing decline of Henry's Eliza as well as speculation on Cassandra's potential experiences at Manydown where the Bigg sisters' father will die on 24 February. This letter to Martha has 23 lines per page; that to Cassandra on 4 February is 31 lines and 9 February to her overruns into a prescript. Nonetheless Austen concludes to Martha on page three of 16 February: 'Now I think I may in <u>Quantity</u> have deserved your Letter. My ideas of Justice in Epistolary Matters are you know very strict'. With retrospective knowledge, we must conclude that Austen can thus concentrate instead on writing *Mansfield Park*. In 4 February Austen 'fears' for Cassandra that 'this week must be a heavy one', missing Martha 20 miles away in Kintbury. Austen presumes to know Martha's mind and movements as she does Cassandra's. She herself is in the throes of reading *Pride and Prejudice* out loud and wants to include them both, having walked to Alton 'like an old Feby come back again'.

Despite her presence in letters to Cassandra, only four letters to Martha now survive. Before her marriage, Martha's life was if anything even more peripatetic than Cassandra's and this would be one explanation for the small number of letters preserved. After the three moves from Enbourne, Deane, and Ibthorpe, Martha lived in Bath, Southampton, and Chawton with the Austens but spent time with family in Kintbury and Steventon. The four letters were received at Ibthorpe (12–13 November 1800), at Barton Court, Kintbury home of the Dundases (29–30 November 1812 and 16 February 1813) and in Bath at a Dundas-rented house (2 September 1814). Martha also visited London and fulfilled proxy shopping commissions there (6 June 1811). If other letters were initially pre-served, they were finally in the hands of Frank's children and the 1800 letter was sent by Frank himself to an American admirer of Austen in 1852 (Le Faye 2011, p. 384). Other letters may have been redistributed and on Frank's death Austen's letters to his first wife Mary were destroyed by their daughter Fanny (Modert 1990, p. xxi).

As with Eliza, we could look to the Juvenilia for substitute correspondence. 'Frederic and Elfrida', the first 'novel' in Volume the First is dedicated to Martha by her 'sincere Freind' as 'a small testimony of the gratitude I feel for your late generosity to me in finishing my muslin Cloak'. The eponymous characters are related to one another since 'The Uncle of Elfrida was the Father of Frederic' and the dedication may also have been made in recognition of Martha's sister Eliza whose uncle was the father of her husband Fulwar: the two couples shared initials and a familial relationship. These real-life cousins were already married when the Lloyd women moved from Enbourne to Deane in 1789 but Austen would have been aware of the match through ongoing communications with the Reverend George Austen's former pupils. The character of Rebecca in the novella is marked out as an expert on muslins, as the dedication suggests Martha is, with the word 'muslin' inserted superscript in the manuscript of the dedication. The 12-year-old Austen has clearly been observing the marriage market from an already jaundiced perspective. In 'Frederic and Elfrida', her counter-heroine Charlotte sits down to a meat feast before deciding to commit suicide after obligingly becoming engaged to two men at once. Aged 36, Rebecca must wait a little longer to marry Captain Roger aged 63 and the 'Qualities' of her mind 'amply atone for the Horor, with which your first appearance must ever inspire the unwary visitor'. The lunatic chronology of the novel allows Rebecca to acquire an 18-year-old daughter who almost overturns the story when she attracts Frederic and treats Elfrida like an old woman. Having fainted excessively, Elfrida concedes and marries Frederic after his initial 'Damme' of refusal.

The dedication to 'Frederic and Elfrida' is written in a slightly different hand and it has been suggested that it was a later addition to a piece originally com-posed in 1787 (Southam 1962, p. 232; *J*, p. xxviii; p. 373). It was perhaps a creation waiting for a recipient with Austen practising her craft as she would the dutiful embroidering of a sampler. Gifts of handwork to the Lloyds and to the Bigg sisters accompanied by dedications are also recorded (Taylor 2015) but both the Juvenilia and the letters as sisterly gifting have this more challenging countercultural function. Martha was 10 years older than Austen and presumably still expecting to marry but Austen wanted unashamedly to share her joking representation of their futures. Ten years later, the loss of Tom Fowle who was both Fulwar's brother and Cassandra's fiancé would have promoted their connection as well as triggering the excision of evidence dating from 1797. The coincidental loss of Mr W. between 1796 and 1798 seems to have been a final blow to Martha's own prospects.

From these early beginnings, Martha became a confidante on the subject of Austen's writing. She has had enough access to the text potentially to memorise 'First Impressions' (11 June 1799) and is told when *Pride and Prejudice* is sold (29–30 November 1812). She is also involved in the dedication of *Emma* to the Prince Regent regarding Austen's wish to conceal James Stanier Clarke's request. In 26 November 1815 Austen observes that Martha will be 'thoroughly convinced of my being influenced now by nothing but the most mercenary motives'. In the context of their letter lives this pronouncement is then wonderfully deflated by the information that Harriet Palmer, who cares for Charles's children after the death of her sister, has been repaid nine shillings on Martha's behalf: 'there was no more oweing'.

Martha is both sister and partner to the Austens but was herself called upon by her own sisters Eliza Fowle and Mary Lloyd Austen and by Mrs Dundas, an invalid family friend living at Barton Court in Kintbury. Mrs Dundas was an 'almost permanent invalid' (Sawtell, 1984, p. 310) until her death in 1812 aged 59 with Martha in residence, and Martha subsequently spent time with the family in Clifton and Bath. In 7–9 October 1808 from Southampton, Austen tells Cassandra that Martha will not remain at Castle Square for long because Mrs Dundas cannot do without her. It is unclear whether Mrs Dundas was regarded as a dependant through sickness or a benefactor through wealth, and there are cryptic allusions possibly expressing jealousy on the subject of Martha as companion. Martha was perhaps drawn to the elegancies of life at Barton just as Austen felt divided in her enjoyment of life at Godmersham. In 30 January 1809, Austen sends a message from Martha about her 'very particular satisfaction' in going first to Barton and then to 'Town'. This is so 'acceptable' and that fact so well-known to Cassandra that Austen 'need not dilate on the subject'. In 6 June 1811, the newly-published Austen negotiates a joint return from London with Cassandra who is also in thrall to family arrangements but by this time there is enjoyment to be found in moving chess-piece sisters around including also Anne Sharp. Martha is now rich enough to afford to send a breakfast set as a present to Chawton and is perhaps, like the Austen sisters, in receipt of a 'Fee' from her wealthier friend.

Austen's letter to Martha of 29–30 November 1812 wishes for Mrs Dundas's 'complete recovery' and commends Martha's 'arduous, busy, useful office' but the older woman has already died. The letter also announces the sale of *Pride and Prejudice* and goes on to debate the present of a shawl from Martha to Miss Benn, suggested by Austen and Cassandra, as well as pleading for Martha to return to send out a Christmas turkey. In 24 January 1813, Austen assumes that Martha is at Barton dealing with the aftermath of the death but 'best pleased to be mistaken' although Martha is with her sister at Steventon by the twenty-ninth. In 20 May 1813 it has been suggested that Austen refers to Martha's receiving a portion of a lottery win which could have been one sixteenth of £20,000 unless this is a cryptic allusion to some benefit from Mrs Dundas's estate. In her letter of 23 June 1814, Austen has envisioned Martha in the sisterhood by observing ambiguously to Cassandra the virtue of avoiding travel in the heat: 'she is as glad of the change as even You & I should be – or almost'. By 2 September 1814, Austen is writing from Hans Place to Pulteney Street in Bath where Martha is staying with Janet Deans Dundas and her family. Martha is by now 'too <u>rich</u> I hope, to care much for Letters' but must be reminded of Mrs Digweed and also of Mrs Hill, formerly Catherine Bigg.

When the Lloyds moved to Ibthorpe they were further removed from Steventon and this may have signalled the beginning of the Austens' friendship with the Bigg sisters. We learn in 9–10 January 1796 that Alethea Bigg met Tom Lefroy and danced with James at a ball at Manydown, the Bigg family home, only six miles from Steventon. In 14–15 January 1796 Austen tells Cassandra that she could not call on the Biggs because the weather was not 'tolerable'. In 18–19 December 1798 Austen is preparing to go to Manydown but will return by Monday and this is intertwined with news of Frank and, as predicted, a 'very thin' ball in the company of Catherine Bigg (24–26 December 1798). In 8–9 January 1799 Austen meets the Biggs at a dinner party at Deane and enjoys the company of 'the Manydown party'. She has already decided not to like another Alethea, who is cousin to the eldest Bigg sister Margaret's husband Henry Blackstone. In 11 June 1799 from Bath, Austen is indignant on Cassandra's behalf in one of her early pre-script postscripts shown in Figure 1.4:

> They do not seem to trouble You much from Manydown. I have long wanted to quarrel with them, & I believe I shall take this opportunity. – There is no denying that they are very capricious! – for they like to enjoy their elder Sisters company when they can.

Elizabeth, Catherine, and Alethea are the sisters closest in age to the Austens; Margaret and Jane, the elder two are married by 1795 and presumably call on the younger for support. Dorothy has died in 1793 and another sister died in infancy. While Austen is still highlighting their capriciousness, she defines Mrs Evelyn as someone 'The Biggs would call . . . a nice Woman' (11 June 1799) suggesting a shared joke about their conversational style and perhaps its limitations.

Elizabeth marries in 1799 but is a widow with one son by 1802 and returns to live at Manydown with Alethea until their brother Harris succeeds to Manydown in 1813. When Cassandra visits to support them, Austen observes that Alethea is still mistress (9 February 1813) because she has never left to be married. Like the

Dashwoods they must, however, vacate the house, and Elizabeth and Alethea then live together in Winchester. Catherine Bigg marries Herbert Hill in 1808 and bears five sons and a daughter. In late February 1815 to Anna, Austen charts the sisters' movements with Elizabeth and Alethea just leaving Catherine at Streatham and Margaret arriving ready for 'Mrs Hill . . . to lye-in of a Daughter', in fact her fourth son Alfred. Catherine's husband is more than 25 years her senior and on a visit to their house Austen notes to Martha 'a melancholy disproportion between the Papa & the little Children' (2 September 1814). This friendship and circulating correspondence is thus significant for sisterhood. In letters exchanged before and after the death of Elizabeth Austen, Austen receives a 'Broche' from Catherine and asks Cassandra to thank her for this 'very kind & welcome mark of friendship' (7–9 October 1808). She is subsequently told in confidence by Alethea of Catherine's marriage (15–16 October 1808). The affianced sister is then 'poor Catherine' (24–25 October) to be thought of at her wedding while Martha is promoted to 'friend & Sister under every circumstance'.

The women have all remained friends despite the three Biggs' failing to persuade Austen to maintain her engagement to their brother Harris for more than a few hours in 1802. The only evidence of this event in Austen's letters comes in 26 June 1808 where Austen convinces Edward that she must be back in Southampton for 'our Friends' 'visit' for a 'private reason'. This is also the letter where she tetchily points out that a 'Legacy' would be their 'Sovereign good'. Austen may have been recalling that she could have been mistress of Manydown with no need for a legacy and that she could have offered sisters from both sides a home but this reaction is primarily against an assumption of wealth by Elizabeth Austen. Austen has already planned her 'early return' from Godmersham in 20–22 June 1808 to be 'sure of seeing Catherine & Alethea'. The negotiation for presence includes a planned 'snug fortnight' for 'you & I & Martha' while Mrs Austen is at Steventon 'either with or without them'. This is a sisterly hierarchy in which Mrs Austen is removed, Martha is essential, and the Biggs are an ambiguous treat because of their own associated dependency. Austen dares to hope for their presence but does not want to anticipate the disappointment of their absence.

The Biggs must make new homes after the death of their father and there are other coded messages in the letters suggesting their association with the Austens. When Cassandra visits in 1813, Austen envisions her sister in that grander home from their early life with its associated changes of dress:

> I thought of you at Manydown in the Draw^g room and in your China Crape; – therefore, you were in the Breakfast parlour in your Brown Bombasin; if I thought of you <u>so</u>, you would have been in the Kitchen in your Morning stuff. (4 February 1813)

She sends a prescript message to Alethea that she is 'still in my Debt' querying their friend's 'notions of Letter writing & Note writing' (9 February 1813) as she does in the last letter in 1817 where 'the Epistolary debt' (24 January) is again on Alethea's side. The 9 February letter envisions 'Candour & Comfort & Coffee & Cribbage' as a shorthand representation of times spent at Manydown where Cassandra is visiting for the last time. Elizabeth and Alethea are about to form the new sisterhood of widow and spinster in which Austen and Cassandra have been living since 1805. The 25 September 1813 letter to Frank from Godmersham suggests Alethea and Elizabeth are expected to visit Cassandra, Mrs Austen, and Martha with Henry's 'company' for a few days. Beginning in Henrietta Street with all her 'might' Austen suggests putting the sisters in 'our own Room' at Chawton (15–16 September 1813) despite the complications of Henry's (un)planned movements. Austen perhaps feels herself distanced in Kent when she learns that the female visitors are staying on: 'a good plan however – I c^d not have settled it better myself' (11–12 October 1813). She adjusts her own plan to hope that 'they will ask Martha to visit them' and this is juxtaposed in the letter with the proposed naming of a heroine after Charlotte Williams whose father rented out the Winchester house in which Alethea and Elizabeth will now live (Le Faye 2011, p. 586). In 6–7 November 1813, Cassandra and all three sisters are envisioned seeing the sights via Streatham in Henry's carriage with Austen stationary at Godmersham trying not to be 'foolishly minute'.

On 13 March 1816 the Bigg sisters' visit to Chawton by post chaise is reported to Caroline but this is a precursor to Austen herself being drawn to Winchester for medical treatment where she lodges in a house found by Elizabeth who is their daily visitor (27 May 1817). In a postscript to Anne Sharp, Austen mentions 'we shall not have Miss Bigg, she being frisked off like half England, into Switzerland' (22 May 1817). Alethea's January 1817 last letter was received at Streatham and carried back to Winchester. It is unclear whether she saw Austen again but the letter kept as a memorial is now untraceable since being copied by Mary Augusta Austen-Leigh for the second edition of the *Memoir* (Modert 1990, p. 61). Alethea died in 1847 and Elizabeth in 1855 so it has been assumed that the memento was lent out by William Heathcote in 1871 before being mislaid (Le Faye 2011, p. 432). The sisters succeeded to greater affluence themselves in the further move to Hursley Park where William inherited from his uncle but the letter survives at another remove, standing in for the lost friend and for the shared lives of the Bigg-Lloyd-Austen women.

Austen's many experiences of being a sister overflowed from her letters into her fiction. John Mullan observes that sisters make up the domestic architecture of the novels (2012, p. 26) but one strand within the marriage plots is also the acquisition of sisters and the exploration of other sisterly relationships. It has been suggested that 'the marriage is grafted onto the sororal union' in *Sense and*

Sensibility and *Pride and Prejudice* (Hudson 1992, p. 61) although in *Emma* and *Mansfield Park* marriage partners are discovered similarly close to home. This section examines the ways in which the sisterhoods of the letters are reconfigured within the novels. Marriage is a form of displacement (Levin 1992, p. 34) that creates new familial spaces and widens the pool of available candidates for sisters. As in life, there are missing sisters, extra-familial sisters, and sisters who are false to the sisterhood.

Austen draws her boundaries wide when she observes in *Northanger Abbey* that '[t]he advantages of natural folly in a beautiful girl have been already set forth by the capital pen of a sister author' (p. 112): by Frances Burney in her epistolary novel *Evelina*. In the novel itself Catherine befriends Eleanor Tilney, a woman looking for a sister and correspondent (p. 236), and the false would-be sister Isabella Thorpe is unmasked and displaced. Despite her early pursuit of Catherine, Isabella gains no sisterly relationship social or marital since she marries neither James Morland nor Frederick Tilney. Her scheming and calculation of the sisterly relationship is explored again in the character of Mary Crawford.

The roles of familial and social sister are also under examination in *Sense and Sensibility* where Lucy Steele is quick to claim Fanny Dashwood as Elinor's sister. Her contention that Edward 'looks upon yourself and the other Miss Dashwoods, quite as his own sisters' (p. 149) is, however, pure spite. Fanny Dashwood uses a different tactic to divide Elinor from Edward describing the Dashwood sisters as 'half blood, which she considered as no relationship at all' (p. 9) unlike the Austens in their regard for the Walters. In the 'indelicacy' of John and Fanny arriving at Norland (p. 6), there is an echo of James and Mary occupying Steventon where, from 1801, the Austens were themselves 'degraded to the condition of visitors' (p. 9). Mary Lloyd Austen's sister has successfully married her cousin Fulwar but it is cousinship that exposes Elinor to Lucy's duplicity in the novel. Sir John Middleton has at least offered the Dashwoods a home on the basis of a cousinly connection but Mrs Jennings has introduced the Steele sisters on the grounds that they are 'all cousins and must put up with one another' (p. 137).

As in the tart observations of the letters, distinctions are observed between the two Steele sisters: 'Lucy was certainly not elegant and her sister not even genteel' (*S&S*, p. 263). This description was revised from 'scarcely elegant' in the first edition, sinking Lucy further as a gentlewoman and critiquing the judgement of the Middleton-John Dashwood circle. Anne Steele's confidential friend Martha Sharpe seems to be a joke combination of two real-life epistolary sisters – Martha Lloyd and Anne Sharp – with Austen eavesdropping on them in the character of Lucy 'hiding in a closet, or behind a chimney-board' (p. 311). When Miss Steele is distracted by the Richardsons, 'very genteel people' with 'their own coach', there is a further joke at the expense of the brother author who was a manipulator of women's letter writing. The 'monstrous deal of money' (p. 312) made by

Mr Richardson undermines his gentility but his keeping a coach pinpoints both his income and the less than genteel expression of it put forward by Anne.

Lucy's proffered role as a sister is examined in the resolution of the triangular relationship with Edward. Although suffering herself, Marianne pre-empts this outcome when she offers Edward 'the affection of a sister' during Lucy's coincidental visit to Berkeley Street (*S&S*, p. 275). In the following chapter, the Steele sisters usurp Elinor and Marianne's place as visitors at the John Dashwoods, precipitating Lucy's revelation of her long-standing engagement to her supposed sister Fanny. After her subsequent marriage to Robert, Lucy describes herself as 'Your sincere well-wisher, friend and, sister' in a letter to Edward and he blushes over her correspondence: 'In a sister it is bad enough, but in a wife!' (p. 414). Lucy, however, inveigles herself back into the favour of Mrs Ferrars and survives by her own contrivance. Marianne revalues her sister's civility and forbearance as 'my nurse, my friend, my sister!' (p. 391) and they remake their community at Delaford away from Mrs Ferrars and Lucy with the diplomatic connivance of Mrs Dashwood.

The search for marriage partners for an increased number of familial sisters in *Pride and Prejudice* brings other women into the circle. Miss Bingley looks forward prematurely to Miss Darcy being 'our sister' (p. 132) although by the end of the novel Georgiana is writing to Elizabeth and '[f]our sides of paper' is 'insufficient to contain all her delight, and all her earnest desire of being loved by her sister' (p. 425). Charlotte Lucas is a sisterly friend for circumstantial and geographic as well as empathetic reasons but her opinion that 'Happiness in marriage is entirely a matter of chance' (p. 25) is regarded by Elizabeth as unsound. Charlotte's 'pure and disinterested desire of an establishment' relieves her family of the burden of her maintenance as 'an old maid' (p. 137) and initially Elizabeth's 'disappointment in Charlotte made her turn with fonder regard to her sister' (p. 144). To herself, Charlotte describes marriage as 'the only honourable provision for well-educated women of small fortune' (p. 138) and she wisely mentions 'nothing which she could not praise' (p. 166) in letters after marriage. As perhaps Austen did at Streatham, Elizabeth rekindles her understanding with Charlotte on her visit to Hunsford with its organised domestic geography. The two elder Bennet sisters unite by living on estates in 'neighbouring' counties and in further rescuing their sister Kitty. Miss Bingley is now related to all five Miss Bennets but swallows her mortification in return for visiting rights to Pemberley, claiming to be fonder of Georgiana and paying off 'every arrear of civility to Elizabeth' (p. 430).

Mansfield Park represents a shift in sisterly relations and leaves those exiled from its resolution unforgiven. The mature novel, written wholly in Austen's thirties, manipulates the condition and relationships of sisters through family bonds and marital aspirations, distinguishing cousinship and the search for a life partner. At the beginning of the novel, Lady Bertram has 'two sisters to be benefited by her elevation' but Mrs Norris, the eldest Miss Ward, settles for her husband because there are 'not so many men of large fortune . . . as there are pretty women to deserve them' (p. 3). Austen has updated the opening words of *Pride and Prejudice* so that women are now in pursuit of a scarce resource rather than men being in want of them. Lady Bertram has been lucky in the marriage market and has 'captivated' Sir Thomas and his large income with only seven thousand pounds of her own which her lawyer uncle deems to be 'at least three thousand pounds short of any equitable claim' (p. 3). Austen parodies Charlotte Lucas's philosophy in the character of Maria Bertram complete '[i]n all the important preparations of the mind' (p. 236). She is 'prepared for matrimony by a hatred of home, restraint and tranquillity; by the misery of disappointed affection and contempt of the man she was to marry. The rest might wait' (p. 236). The marriage bargain is completed by coming full circle from the circumstances of Maria's Aunt Norris, married out of desperation after her dozen-year wait. At the Rushworths' wedding, 'no one would have supposed . . . that she had ever heard of conjugal infelicity in her life, or could have the smallest insight into the disposition of the niece who had been brought up under her eye' (pp. 237–238). The end of the novel presents Mrs Norris and Maria Rushworth in a re-formed community in exile rather than the rekindled if pragmatic understanding between Elizabeth and Charlotte.

Mary Crawford meanwhile manipulates three sisterly roles in her relationships with Henry, Mrs Grant, and Fanny. When Henry proposes to marry Fanny rather than to pursue his 'idle designs' (*MP*, p. 338), he sees a new triumvirate of himself, Fanny, and Mrs Grant with 'an equal claim' to Mary: 'Fanny will be so truly your sister!' (p. 342). In her early voice, Mary reclaims a half-blood relationship to Mrs Grant 'a sister without preciseness or rusticity' (p. 47) who offers a convenient escape but no competition; for Mrs Grant, Mary is 'her dearest object' (p. 48). Mary is repeatedly and emphatically declared a good sister to Henry but a dangerous sister to women especially to Fanny and effectively to the Bertram sisters too. In a letter to Portsmouth, Mary recounts a meeting with the Bertrams that she used as an occasion to speak to them of Fanny 'as a sister should' (p. 456). Mary's encouragement of Henry has previously caused Julia and Maria to become enemies as theatre participants and during the Sotherton visit. When she accepts the necklace from Mary which is insinuated on her by Henry, Fanny concludes, 'Miss Crawford, complaisant as a sister, was careless as a woman and a friend' (p. 302). When the Crawfords leave Mansfield, Edmund is surprised that Fanny does not 'regret' Mary but 'Alas! it was this sister, this friend and companion, who was now the chief bane of Fanny's comfort' (p. 423). The Crawfords instead represent the dissolution of all Fanny's hopes. If Fanny were to accept Mary as a sister this would mean dividing herself from Edmund and in effect compounding their relationship as brother-sister-cousin. Indeed the threat that they will be kept apart is sustained until late in the novel and despite losing the

Crawfords as a result of Maria's elopement. Mrs Norris predicted of Tom and Edmund early in the novel, that Fanny 'will never be more to either than a sister' if the Bertrams 'breed her up with them' (p. 7). On arriving in Portsmouth before his final realisation and regeneration, Edmund exclaims: 'My Fanny – my only sister – my only comfort now' (p. 515).

In outline, Fanny Price has sisters – but not sisterhood – thrust upon her in a novel where genetic sisters fail to create new communities over two generations. Mrs Norris occupies a family place as a result of her husband's living and is influential over her own nieces who are not sisterly. Fanny is ambiguously adopted and takes the role of companion to Lady Bertram as a result of Mrs Norris's gesture towards their third sister. Fanny is then forced into a further relationship with Mary Crawford, a more refined version of Lucy Steele, who connives to secure the match that would make them sisters through Henry. When Fanny is exiled to Portsmouth to consider her options in the third volume of the novel, she encounters the ghosts of two lost sisters: Mrs Price now worn out as the wife of a half-drunk lieutenant and her dead daughter, Fanny's sister Mary (*MP*, pp. 445–446). The memory of Mary reconciles Fanny to her role in the family and Fanny can then renovate sisterhood when she cultivates her own familial sister Susan. Susan assumes Fanny's place at Mansfield, and Edmund then loses his 'only sister' by marrying her.

After this darker context for sisterhood, new questions of women's community are asked insistently in *Emma* where, in default of equivalent society, the heroine is asked to choose between an impoverished female trio and the attendees of a girls' school. This choice is triggered at the beginning of the novel by the marriage of Miss Taylor who although 'little short of a mother' (p. 3) is also on an 'equal footing' and enjoys 'perfect unreserve' (p. 4) in a sisterly relationship with her former pupil. As Mrs Weston, she is a partial observer when she declares in conversation with Mr Knightley that Emma is a good daughter, kind sister, and true friend (p. 40). He, however, expresses concern about Emma's choice of a companion in Harriet Smith whose 'ignorance is hourly flattery' (p. 39), and candidates to be Emma's sister increase with Mr Knightley's own exclamation that '[his sister-in-law] Isabella does not seem more my sister' (p. 41). The community offers a more straightforward alternative sister from the trio but Emma rejects Jane Fairfax ostensibly because of the other woman's cool detachment and her superior accomplishments. There is a key to this rejection, however, in Emma's thoughts about Jane and her reserve. In a concise survey of social niceties redolent of Austen's letters, Emma complains that she will 'have to pay civilities to a person she did not like through three long months! – to be always doing more than she wished and less than she ought!' (p. 177). Prompted by Frank Churchill, Emma half-perceives the reasons for the lack of community between her and Jane. She has, however, lighted on the wrong love interest and contributes substantially to Frank's cruelties.

Jane is also excluded from notice because of her place in the home of the Bateses. The social position of Miss Bates is becoming more indeterminate because of the death of her rector father and the dependence of her elderly mother but she nonetheless enjoys 'a most uncommon degree of popularity for a woman neither young, handsome, rich or married' (*E*, p. 20). Spinsters have scarcely rallied since Elizabeth Watson's advice to another Emma to marry because 'it is very bad to grow old and be poor and laughed at' (*LM*, p. 82) and Austen has recently raised with Fanny Knight the single woman's 'propensity for being poor' (18–20 November 1814). Through Miss Bates, Austen explores her own status in the aftermath of her father's death in 1805 even to the presents of fruit and meat that arrived at Chawton Cottage from brother Edward like the fictional apples and pork from Donwell and Hartfield. The wider community rallies, and even Frank Churchill points out in his duplicitous way that Miss Bates 'is a woman that one may, that one *must* laugh at; but that one would not wish to slight' (*E*, p. 281). Miss Bates seems destined to fall lower than the Austens to the level of Miss Benn in Chawton but will be rescued by Jane's marriage although Austen herself told her family that the new Mrs Churchill would not live more than ten years (Le Faye 2011, p. 241). Perhaps there is some gentle mockery in compliment to the sisterhood when first Fanny Price and now Emma are sisters to their husbands before they become wives. Emma indeed finds herself, through marriage, sister to her own sister and it is Mr Knightley who becomes a geographically dependent live-in companion.

Persuasion was not, of course, subject to the 'scratching out' or final revision recommended to Anna but it is notable in the novel that Elizabeth Elliot is repeatedly coupled not with her sister but with Sir Walter in their 'cold composure' and 'heartless elegance' (p. 245). As a heroine, Anne Elliot seems most likely to share Austen and Cassandra's singleness. Anne is 'nobody with either father or sister; her word had no weight; her convenience was always to give way' (p. 6) and she must actively seek social sisterhood. The novel offers Anne a new community and new sisters as a result of her perseverance even though she lacks a Cassandra or a Martha, or indeed cousins and nieces. In Mrs Clay, Elizabeth finds a companion by 'turning from the society of so deserving a sister' (p. 17) to a widowed version of Harriet Smith with devious plans for remarriage. Anne is equally down-graded by her hypochondriac younger sister Mary and esteemed by the Musgroves only as a willing ear or player of country dances on the piano. She is finally valued out loud as 'so proper so capable' (p. 123) by Wentworth at the very moment when he comes to regard himself as tied to Louisa after her fall. Excluded even from this sisterly contribution by Mary's neediness, Anne rekindles a school sisterhood with Mrs Smith who is somewhat clumsily instrumental in uncovering the motivations of cousin and heir Mr Elliot. The act of reaching out to another woman and of representing women's constancy to Captain Harville promotes Anne's final happiness. After marriage, she can dispense with now 'innoxious cousins' (p. 267), leaving Wentworth to forgive the sister-mother Lady Russell while Anne finally joins a sisterhood of Navy wives. With Mrs Croft and the invalided Captain Harville she shares 'the kind-hearted intercourse of brother and sister' (p. 267) and this finally remedies the absence of sisters at sea or at school (p. 33) that excluded them from the lost engagement.

The role of sister and of sisterhood is questioned and refashioned in Austen's letters and fiction where she seeks, finds, and fails to find sisters through friendship and community. The letter is an established writing vehicle for women, and Austen began her examination of the sisterly contract and its letter networks from her earliest writings. She read and discussed novels themselves written in letters. The unfolding life of this 'merciless sister' and published author is examined in the next chapter by exploring Austen's use of letters as narrative in her early novels before reconsidering the place of letters in her mature works. She continued to write letters in life while her epistolary fiction evolved into novels about letters.

5

Novels in Letters

Letters into Novels

The letter was not just part of the structure of Austen's life; it also structured her early ventures into fiction. During the early period when there are no letters extant, Austen exercised her powers in fictional letter writing as she does in 'Amelia Webster', 'The Three Sisters', and 'A Collection of Letters' in Volume the First of her earliest writings. These pieces, re-copied and preserved as books with a contents page and page numbers, demonstrate an engagement not just with the form of the novel but with the letter manual and the epistolary novel. 'Love and Freindship' and 'Lesley Castle' in Volume the Second are more sophisticated, less reductive, and more satirical, and Austen initially persevered with the form. This chapter considers the place of *Lady Susan* and the presumed epistolary version of *Sense and Sensibility* as explorations of the letter as fiction. The chapter also weighs up the potential for the original draft of *Pride and Prejudice* being in epistolary form and uses this as a springboard for the discussion of letters as narrative devices of plot and character within the mature novels. The letter forms both the fabric and architecture of the novels even after the epistolary form is abandoned, and the epistolary nature of the Juvenilia learned from manuals, novels, and the lived practice of letter writing can still be traced in the form of the full-length works. As Norman Page observes, letter writing was a 'way of life as well as a device of art' (1972, p. 171) and the deployment of letters as art becomes a pivot for the letter as biographical evidence of a life.

Among the documentary evidence of Austen's life is a note to the future compiled by Cassandra. Using this memorandum (Chapman 1954, facing p. 242) and with additional conjectural detail, Austen's early works have been dated (Sutherland 2005b, pp. 20–22).The letters within the Juvenilia were written by 1793 and the more ambitious epistolary novella *Lady Susan* by 1795. 'Elinor and Marianne' was written in 1795 and 'First Impressions' in 1796–1797 in time for the Reverend George Austen's approach to publisher Cadell dated 1 November 1797. It has been suggested that Austen was an epistolary novelist until 1797

The Life of the Author: Jane Austen, First Edition. Catherine Delafield.
© 2023 John Wiley & Sons Ltd. Published 2023 by John Wiley & Sons Ltd.

(Bray 2003, p. 115) and even that one third of her major fiction was epistolary (Galperin 2003, p. 21). By 1797 'Elinor and Marianne' was already being redrafted in third-person narrative form and 'Susan', the early version of *Northanger Abbey*, was written in 1798–1799 when Austen was aged 23. The epistolary Juvenilia were written for manuscript circulation because Austen was writing letters and reading letter manuals but she was also reading epistolary novels with a critical eye. The novels in their original and redrafted forms were thus influenced by her daily correspondence as well as her authorial ambitions.

Since their wider appearance in print, the Juvenilia have come under closer study revealing their use of disruptive voices, the awareness of an audience, and a critical engagement with models of contemporary writing. When the first half of Chapman's *Minor Works* (1954) was updated as *Catharine and Other Writings* (Doody 1993), its new title prioritised the text most like that of the mature published novels. Among its symbolic qualities, the 'Bower' of 'Catharine, or the Bower' operates as letters do at a public/private boundary (Leffel 2011) and at the boundary of Austen's choice of narrative form. Subsequent editors have emphasised how a named or calibrated audience of dedicatees positions the Juvenilia like letters. Critics have explored intertextual relationships with manuals and the epistolary form of the novel but have also pointed out that the unrestrained exuberance of the youthful or teenage writings was retained and sustained in private manuscript circulation within Austen's actual letters (Southam 1964; Fergus 1998b; Sabor 2006; Alexander 2014; Sutherland 2017c).

The Juvenilia explore the agency of letter writing as part of life and as art. The letter promotes three marriages in 'Amelia Webster', reveals a counterplot in 'The Three Sisters' and offers Laura a vehicle for life writing in 'Love and Freindship'. These pieces are developing into the programmed complexity of the longer *Lady Susan* while already demonstrating the logistical issues to which Austen attributes her abandonment of the epistolary form. Even without the use of the letter as narrative, the dedications transform the Juvenile writings into texts with an audience. These family manuscript productions were targeted, as discussed in Chapters 3 and 4, like letters themselves. Christine Alexander observes that being unfinished is part of the joke (2014, p. x) but this is also part of the lived reality of correspondence.

The epistolary 'Amelia Webster' dedicated 'by Permission' to Mrs Austen 'by Her humble Servant / The Author' results in the marriage of three couples within seven letters. The conventions of the fictional and factual letter collide with hilarious precision. Flourishes from the form of the letter embroider the skeletal plot and occupy more of the text than actual events as when Matilda writes to Amelia of her 'amiable Brother', 'never did I see a finer form, save that of your sincere freind / Matilda Hervey' (*J*, p. 58). Her brother George proposes that Henry Beverley marry Matilda: 'She will have two thousand Pounds and as much more as you can get. If you don't marry her, you will mortally offend/George Hervey' (p. 58). Amelia writes in the second sentence of two in her first letter to Matilda: 'I have a thousand things to tell you, but my paper will only permit me to add that I am yr affect. Freind' (p. 58) and demonstrates in the second sentence of her second letter (p. 59) an earlier use of a technique deployed in *Sense and Sensibility* when Lucy Steele writes to Elinor, 'My paper reminds me to conclude'. Epistolary fiction is itself under examination by the 11 year-old Austen when Benjamin Bar's letter to Sarah Hervey in 'Amelia Webster' employs one of the more improbable elements of letter transmission used in Richardson's *Pamela*. A hollow oak one mile from Bar's home and seven miles from Sarah's is chosen for the exchange of their letters because Benjamin believes the walk will be beneficial to his correspondent. This 100-word logistical discussion is the longest letter of the piece (p. 59) and questions with amusement the employment of the letter form by Richardson. The manuals had advised, in conjunction with Dr. Johnson, that '[t]rifles always require exuberance of ornament' (Johnson 1779, p. iv), and Austen later uses the whole of a much longer letter in 'Love and Freindship' to describe answering a knock at the door (*J*, pp. 106–107).

'The Three Sisters', also in Volume the First, is an 'unfinished novel' in four longer interacting letters 'respectfully inscribed' to Edward Austen probably on the occasion of his marriage to Elizabeth, one of the three Bridges sisters who were all married in 1791. In this piece, daughters are regarded as interchangeable in a marriage situation reminiscent of Mrs Bennet's. Georgiana Stanhope writes to her friend 'Miss XXX' that her mother's resolution 'is generally more strictly kept than rationally formed' (*J*, p. 78). Austen analyses the art of epistolary construction by introducing offstage correspondents and parallel accounts of events. Mary Stanhope writes to 'Mrs . . .' that Mr Watts is 'quite an old Man, about two and thirty' with 'a large fortune . . . but then he is very healthy' (p. 74). Through the letters, Georgiana and third sister Sophia reveal with some brutality that they want to avoid Watts's being palmed off on one of them by their mother. As in Austen's other Juvenilia, the plot turns on an exuberant and obsessive need for acquisition. In this case, Mary demands a new and gaudy carriage in addition to jewels, new furniture, and servants and an extensive round of visits and engagements. The voices of the sisters are a cruder representation of the free indirect perspectives explored within the later novels. Austen is testing the differentiation between points of view when Mary finally agrees to marry Mr Watts and Georgiana reveals the younger sisters' bluff to her correspondent; they have claimed that they would accept Watts if Mary refuses him.

These two epistolary works present the social and matrimonial concerns of the published novels in extreme burlesque form. They are also already beginning to explore the possibility that the letter is not a flexible enough vehicle for narrative in the longer form of the novel. After the brief and plot-hungry 'Amelia Webster' and designedly unfinished 'The Three Sisters', Volume the Second contains 'Love and Freindship', the 'novel in a series of letters' dedicated to sister-cousin Eliza. Given the dating of the text (13 June 1790; *J*, p. 141) and of Edward's marriage (December 1791) it was probably written before 'The Three Sisters'. The letter in this mode was a type of autobiography as sociable exchange, a format used, for instance, by Mary Delany to her friend the Duchess of Portland (Delafield 2020, pp. 82–83). It has been pointed out that letter manuals 'provided the intriguing prospect of reading about the dissolute in a morally sanctioned mode' (Mitchell 2016, p. 442) and in 'Love and Freindship' the letter is cover for a series of zany adventures narrated from the viewpoint of one of the characters. Austen has come to understand in her mid-teens that the letter might indeed sanction accounts of a departure from convention and she happily exploits the potential for rebellion in the form of a request for autobiography. This is a joke about the letter's covert opportunities as life writing rather than about the letter form itself or about the possibilities of the epistolary novel.

Another 'unfinished novel in letters' was dedicated to cousin Eliza's later second husband Henry and makes direct fun of epistolary convention. 'Lesley Castle' includes the parallel correspondences of Charlotte Luttrell and her sister Eloisa, and Austen once more enjoys the problem of women having to narrate themselves, especially over the relative sizes of the tall Lesleys and their diminutive and vulgar new stepmother. The melancholy Eloisa is keen to find a 'Freind . . . independant of my Sister' to 'speak with less reserve than to any other person' (*J*, p. 168) and spends much of her only letter promoting her own misery so that her flirtatious female correspondent can reflect back this 'Bewitching Sweetness' (p. 171). Following an untimely fatal injury to the groom, Eloisa's wedding has had to be cancelled and only a few weeks later Charlotte has been chivvying her sister into entertaining a new suitor (p. 156). Charlotte is comically obsessed with the eating and drinking associated with marriage and, having prepared the now redundant 'Wedding dinner', is mortified to have 'been Roasting, Broiling and Stewing both the Meat and Myself to no purpose' (p. 146). The use of five correspondents represents the beginning of Austen's manipulation of voices within a narrative. Eloisa exchanges letters with her new friend Mrs Marlowe whose name echoes Richardson's doomed Clarissa Harlowe, and Charlotte has 'two confidential Correspondents' (p. 168) in Margaret Lesley and Margaret's new stepmother Susan. The situations of the Lesleys and Lutterells are narrated and re-narrated through letters with comic effect. Of the ten letters, four are from Margaret to Charlotte with three in return. Eloisa and Emma Marlowe write one letter each and Susan Lady Lesley writes once to Charlotte. When Charlotte writes to her school friend Margaret about writing to her friend Susan Fitzgerald to seek information about the marriage of Margaret's father, Susan's reply is enclosed: 'I was myself present at the Ceremony, which you will not be surprised at when

I subscribe myself / Your Affectionate Susan Lesley' (p. 149). Eloisa writes to Emma Marlowe about Charlotte who writes to Margaret about Eloisa. Margaret writes to Charlotte about Susan who writes to Charlotte about Margaret. The letters are dated between 3 January and 13 April 1792 meaning that 'Lesley Castle' was probably composed in that year (*J*, p. xxix). The joke cannot be sustained but Austen was experimenting here with contrasting viewpoints and dynamic linear progression.

In the 41 letters of *Lady Susan*, Austen moves on to develop further the alternative viewpoints and real-time exchanges of 'The Three Sisters' and 'Lesley Castle'. 'Lesley Castle' has explored the potential for the relationship between correspondents to be a significant component of the plot. In the later novella, Lady Susan writes 12 of her 16 letters to her largely passive co-conspirator Alicia Johnson, and Catherine Vernon writes 11 letters revealing her suspicions of Lady Susan to her mother Lady de Courcy. It is these letters that essentially provide the thrust of the plot from different viewpoints. The tone is brutally comic and letters forward both plot and character.

In Letter 1, Lady Susan writes to her mostly invisible brother-in-law to propose or insist on a visit to Churchill and the 'delightful retirement' (*LM*, p. 3) of the Vernons' home but writing to Alicia in Letter 2 she describes the country village as an 'insupportable spot' (p. 5). In Letter 29, she scorns Reginald to Alicia and then in Letter 30 writes to him a delicately balanced argument in favour of their future union. In Letter 5, there is a casual plot to mislead Alicia's observant husband who must be deceived 'entirely; – since he will be stubborn, he must be tricked' (p. 9). Lady Susan will therefore write letters under cover for Alicia to forward to her lover Manwaring who is married to Mr Johnson's ward. In Letter 29, Lady Susan coldly describes Mr Johnson as 'too old to be agreable, & too young to die' (p. 62) echoing Mary Stanhope's description of Mr Watts in 'The Three Sisters'. In Letter 28, Alicia congratulates herself on her epistolary influence, 'pleased to find that my Letter had so much effect on you' (p. 89), but Lady Susan is later thwarted and diverted in her aims to keep Manwaring apart from Reginald when Letter 30 'which was intended to keep him longer in the Country, has hastened him to Town' (p. 66). The letters become shorter as the time frame narrows in the final third of the novella and Lady Susan is unmasked by a faulty delivery. Reginald carries a dismissive note about him to Alicia by way of introduction but is intercepted by a visit from Mrs Manwaring and this accident also cuts off a source of narrative when Alicia is forbidden to communicate with her friend.

This approach develops and adds greater complexity to the multiple viewpoints employed in 'Lesley Castle'. Even before its abrupt conclusion, *Lady Susan* toys with the logistics of the epistolary form. It is surely no coincidence that the husband/guardian who unmasks the plot in Letter 32 is Mr Johnson, as is the acknowledged author of epistolary guidance in *The Complete Art of Writing Letters*

(Johnson 1779) who quotes Dr Johnson from *The Rambler*. Letter 11 is read aloud in Letter 12; Letter 13 encloses Letter 14 replying to Letter 12 and is returned in Letter 15. The school principal Miss Summers's letter arrives offstage and the illicit Manwaring letters circulate in the background. Letters 22–25 have a timing problem as they are written, sent, read, and received over only two hours. Letter 38 mentions that Reginald has written to Mr Johnson, and the opening of Letter 40 demonstrates that there is a missing letter written in the morning of the same day from Lady de Courcy to her daughter Mrs Vernon. The impracticalities come to a head when Reginald asks Lady Susan why their relationship should be prolonged and he has to write a letter about this: 'Why would you write to me?' he asks when her 'misconduct' is 'unanswerably proved' (*LM*, p. 69). These are issues that expose the epistolary form described as 'morally anarchic' by Deborah Kaplan (1987a, p. 169). Kaplan suggests that Lady Susan is able to exploit female networks in the novella (p. 168) but that the text is 'fractured by these competing perspectives' (p. 174) both here and in the preceding drafts 'Elinor and Marianne' and 'First Impressions'. The timing of these epistolary compositions has also been interpreted as significant to Austen's development as a novelist. Brian Southam regards the third-person narrative of 'Catharine' (1792) as an experiment and he views the epistolary novel as the 'less demanding form' (1964, p. 46) to which Austen returned until 1797.

While Austen's authorship remained within the family circle, manuscripts were circulating among an audience familiar with both the epistolary novel and with Austen's early writings. There is humour within the anarchy when Lady Susan will not allow Manwaring to lodge nearby for fear of damaging her reputation: 'Those women are inexcusable who forget what is due to themselves & the opinion of the World' (*LM*, p. 31). The rhetoric of the Juvenilia is deployed by Lady Susan and reported by Mrs Vernon to her own mother when Frederica is under threat: 'Am I capable of consigning <u>her</u> to everlasting Misery whose welfare it is my first Earthly Duty to promote?' (p. 52). There is also, however, a sense of the composition of actual letters when Mrs Vernon observes tersely, 'if she chuses to come, no want of cordiality on my part will keep her away' (p. 61). Some of the phrasing is already anticipating the mature novels; 'it required some consideration to be tranquilly happy' (p. 47) seems closer to *Pride and Prejudice* than to 'Lesley Castle' suggesting the extension of epistolary voices outside the epistolary form is already under development.

The omniscient narrator of the conclusion to the novella draws attention to the unreliability of Lady Susan's voice regarding the happiness of her second marriage 'for who would take her assurance of it, on either side of the question?' (*LM*, p. 77). This narrating voice is, however, mischievous in its conclusion that 'She had nothing against her, but her Husband & her Conscience' (p. 77). This is an early version of the conclusive uncertainty of the later novels where scheming women secure their futures. Like Lady Susan, Lucy Steele prospers through 'no other sacrifice than that of time and conscience' (*S&S*, p. 426) and 'artful' Mrs Clay plays a longer double game to secure her role as the next Lady Elliot (*P*, p. 273). When Mary Crawford gives Maria Rushworth's elopement with Henry 'no harsher name than folly' (*MP*, p. 526), she scorns 'cold prudence', gambling as she did during the earlier game of Speculation when 'The game was her's, and only did not pay her for what she had given to secure it' (p. 282). In the earlier work, Lady Susan's letters demonstrate that she despises Manwaring, Reginald, and her eventual second husband, and Alicia Johnson is more surely her lover-prey. Theirs is an early exploration of female social dependency explored and exploited in letters. In Letter 22, Lady Susan tells her friend she will 'releive' herself by writing to her (*LM*, p. 42) and, like Lady Susan, Alicia maintains the doubleness of her life and opinions, declaring at the point of discovery that 'Facts are such horrid things!' (p. 67). Lady Susan's final contribution in her own voice is cruel and dangerous in a more realistic setting than that of the rebellious Laura. She declares in Letter 39 to Alicia that she is 'tired of submitting my will to the Caprices of others' (p. 72). She looks forward to Alicia's widowhood and pronounces herself unchanged: 'I yield to the necessity which parts us. . . . Adieu dearest of Friends. May the next Gouty Attack be more favourable – & may you always regard me as unalterably Yours / *S. Vernon*' (pp. 71–72).

In a seminal work on epistolarity, Janet Altman describes the result as a mosaic (1982, p. 187), creating meaning from the formal properties of letters (p. 4) and the 'structured interplay' between them (p. 183). It was however a perception of the 'gaps and traps' (Altman 1982, p. 212) such as absence, remoteness from events, and the descriptive role of letters composed in real-time that caused Austen to look for another form of narrative. Editing and presence disrupt the reading of Austen's letters as life writing. The conclusion of *Lady Susan* observes that the 'meeting' and 'separation' of 'parties' (*LM*, p. 75) disrupts narrative. Joe Bray describes how the later novels reconcile different points of view (2003, p. 116) but concludes that 'letters remain central to her art' and are 'part of the fabric of her novels' (p. 131).

The *Lady Susan* conclusion that signals a change of voice may express Austen's frustrations at the time of the original composition in 1795 but may also be the result of her making the existing fair copy of the novella in 1805. The epistolary 'Elinor and Marianne' was also written in 1795 and 'First Impressions' in 1796–1797. In returning to revise 'Elinor and Marianne' in 1797, Austen acknowledges the need for more flexibility and the opportunity to use a range of voices within a narrative frame. Letters were nonetheless available to give voices new contexts and new consequences, and for the development of free indirect speech.

It is Cassandra's memorandum that suggests that 'Elinor and Marianne' was written in 1795 immediately after *Lady Susan*. There was at this time a brief vogue for contrast novels (Butler 1975, pp. 128–130; Kirkham 1983a, pp. 85–86) and in 1795 Maria Edgeworth published her *Letters for Literary Ladies* including 'Letters of Julia and Caroline' (1795), an epistolary 'moral tale' about the dangers of sensibility. As Edgeworth's first published work, 'Letters' was bound in with letters, believed to be autobiographical (Narain 1998), that were exchanged between two men about women's education. *Letters for Literary Ladies* was published anonymously but it is possible that Austen could have been aware of its authorship and origins. Before their removal to Ireland in 1783, Edgeworth's father Richard had been a neighbour of the Leigh-Perrots in Berkshire (Le Faye 2004, p. 118). 'Letters of Julia and Caroline' consists of seven letters; one is a reply from Julia to Caroline, the other five to Julia are replies from Caroline only, and the final letter is from Caroline to Julia's estranged husband. Julia pinpoints their differences in Letter I when she writes to her friend: 'In vain, dear Caroline, you urge me to think; I profess only to feel . . . I have no system: that is the very difference between us' (Edgeworth 1795, p. 3). Julia is reflecting back Caroline's request for a 'system' not included in the text as published, and Julia's insistence that 'I leave everything to fortune; you leave nothing' (p. 11) echoes Marianne in *Sense and Sensibility*. In Austen's novel, Elinor challenges her sister about expecting a letter from Willoughby when they are at Mrs Jennings's house in London but must then defend herself against having 'nothing to tell'. Marianne takes haughty exception to this: 'We have neither of us anything to tell; you, because you communicate, and I, because I conceal nothing' (*S&S*, p. 193).

In Edgeworth's piece, the progress of Julia's life is traced in the letter-responses of her friend with no sense of the logistics and transmission involved. Julia should have married Caroline's brother Mr Percy and, five years after Julia's ill-advised marriage to Lord V, Caroline writes: 'I am your friend, nor would the name of sister have increased my friendship' (Edgeworth 1795, p. 39). From her friend's viewpoint, it appears that Julia thrives on praise and Caroline suggests that praise is equally to be earned from domestic virtue. By Letter VI, Julia has eloped from her unsatisfactory marriage and Caroline has burned her previous letter. In default of further letters from Julia, Caroline adopts her friend's melodramatic tone when she protests: 'In misfortune, in sickness, or in poverty, I never would have forsaken you; but infamy I cannot share! . . . I went to the brink of the precipice to save you; with all my force I held you back; but in vain' (pp. 63–64). The next and final letter encloses a note of remorse from Julia who has died embracing her child.

This sequence in epistolary format offers a representation of sensibility as Austen could have explored it in 'Elinor and Marianne'. She and Edgeworth in parallel examine this combination of narrative form and content. In 'Love and Freindship' (1790), Austen has given Laura a voice and free rein to faint 'on the Sofa' (*J*, p. 117) but five years later, with *Lady Susan* as a stepping stone, she begins to explore consequences in a realistic setting. It may be that sustaining Marianne's voice became unfeasible at longer length and so *Sense and Sensibility* allows greater access to the reflected more rational narrator of sense. Edgeworth's crossover moment in 'Letters of Julia and Caroline' may also have suggested a way in which the realistic interaction of two viewpoints could be developed by Austen beyond the contrasting characters of Lady Susan and her sister-in-law Catherine Vernon. As Edgeworth did in 'Letters', Austen's revision controls access to the victim of sensibility and Elinor's becomes the dominant narrative voice. Marianne is not sacrificed to sensibility but taken only to the brink of death by her over-indulgence unlike Edgeworth's Julia and the doomed Sophia in 'Love and Freindship'. By the time of her revision for publication, Austen has reconciled an approach to the contrasting characters when she uses her authorial voice to observe: 'Their means were as different as their objects, and equally suited to the advancement of each' (*S&S*, p. 120).

Cassandra's assertion 'I am sure something of this/same story & character had been/written earlier & called Elinor & Marianne' (Chapman 1954, facing p. 242) has sparked debates over the potential form of Austen's first two published novels. Without the original drafts of *Sense and Sensibility* and *Pride and Prejudice*, the argument about their reliance on epistolary originals can only be conducted through the published versions of 1811 and 1813 but an exploration of the letter's role in these earlier works also illustrates how the letter becomes a plot device in the later novels. Actual letters can be seen to progress the plot at the same time as the consideration of lost letters fuels the debate over the novels' epistolary form.

In his *Memoir*, James Edward Austen-Leigh seems to refer almost verbatim to Cassandra's memorandum (1871, p. 47) but a letter from his sister Caroline also observes that *Sense and Sensibility* was 'first written in letters – & so read to her family' (Sutherland 2002, p. 185). Mary Lascelles pronounces the opinion that point of view was easier in third-person narrative than in an epistolary novel (1939, p. 203). She assumes that 'Elinor and Marianne' was light-hearted when read aloud whereas *Sense and Sensibility* was grave (p. 13) and 'First Impressions' more serious and ambitious (p. 14). It is interesting that Lascelles believes from her own reading of the letters that Cassandra had read 'First Impressions' but not *Pride and Prejudice* (p. 31). In his study of Austen's irony, Marvin Mudrick makes frequent use of the letters to reinforce points when he claims that Mary Crawford and Emma are representations of the actual Austen (1952, pp. 169–170, p. 194). With regard to the Juvenilia, however, he considers the 'letter form as a licence for absurdity and irrelevance' (p. 6) deployed to expose delusion (p. 18). Brian Southam (1964) and D. W. Harding (1965) are the chief champions for *Pride and Prejudice*'s epistolary origins. Southam declares Elinor an unlikely epistolary heroine on the basis of 'temperament and circumstances' (1964, p. 56) whereas *Pride and Prejudice* has 'a very credible system of letters to carry much of the story in an epistolary version' (p. 62).

The contrast model of 'Julia and Caroline' seems to suggest that Elinor and Marianne would be correspondents for an epistolary form of the surviving plot. Such a structure would, however, make the exploration of Lucy Steele's manipulation of Elinor less visible and of course the sisters are never physically apart. Harding discounts the possibility rather on the basis of Caroline Austen's faulty memory and declares in his introduction to the *Memoir* in the Penguin edition of *Persuasion* that *Sense and Sensibility* 'in the form of letters is improbable' but that 'an original letter form can much more plausibly be traced' (1965, p. 269) in *Pride and Prejudice*. Surely, however, on the model of the recently completed *Lady Susan* there could have been parallel sets of correspondence by Elinor and Lucy recounting events from their viewpoints. Lucy's correspondence is one of her distinguishing traits discussed in the revised novel. There is also a tantalising glimpse of Elinor finding 'fault with every absent friend' (*S&S*, p. 405) who fails to write with news of Edward's apparent marriage to Lucy. Various suggestions have also been made about potential scenes in the novel being originally in the form of letters including the John Dashwoods' discussion of Mrs Dashwood's future income (pp. 10–15; Klenck 2005, p. 43), Brandon's account of Eliza (pp. 232–240; Leduc 2015, p. 508), and Willoughby's visit to Cleveland (pp. 359–376; Klenck 2005, p. 49).

This argument for and against epistolarity has also been explored on a purely statistical basis. It is claimed that there are 21 letter scenes in *Sense and Sensibility* and 44 letter scenes in *Pride and Prejudice* (Klenck 2005, p. 40). A survey of *Sense and Sensibility* traces 45 letter references (Leduc 2015, p. 29), updating counts of 22 by Harding (1998, p. 215) and Sabor (2011). It is suggested that there are 40 actual letters and references to 200 others in the six mature novels (Bender 1967, p. 28), and that Mary Crawford is the most prolific letter-writer because five of her letters appear on the page (p. 45). Harding supplements his discussion of 'the supposed letter form of *Sense and Sensibility*' by comparison with the other five mature novels and even offers lines of letter text as a proportion of the overall lines of text for each novel. On both counts, *Pride and Prejudice* emerges as the novel where the letter predominates with 52 letters and nearly 6½% of the text. In light of the discussion of the letter in the mature novels to follow, it is *Mansfield Park* that presents the next highest proportion of letter text at just under 3% from 49 letters; the other novels are between 1 and 2% (Harding 1998, p. 215). At Harding's count, *Emma* with its traces of 53 letters still contains more letter references than *Sense and Sensibility* even with Leduc's re-count. Revisiting *Pride and Prejudice* using the Leduc methodology brings the letter count up to 65.

This mechanical accounting goes some way towards identifying the vestiges of the letter form within the novels. The mechanics of the conversion done by Austen are only to be found in hints supplied by letters to Cassandra and Martha. 'First Impressions' was still circulating in manuscript in 1799 (Austen to Cassandra, 11 June) then was altered and contracted, according to Cassandra's memorandum, in the process of becoming *Pride and Prejudice* by 1812 when Austen announced to Martha that it was sold. 'Elinor and Marianne' was converted in 1797 once 'First Impressions' was completed. If Austen made a concerted effort to remove the epistolary traces in *Sense and Sensibility*, she seems to have found the retention of epistolary elements more palatable when she revised *Pride and Prejudice*. In the interim, she had written 'Susan' (1798–1799), later *Northanger Abbey* and 'The Watsons' fragment (1804) and gained even more facility in the deployment of letters as an instrument of plot and character within third-person narrative. In terms of the epistolary novel, *Sense and Sensibility* and *Pride and Prejudice* are thus transitional. Their current form marks them as novels of Austen's maturity but their creation links them more closely with the Juvenilia and *Lady Susan*.

Sense and Sensibility assumes shared knowledge of novels of sensibility and encourages that intimacy. Willoughby's 'manly beauty and more than common gracefulness' (p. 51) and his description by Margaret as 'Marianne's preserver' (p. 55) are a normalisation of the burlesque of the Juvenilia. Elinor fears that Marianne will extract all the 'melancholy order of disastrous love' (p. 67) from Colonel Brandon's story of Eliza, and Marianne later claims extravagantly that 'misery such as mine has no pride' (p. 215). Elinor by contrast is defined by the absence of such exaggerations. In a passage possibly originally in letter form back to Norland, Marianne complains of Elinor's 'self-command' to her mother, 'When does she try to avoid society or appear restless and dissatisfied in it?' (p. 47) and when that 'self-command' is tested by Lucy, Elinor is 'in no danger of an hysterical fit, or a swoon' (p. 148). Elinor in her turn complains, like Edgeworth's Caroline, of Marianne's 'systems' in their 'unfortunate tendency of setting propriety at nought' (p. 66) in an exchange with Colonel Brandon that could again have been recounted by letter. At the end of the novel, the scenarios of the Juvenilia are contradicted when we learn that Willoughby has not 'fled from society, or contracted an habitual gloom of temper, or died of a broken heart' (p. 430). We learn also that despite jealousies between Fanny and Lucy and disagreements between Robert and Lucy 'nothing could exceed the harmony in which they all lived together' (p. 428) and this reads like the voice of Lucy in a letter. The more subtle form of irony is emerging and directed at the less dashing figure of Edward: 'after experiencing the blessings of *one* imprudent engagement, contracted without his mother's consent, . . . nothing less could be expected of him in the failure of *that*, than the immediate contraction of another' (p. 409).

The physically available letters within the novel are those between Willoughby and Marianne and between Edward and Lucy. The latter are authorised to correspond by their engagement, however secret, while the former are not. Mrs Dashwood tells Elinor after Willoughby's precipitate departure, 'If I find they correspond, every fear of mine will be removed' (*S&S*, p. 93) and Colonel Brandon later associates correspondence with an impending marriage (p. 197). Lucy can receive letters because she is engaged to Edward and both she and the future Mrs Willoughby exploit correspondence to unsettle the Dashwood sisters. Having received no letters at Mrs Jennings's house, Marianne writes to Willoughby three times before their chance encounter. After her 'desperate calmness' (p. 205) in writing for one last time, his reply is 'impudently cruel . . . deep in hardened villainy' in language Elinor is surely borrowing from sensibility tempered by her concerns at the 'impropriety of their having been written at all' (p. 209). She reads the whole in review in an approach reminiscent of the shared and circulating letters of epistolary novels although she later learns from Willoughby that the final letter was 'servilely' copied: his wife's 'style of letter writing . . . her own happy thoughts and gentle diction' (p. 372).

At the end of Volume 1 of the novel, Lucy uses a letter as corroboration to Elinor of her engagement: 'the picture, the letter, the ring, formed together such a body of evidence' (*S&S*, p. 159). The ring has been on view at Barton (pp. 113–114, p. 118), presumably pressed on Edward when Lucy has perceived his attentions inclining towards Elinor, and Lucy shows a letter direction in Edward's hand: 'He was tired, I dare say, for he had just filled the sheet to me as full as possible' (p. 154). This reiterates her epistolary ownership but Elinor sees only the wearily written address portion not his actual words. Lucy claims that 'Writing to each other . . . is the only comfort we have in such long separations' (p. 154) and Elinor recreates her own evidence in her review of the situation through which she comes to sympathise with the 19-year-old Edward tied to an 'illiterate, artful, and selfish' wife (p. 160). Lucy's own writing style is perhaps to be found in her 'overpowering delight . . . in finding [Elinor] *still* in town' (p. 247). The speech includes a great deal of 'emphasis' equivalent to repeated underlining in a letter, of which Austen herself was of course fond. Elinor is adept as a reader of Lucy's letters later in the novel, recognising the 'real design' of 'my paper reminds me to conclude' (p. 315) when the letter is duly passed on to Mrs Jennings for reading aloud. Elinor has not, however, 'recognised the whole of Lucy in the message' (p. 402) sent, as Mrs Ferrars, via Thomas. In a residual document from 'Elinor and Marianne', Lucy has already dismissed Edward by letter from the very altar and Edward subsequently shares this communication with Elinor out of sequence along with its postscript about destroying the items of 'evidence' (p. 414). Edward has 'blushed over pages of her writing' and 'this is the only letter . . . of which the substance made amends for the defect of the style' (p. 414).

In developing from 'First Impressions', *Pride and Prejudice* betrays some of its original proximity to the Juvenilia. Mr Darcy, for instance, 'soon drew the attention of the room by his fine tall person, handsome features and noble mien; and the report which was in general circulation within five minutes after his entrance, of his having ten thousand a year' (p. 10). The sight of officers is the first priority for the younger Bennets unless 'a very smart bonnet or a really new muslin . . . could recal them' (p. 80) and Bingley is 'the slave of his designing friends' (p. 151). Lydia is preserved 'from irremediable infamy' (p. 371) and Mr Bennet is saved 'a world of trouble and economy' (p. 418) when Darcy is revealed as the family's benefactor.

Letters are presented as forwarders of the plot and an account of Jane's to Elizabeth at Lambton gives a sense of letter writing in life with 'an account of all their little parties and engagements, with such news as the country afforded' before the 'latter half . . . dated a day later' with its news of 'poor Lydia' (p. 301). In the middle of the letter an 'Adieu' is followed immediately by 'I take up my pen' to request Mr Gardiner's aid (p. 304). This is reasonably a letter-survival from 'First Impressions' but the progression to free indirect speech from the letter form may also be detected as, for instance, in Elizabeth's comments after the Netherfield Ball: 'had her family made an agreement to expose themselves as much as they could during the evening, it would have been impossible for them to play their parts with more spirit, or finer success' (p. 114). This could have been an account written to an absent correspondent as could Elizabeth's observation on Mrs Bennet: 'more alive to the disgrace, which the want of new clothes must reflect on her daughters nuptials, than to any sense of shame at her eloping and living with Wickham, a fortnight before they took place' (p. 343).

Other evidence of retained letters can be traced in support of the Southam/ Harding argument. There is a letter-type conversation between Mrs Gardiner and Elizabeth about Wickham (*P&P*, pp. 163–164) and comments on the projected effusions of travellers to the Lakes suggest a letter exchange (pp. 174–175). The survival of this aunt–niece correspondence forms part of the final explanations (pp. 355–360) and Mr Gardiner writes his version of the Wickham settlements to Mr Bennet (pp. 345–346). Letter-writing exposes Miss Bingley's character both in her treatment of Jane and in her pursuit of Darcy. In the sociable space for letter writing at Netherfield, she indulges in 'a curious dialogue' about Darcy's letter-writing skills (p. 51). Women's letter writing is contextualised when an evening at Hunsford is spent 'telling again what had already been written' (p. 179). As in *Lady Susan*, the letter as an object promotes plot development. Re-reading Jane's letters at Hunsford stokes Elizabeth's exasperation with Mr Darcy (p. 210) immediately before his proposal. At its broadest level, Elizabeth and Jane are apart enough for the plot to be forwarded by means of letters as demonstrated above but the delay in conveying the news about Lydia caused by Jane's writing 'the direction remarkably ill' (p. 301) would have been difficult to represent unless this letter was further forwarded for discussion with another correspondent.

The most assiduous writer of letters still visible in the text is Mr Collins and his letters track an evolution in Elizabeth's relationship with her father, preparing her for married life away from the family home. Although Mr Bennet is 'a most negligent and dilatory correspondent' (*P&P*, p. 324) who abominates writing as part of his parental deficiencies, it is worth the effort for the entertainment of Mr Collins's correspondence (p. 404). When Collins writes to introduce himself, he is a 'well-wisher and friend' as Lucy Steele professed herself in rejecting Edward Ferrars, and Elizabeth and her father can agree on her cousin's lack of sense (pp. 60–70). Although no letter refers to Mr Collins's rejected proposal, about which father and daughter also agree, Letter XL from a rejected suitor in *The Complete Letter-Writer* seems to strike a chord: 'I am exceedingly concerned, that I cannot be as acceptable to you, as I have the good fortune to find myself to your honoured parents' (1776, p. 155). Collins's letter commiserating on Lydia's elopement and congratulating himself on his own escape is described as a curiosity, read by Elizabeth and Jane in Mr Bennet's absence and then left hanging in the text (*P&P*, pp. 327–328). It reads like one of cousin Edward Cooper's letters of 'cruel comfort' would. After early agreement between father and daughter and intermediate neutrality over Collins's letters, the extracts from his final warning letter about Lady Catherine's unfriendly eye on a match with Mr Darcy (pp. 402–403) make Elizabeth reluctant to appreciate the joke and she is no longer 'diverted' by her father's wit and pleasantries.

It is, however, Darcy's long letter of explanation that dominates the text and the plot of the novel. This letter is displaced from any previous epistolary narrative because its composition and reading are integral to future events. The letter has a pivotal function between a frivolous interest in Darcy's cousin and the more serious consideration to come: 'Colonel Fitzwilliam was no longer an object. She could think only of her letter' (*P&P*, p. 232). It is read and reread as a process of redefinition and Elizabeth is effectively still reading both Darcy and his letter when she reaches Pemberley and then beyond to their final reconciliation.

In the grounds of Rosings, Elizabeth is presented with a very material document: an 'envelope containing two sheets of paper, written quite through in a very close hand. – The envelope itself was likewise full' (pp. 218). Darcy has dated his letter 'eight o'clock'. It is to be put into Elizabeth's own hands and if that were not personal enough, the letter ends 'God bless you' (p. 225). The description of Elizabeth at this point creates the impression that she is reading the letter in a time lag, after the reader of the novel 'with an eagerness which hardly left her power of comprehension, and from impatience of knowing what the next sentence might bring, was incapable of attending to the sense of the one before her eyes' (p. 226). She rereads the Wickham section and in the process rereads Wickham when she recognises the previous 'impropriety' of his 'communication to a stranger' (p. 229) and she knows the letter by heart by the time she informs Jane about Wickham's conduct (p. 249). Mrs Gardiner's letter read on a bench in the seclusion of a 'little copse' (p. 355) appears verbatim but is not shared with Jane whereas the Wickham portions of Darcy's 'explanatory letter' (p. 370) are read again through Jane's eyes when Bingley and Darcy revisit Longbourn. In the final chapters of the novel, the letter is then effectively re-received when Elizabeth is 'Proud that in a cause of compassion and honour, he had been able to get the better of himself' (p. 361). The letter has thus taken on a character outside its narrative role, further elaborated by Elizabeth and Darcy's discussion of her changed sentiments after Mrs Gardiner's letter emboldens her to speak. Darcy is concerned about Elizabeth's having 'the power of reading again' (p. 409) but she is able to relive the process of the letter from bitterness to charity. The letter needed to be written but Darcy now wishes it destroyed whereas Elizabeth believes that every 'unpleasant circumstance' can be forgotten because of the changed 'feelings of the person who wrote, and the person who received it' (p. 409). The letter is not just a narrative vehicle but an evolving and plot-significant document to be revisited and repositioned in context. With the revision of 'First Impressions' and first impressions, it will no longer be hidden in the distant oak tree deployed in 'Amelia Webster'.

The device of the letter operates within the realistic representation of actual life but remains an element of the novels' overarching structures as discussed below. The published novels demonstrate that letters have created the voices heard through free indirect speech, and voices have consequences. It is the letter that reinforces Fanny Price's role as the still centre of *Mansfield Park*; it is Emma's failure to read the letters in front of her that frames the narrative of the novel in her name.

Using the conjectured timing of composition, *Northanger Abbey* becomes the first of the novels designed without an epistolary form. Park Honan describes the 'creaking letter form' being dropped for the composition originally entitled 'Susan' (1987, p. 139). At the same time, the novel revised and originally sent for publication in 1803 assumes knowledge of the reading matter underpinning the Juvenilia, if not the actual Juvenilia themselves, in its choice of discourses, novels, and suitors. 'Friendship' as 'the finest balm for the pangs of disappointed love' (*NA*, p. 25) is a new epigram for the work dedicated to Eliza de Feuillide. Just as Isabel in 'Love and Freindship' has seen more of the world than Laura, Isabella Thorpe is 'four years better informed' (p. 26) than Catherine Morland who 'from fifteen to seventeen' is 'in training for a heroine' (p. 7). In the brutal world of the Gothic transferred to the brutal world of child-bearing, Mrs Morland lives on to have 10 children 'instead of dying in bringing the latter into the world, as anybody might expect' (p. 5). Catherine herself learns that despite the charm of Mrs Radcliffe's works and those 'of her imitators, it was not in them perhaps that human nature, at least in the midland counties of England, was to be looked for' (p. 205) but she still believes General Tilney 'not perfectly amiable' (p. 206). Frederick Tilney may not be 'the instigator of the three villains in horsemen's great coats, by whom she will hereafter be forced into a travelling-chaise and four, which will drive off at great speed' (p. 133) but the Gothic is identifiable in real life. Catherine is uncivilly expelled from Northanger to travel as 'a heroine in a hack post-chaise' (p. 241) and 'in suspecting General Tilney of either murdering or shutting up his wife, she had scarcely sinned against his character, or magnified his cruelty' (p. 256).

In *Northanger Abbey*, the next stage of Austen's exploration of letters as plot devices and betrayals of character reflects her own learned practices from letters in fact and in fiction. Austen has redeveloped her voice beyond that of an 'imitator' to that of a satirist to offer her own commentary on the available models for narrative. In parallel with Austen's own views of the novel (*NA*, pp. 30–31), Henry Tilney is presented as both a muslin critic and the voice of the letter manual: 'Everybody allows that the talent of writing agreeable letters is peculiarly female . . . assisted by the practice of keeping a journal' (p. 19). Henry teases Catherine that the 'habit of journalizing' forms 'the easy style of writing for which ladies are so generally celebrated' (p. 19). He assumes that dress, complexion, and the 'curl of your hair' will be noted for transmission to 'absent cousins' along with 'the civilities and compliments of every day' (p. 19). The list of subjects incorporates Austen and Cassandra's own letter topics and when Henry describes the 'total inattention to stops' (p. 20), this jokingly introduces Austen's love of epistolary dashes. In critiquing the subject and grammar of women's writing, however, Henry ignores its value within women's social networks. In the novel, Catherine is offered not just a choice of suitors but a choice of correspondents. Her own sister Sarah does not demand Catherine's 'writing by every post' (p. 11) as a heroine's sister should. In Bath, Isabella's 'resolute stilishness' (p. 51) reflects her scheming for a sisterly relationship but Eleanor Tilney is described as having 'real elegance' by contrast with her. Catherine regards 'a desire of corresponding' with Eleanor (p. 141) as the height of sisterhood when Eleanor is shaping to invite her friend to Northanger. When Catherine must write only 'under cover' to Eleanor's maid (*NA*, p. 236) this seems a dereliction because it will circumvent Eleanor's father whatever his faults. There was perhaps a nod to the real-life situation of Austen and Martha's keeping the volume of their correspondence secret from their respective uncles (2 June 1799) during the composition of this novel. Eleanor wants to be able to 'ask for your correspondence as I ought to do' and Catherine's warm-heartedness overcomes pride and convention so that she '*will* write . . . indeed' (p. 236).

Correspondence forwards the plot and provides character for the voices of correspondents as well as presenting the letters as objects for general reading. Letters from the Reverend Richard Morland have confirmed the terms of James's engagement and at Northanger Catherine depends on a network of correspondents but particularly Isabella who is declared 'scrupulous' in keeping her promises: 'she was anxious to be assured of Isabella's having matched some fine netting-cotton . . . and of her continuing on the best terms with James' (*NA*, p. 206). The humorous comparison between these twin concerns is reminiscent of Austen's proxy shopping in Bath complete with her sketch of lace (2 June 1799). After significant delay, one of Isabella's actual letters makes its way into the text (*NA*, pp. 222–224). It has, however, been pre-empted by another from Catherine's brother James (pp. 207–208) that arrives 10 days after the journey to Northanger and after Catherine has been disabused of General Tilney's fiendish behaviour towards his late wife. James's letter is shared with and interpreted by the Tilneys. It gives context for the 'shallow artifice' of Isabella's subsequent letter that might otherwise have been misinterpreted. Isabella has resented the letters from Fullerton about income; she now succeeds Lucy Steele and prefigures Mary Crawford in her manipulation of the form. Catherine reads aloud 'the most material passages' of the later letter 'with strong indignation' (p. 224). Catherine can dismiss Isabella in this new guise because the letter reread with the Tilneys 'has served to make her character better known' (p. 224). As in the novels of Austen's maturity, character emerges from a letter read, reread, and discussed in context.

Mansfield Park gives opportunities for epistolary communication by separating its heroine from her family but it is only when she returns to them that the importance of the letter becomes paramount. The novel is structured around Fanny Price's epistolary relationships with four correspondents: her brother William, her neighbour and rival Mary Crawford, her cousin Edmund, and her aunt Lady Bertram. Austen was drawing on her own experience of writing to her sailor brothers for the only satisfactory correspondence in Fanny's life and this is a constant through the novel. In her own letters, Austen commends a lawyer advising her brother Edward for 'such thinking, clear, considerate Letters as Frank might have written' (5–8 March 1814). In 6–7 November 1813, she reports Charles's 'nice long Black & red letter' crossed in different colours to give full value for the postage. When Fanny first arrives at Mansfield, Edmund provides 'paper and every other material' (*MP*, p. 17) for her letter to William and his father will frank it (p. 18). Mary Crawford reflects on the 'one style' of masculine letter writing: 'Henry . . . in every respect exactly what a brother should be . . . has never yet turned a page in a letter' (p. 70). Mary expects men to write like women but will later exploit and pervert her letter connection with Fanny to give Henry an environment for harassment. Edmund again supports his cousin by seconding William's 'excellence as a correspondent' (p. 70) and drawing Fanny out on her brother's accomplishments.

Fanny herself is as scrupulous in letter writing and receiving as she is in her duty and principles (*MP*, p. 307). Letters contextualised by Austen's own about Frank (28 December 1798) announce that William is 'made' a lieutenant. Unlike in life, the letters reported in the novel are unmitigated by female concerns and ownership because they form part of Henry Crawford's manipulation of events. The 'very great happiness', delight, and 'general joy' (*MP*, p. 346) are quoted from the stilted correspondence of men whose letters are mediated by Henry. The outcome of this is Henry's unwelcome proposal and Fanny differentiates clearly between the two actions: 'He had previously made her the happiest of human beings, and now he had insulted her' (p. 350). After a note from Mary urging acceptance of Henry's proposal, she accepts congratulations on William's behalf but adds, 'The rest of your note I know means nothing' (p. 355). Fanny's reply is polite and programmed. Although 'obliged' and honoured she can still baldly state, however, 'I have seen too much of Mr Crawford not to understand his manners' (p. 355). She thinks her own note 'ill-written' with 'no arrangement' (p. 356) but it is blunt and principled and designedly ends the second volume of the novel as published.

The appearance of propriety is exploited through correspondence as part of Mary's villainy. Having a conniving sister solves the issue of proper correspondence between men and women that caused Mrs Dashwood's anxiety over the putative engagement between Marianne and Willoughby in *Sense and Sensibility*. Once Fanny is sent to Portsmouth to consider her options, she is pinned there as a recipient of Mary's letters and Henry's attentions. When the Crawfords leave Mansfield, Mary's 'apparent affection' for Fanny predicates correspondence and the included lines from Henry are 'quite as unpleasant as she had feared': 'Miss Crawford's style of writing, lively and affectionate, was itself an evil, independent of what she was thus forced into reading from the brother's pen' (*MP*, p. 434). At the same time Fanny is manipulated by both parties into reading the letters out loud to Edmund and so 'compelled into a correspondence which was bringing her the addresses of a man she did not love, and obliging her to administer to the adverse passion of the man she did' (p. 434). In Portsmouth, she regrets letters before she regrets her rejection of Henry. When there is a 'longer interval' between letters after 'the rapid rate in which their correspondence had begun', Mary writes at some length about having spoken of Fanny to Maria Rushworth 'as a sister should' (p. 456) supplying 'great food . . . for unpleasant meditation' (p. 457). Despite her unease, Fanny nonetheless values the letter as Austen and Cassandra did for regularity, shared family news, and making the absent present: 'it connected her with the absent, it told her of people and things about whom she had never felt so much curiosity as now, and she would have been glad to have been sure of such a letter every week' (p. 457).

Correspondence with Edmund proves hardly less painful. Fanny's most valued letter is her cousin's unfinished note accompanying the gift of the chain that would allow Fanny to wear William's amber cross at her coming-out ball. Edmund actually visits her on purpose in the east room and is stopped in the act of writing by her appearance. In this scene, Edmund promotes the triangular relationship with Mary when he persuades Fanny to use the cunningly gifted necklace from Mary/Henry and so to avert any coolness between his 'two dearest objects . . . on earth' (*MP*, p. 306). Fanny would prefer to unite her 'dearest objects' Edmund and

William, of course, and stores the 12-word note with the chain as both memorabilia and provenance: 'Two lines more prized had never fallen from the pen of the most distinguished author – never more completely blessed the researches of the fondest biographer' (p. 308). The note reinforces Mary's earlier judgement of the masculine writing style and comments retrospectively on Cassandra's role as inadvertent keeper/editor of Austen's own letters. In Volume 2 of the novel, 'The enthusiasm of a woman's love is even beyond the biographer's' and even Edmund's handwriting conveys 'blessedness' especially in the 'felicity' of the words 'My very dear Fanny' (p. 308).

In the latter part of the novel Edmund proves himself more satisfying than Henry as a male correspondent in volume if not in content. Fanny must wait for his much longer letter until seven weeks after she arrives in Portsmouth and this letter postpones her return to Mansfield so that Fanny 'will never wish for a letter again' (p. 491). It also reasserts that, in spite of Mary's 'too lively mind', Edmund 'cannot give her up' (p. 489). Edmund further confirms Fanny is 'very much wanted' (p. 491) by Lady Bertram and missed by him and after her initial irritation at her cousin's procrastination, Fanny concludes, 'It was a letter, in short, which she would not but have had for the world, and which could never be valued enough' (p. 492). It has retention claims very different from the earlier note.

In the same chapter the anguish of these cousin-correspondents is accompanied and contrasted by an initially comic reflection on women's letter writing introducing Fanny's correspondence with her aunt. Early on in the novel when Sir Thomas goes to Antigua, Lady Bertram is saved from 'all possible fatigue. . . but that of directing her letters' (*MP*, p. 39) and in Portsmouth Fanny prioritises her 'correspondence with her aunt Bertram' (p. 457) over Mary's as a means of making the absent present. Edmund's long letter concludes with news of the Grants going to Bath and this is a prelude to the surprising information that Lady Bertram 'rather shone in the epistolary line' with her 'common-place, amplifying style, so that very little matter was enough for her' (p. 493). Austen jokes at the expense of herself and her correspondents. 'Every body at all addicted to letter writing, without having much to say, which will include a large proportion of the female world at least, must feel with Lady Bertram' when the 'epistolary uses' of Dr. Grant's gout 'fall to the share of her thankless son' (p. 493). She sees the information 'treated as concisely as possible at the end of a long letter, instead of having it to spread over the largest part of a page of her own' (p. 493). The extradiegetic commentator then observes 'a rich amends' from the 'alarming intelligence' (p. 493) of Tom Bertram's 'dangerous illness' that will provide 'occupation for the pen for many days to come' (p. 494). The 'amplifying style' of the resulting letter is, however, less 'warm and genuine' than Fanny's feelings on receiving it. Lady Bertram in her 'frequent accounts' with 'the same medley of trusts, hopes and fears' is only 'playing at being frightened' until Tom actually arrives and 'a letter which she had previously preparing for Fanny, was finished in a different style, in the language of real feeling and alarm; then she wrote as she might have spoken' (p. 495).

In a further triangulation of correspondence, Tom's dangerous illness also provokes Mary Crawford's unfeelingly tasteless letter in which she completely misrepresents Fanny. Mary has to seek information from Fanny because the Grants are away, closing down a direct channel of communication and adds, 'I see you smile and look cunning . . . If he is to die, there will be *two* poor young men less in the world' (p. 502). This seems to glance back at some of the Juvenilia's exuberance now buried in Austen's own correspondence where she offers Cassandra 'a dead Baronet in almost every Letter' (8–9 September 1816). Mary provides a clue to Henry's pending desertion because he returns from Richmond during the letter as she is folding it, causing her to write on after her initial close. Experience of reading Austen's letters suggests the significance of information supplied on the last quarter of the sheet as this is, albeit within the text of the novel. Austen's family readers might also have been alert to messages of 'unalterable affection' (*MP*, p. 504) that conclude the letter; Lady Susan was 'unalterably yours' as her last contribution to the work in her name (*LM*, p. 72).

The closing chapters of the novel particularise character through correspondence. Fanny refuses the accompanying offer of transportation back to Mansfield – 'She had a rule to apply to, which settled every thing' (*MP*, p. 505) – and the appearance of 'little writing' with the 'air of a letter of haste and business' (p. 506) of Mary's next letter suggests a pre-emptive plan to collect her without notice. Mary tries to cut Fanny off from other communication and even tends toward blaming Fanny for Henry's flight (p. 507, p. 527) but alternative and public communication arrives in the form of Mr Price's newspaper (pp. 508–509). Instead of being forced into Henry's company, Fanny receives another unwelcome/valued Edmund letter. He concludes, 'There is no end of the evil let loose upon us' while she rejoices in 'The evil which brought such good to her!' (p. 513). The letters of Sir Thomas and his friend Mr Harding are used to reconstruct events (pp. 520–521) but the voice of the narrator in the final chapter is surprisingly close in tone to the Juvenilia, suggesting an incomplete engagement with the final moral message of the novel. Tom's recovery, the promotion of Susan to the role of Lady Bertram's companion, and the death of Dr Grant are signalled in the context of an unspecified timeframe for 'the transfer of unchanging attachments' (p. 544) and the entertainment and instruction of mortals and their neighbours (p. 546). When the final chapter opens 'Let other pens dwell on guilt and misery' (p. 533), Austen simultaneously embraces and abnegates her responsibilities, reiterating both the valuable and unwelcome elements of communication experienced by 'My Fanny'.

In Austen's next novel, letters and their absence provide clues to the deception ongoing between Frank Churchill and Highbury as well as that between Emma and herself. After Jane Fairfax's defence of the Post Office, letters are known to be circulating unseen as they once did in *Lady Susan*. The most principled correspondent is hidden but *Emma* is also structured around the receipt, reading, and discussion of letters. Three letters from Frank Churchill in the second, thirty-first, and fiftieth chapters operate as an epistolary exoskeleton for the 55 chapters of the novel although only the last letter is explicitly in the text. Women's letter networks that are integral to the community are manipulated, forming a double deception since the writer is fully aware that letters are written to be shared. In the first half of the novel, letters by Robert Martin and Jane Fairfax create situations in which Emma demonstrates her social aptitude and then betrays her total misunderstanding of the other women in her circle. After Frank betrays an unacknowledged letter connection concerning Mr Perry's plan to set up a carriage (*E*, pp. 373–375), the letters of a child's game are used to send a message to Jane and Mr Knightley's observation here defines the structure of a novel exploiting the epistolary and the alphabet: 'These letters were but the vehicle for gallantry and trick . . . chosen to conceal a deeper game' (p. 377).

The letters in *Emma* are defined by both similarities and differences. They are written from duty, as family communications, and as a marriage proposal, and they must be read carefully for clues about circulating relationships. When Mrs Weston receives a 'highly-prized' (*E*, p. 16) first letter from Frank Churchill, the novel reader also learns that it is 'a handsome letter' four times in one paragraph through a direct quotation from someone representative of Highbury's tea-drinking circle, undoubtedly Miss Bates. Robert Martin's proposal letter arrives in a parcel appearing to be from his sisters and left at Mrs Goddard's possibly in imitation of the music parcel sent by Fanny Knight to circumvent her Aunt Cassandra in November 1814. The letter, that 'would not have disgraced a gentleman' (*E*, p. 53), is dissected and answered but not presented on the page. Emma conveniently dismisses the farmer's epistolary skills as insufficient compensation for his presumed 'clownish manner' (p. 57). Jane Fairfax's reported letter to Miss Bates unpicks a social situation reflective of Austen's own: how to avoid the routine letter and its impact on a visit. Jane Fairfax's regular letter arrives on a different day when Emma expects to be 'quite safe' from it (p. 166). Jane is 'writing out of rule' (p. 169) because she is coming in person and, like Austen herself 'writing out of rule', the letter is 'only two pages' (p. 168). Miss Bates explains that 'in general she fills the whole paper and crosses half' (p. 168) with her excellent writing so this is a matter of Jane's giving good value to her impoverished aunt. Although the letter is closely discussed, Emma makes a distinction when she regains the street: 'though she had in fact heard the whole substance of Jane Fairfax's letter, she had been able to escape the letter itself' (p. 173). The letter has once again been conveyed only through the garrulous conversation of Miss Bates.

Frank Churchill's letter to Mrs Weston following his visit so carefully timed with Jane's is read by Emma although not out loud. She has been 'impatient for a letter' in light of her own feelings as well as 'fancying interesting dialogues and inventing elegant letters' through which their 'affection was always to subside into friendship' (*E*, p. 284). Although apparently containing 'no suspicious flourishes' this letter is absolutely designed to deceive, even down to the compliment to Harriet Smith in 'the very lowest vacant corner' (p. 286). Austen's prescripts to her own letters demonstrate the value of information in those vacant corners where Emma reads – and is meant to read – a reference to herself.

With Frank absent, Jane Fairfax's uncharacteristically vocal defence of the Post Office is a smokescreen over letters unseen and unshared: a return to the issues of correspondence between men and women unauthorised by a prior relationship. Jane must circumnavigate the practical and unsuspicious John Knightley by protesting her need for letters first as a means of exercise and then as a familial duty: 'till I have outlived all my affections, a post-office, I think, must always have power to draw me out' (*E*, p. 317). Jane can claim here that 'negligence or blunder' seldom appears (p. 320) signalling the 'blunder' anagram that will acknowledge the clumsy betrayal of Perry's carriage plans seven chapters later. Jane must then endure a further tussle with Mrs Elton who wants to send her own servant for letters to the Bates household and continues the assault after dinner. Emma also adds to Jane's embarrassment by beginning a discussion about Frank's handwriting while herself mis-guessing Jane's correspondent to be Mr Dixon. When Mr Weston arrives later he redoubles the stress of the 'governess-trade' discussion (p. 325) by announcing: 'I met the letters in my way this morning, and seeing my son's hand, presumed to open it . . . [Mrs Weston] is his principal correspondent, I assure you' resulting in affected laughter about such a 'dangerous precedent' from Jane's tormentor Mrs Elton (p. 330). This set of three chapters closing Volume 2 stands out because of Jane's uncharacteristic volubility and the concentrated discussion of facets of letter writing without any actual letters appearing in the text. Austen has found a more sophisticated application for the dedicated door-knocking letter in 'Love and Freindship' (*J*, pp. 106–107) so that letters driven underground can come dangerously close to the surface.

In the final analysis, letters have contributed to what Mrs Weston describes as 'a system of secrecy and concealment' (*E*, p. 434). When Frank's explanation arrives towards the end of the novel it uncovers other letters including one mistakenly unposted; it was only when Jane returned Frank's letters that the direction of future communications to Mr Smallridge's finally spurred him into action (p. 482). Austen has made Frank's letter even more significant because none of the other letters is in the text. This is not an epistolary novel and yet the letter is at the heart of both society and the deception of that society. The emphasis is even greater when Frank's unparagraphed letter is reread by Mr Knightley in the next chapter.

A letter is finally handed to the reader and it is to 'be waded through' (p. 475) in telling a different story from the one that has been apparent. P. D. James suggests that *Emma* is a detective story by drawing parallels with both the mystery in a self-contained setting (1998, p. 189) and the epistolary explanation (p. 200). When an actual letter appears, Frank is manipulating the form to deal with all his explanations in public and takes little account of his audience. Emma has been solving the wrong mystery all along and has earlier misguidedly hoped for a return to a 'life of civility' (*E*, p. 196) with the arrival of a Mrs Elton. Face to face with Emma in the knowledge of Frank's letter, Jane Fairfax deplores her own 'life of deceit' and the 'cold and artificial' part she has acted (p. 501) notwithstanding her defence of the postal system. Although far from being a novel in letters, *Emma* demonstrates the opportunities and pitfalls of a life of epistolarity.

In *Persuasion*, Austen prepares the reader for Captain Wentworth's grasp of the epistolary opportunity written into her revised ending. At the Musgroves' early in the novel, he and Anne both know that his 'great object . . . to be at sea' (*P*, p. 70) seven years before was the result of their broken engagement. The scene affords them a secret correspondence even though they have been merely civil where once they would have found it 'difficult to cease to speak to one another' (p. 69). Austen compensates for the submersion in men's naval matters by giving Wentworth an extraordinary statement when he explains to his audience that his first command the *Asp* was barely seaworthy. He likens the ship's condition to 'the fashion and strength of any old pelisse, which you had seen lent about among half your acquaintance, ever since you could remember, and which at last, on some very wet day, is lent to yourself' (p. 71). Despite his bitterness towards Anne, he seeks an analogy that will translate into women's understanding and is more successful in this than even Henry Tilney with his knowledge of muslin and journals. Wentworth recognises the value of communication as part of his growing reconciliation with Anne and it is he who ensures that notes on Louisa Musgrove's progress reach her (p. 136). In return Anne makes her impassioned defence of women who cannot tell their own stories because women's feelings are confined to men's authorship (p. 255). The early pelisse analogy has demonstrated that there is the possibility of a shared understanding.

Three specific instances of letters frame the second volume of the novel: Mary writing to Anne, William Elliot writing to Charles Smith, and Captain Wentworth writing to Anne. The relationship between the Elliot sisters has already been defined in a single sentence on letter writing: 'Mary never wrote to Bath herself; all the toil of keeping up a slow and unsatisfactory correspondence with Elizabeth fell on Anne' (*P*, p. 115). Once Anne and Elizabeth are at the same address, Mary, full of complaints and contradictions, betrays herself as a snobbish hypochondriac in a 'thicker letter than usual' because it can be brought to Bath by Mrs Croft (p. 176). There is a long second section because, having signalled its thickness, the letter arrives in 'an envelop, containing nearly as much more' (p. 178), revealing Louisa's engagement to Captain Benwick. Discussion of the letter's contents with her family once more exaggerates the snobbery of father and sister. They concern themselves only with carriage horses and the Crofts' potential location in Bath. The main news of the letter must be discussed by Anne with herself because she has no Tilneys, Jane Bennet, or Mr Knightley available.

Discussion is the key to the value of the letters retained by Mrs Smith concerning the past behaviour of Mr Elliot. The agency of letters is reinforced by these 'document[s] of former intimacy' (p. 220) and 'written proof' (p. 221). The letters are produced in an attempt to save Anne from the plotted marriage but any temptation to regain Kellynch by uniting herself to Mr Elliot is easily resisted because of the renewed presence and freedom of Captain Wentworth already reinforced by Mary's letter. Anne is shocked by the disrespect shown towards her father in Mr Elliot's correspondence but admits that 'her seeing the letter was a violation of the laws of honour' (p. 221). Austen seems to admit that such letters might exist but should not be shared by an unauthorised audience leaving Anne's declaration 'that no private correspondence could bear the eye of others' (p. 221) ambiguous in the context of both the novels and the letters in life.

The third pivotal letter in *Persuasion* was written for the revised ending of the novel and as she opens it Anne recognises that 'On the contents of that letter depended all which this world could do for her!' (p. 257) The letter's composition is disguised in real time as a matter of business and it is written in the sociable space of the Musgroves' White Hart apartment. The novel's original ending described Wentworth awaiting a response from Anne to Admiral Croft's offer to vacate Kellynch Hall on the occasion of her anticipated marriage to William Elliot. The revision uses a letter to force action, presenting another post-proposal document personally delivered with 'glowing entreaty' (p. 257). Unlike Darcy who writes the next day, Wentworth is writing more than seven years after being refused but like the eager and impatient Elizabeth Bennet, Anne 'devours' Wentworth's opportunistically composed words. She is then able to exploit Charles Musgrove's masculine interest in 'a capital gun' (p. 261) to ensure that she can be alone with Wentworth and secure the contents of the letter of which 'nothing was to be retracted or qualified' (p. 262). Anne's overheard conversation has acted as a pre-discussion of his own letter and Wentworth describes his 'irresistible governance' in response to her words causing him to 'seize' a sheet of paper and 'pour out' his feelings (p. 262). He is as impetuous in this as one of the Juvenilia heroines but in adapting the medium of his worn pelisse imagery, he has used the letter to demonstrate that men can be trusted with a pen and with constancy. Austen has rewritten her ending using the analysed and critiqued letter as a plot device once again but this time the contents will remain personal and ostensibly unshared.

The letter has thus evolved into a romantic object and could have remained as its own postscript to Austen's writing were it not for the existence of the fragmentary *Sanditon* in which Austen revisits and reiterates the currency of her burlesque style using women's letters. Austen may, of course, have revised *Persuasion* further before publication. As it is, Clara Brereton in *Sanditon* is described by Charlotte Heywood as 'the most perfect representative of whatever heroine might be most beautiful and bewitching' (*LM*, pp. 168–169) in the epistolary volumes of the circulating library from which she has just emerged. Clara's seducer Sir Edward Denham arrives after 'the duty of letter-writing' has been performed and Austen then refers to Charlotte herself when making 'no apologies for my heroine's vanity' (p. 172). Mr Parker has already announced that 'Women are the only correspondents to be depended on' (p. 161) and that his sisters never fail him. The new resort depends on letters, and information anticipating potential visitors is supplied by a '*short* chain' in 13 letters of 'constant correspondence' emanating from Diana Parker with 'not a link wanting' (p. 187). The ensuing confusion caused by Diana's officious interference is an epistolary novel in miniature not unlike the teenage Austen's 'Amelia Webster'. The discussion of letters in the published novels has provided the grounds for realising that the letter can become a non-communicative device and vehicle for unreliable information much as it can be in life. When Charlotte remarks rather primly that 'the subject had supplied letters and extracts and messages enough to make everything appear what it was not' (p. 201), this could even be read as Austen's final warning to the biographer that 'no private correspondence could bear the eye of others'.

Kathryn Sutherland describes *Sense and Sensibility*, *Pride and Prejudice*, and *Northanger Abbey* as having 'double lives' (2005b, p. 12) resulting from Austen's continuing 'habits of confidential manuscript circulation' (p. 14). In the absence of the original texts, it is tempting for biographers to write about 'Elinor and Marianne' (1795) and 'First Impressions' (1796–1797) as if they actually were *Sense and Sensibility* (1811) and *Pride and Prejudice* (1813). This has a tendency to contextualise the published novels on a different trajectory within Austen's life. The letter hiatus in life in 1797 and then in 1810 and 1812 deprives us of any commentary on the preparation of the novels for publication but the act of revision for Austen is demonstrated by existing manuscripts and by the cancelled chapter of *Persuasion*. The revision of early compositions from epistolary to third-person direct narrative can only be surmised but as discussed in this chapter there are indications of how the letter voices became free indirect speech and how letters remained embedded as narrative devices. David Lodge observes that Austen's point of view evolved from the epistolary novel where immediacy was paid for by uneconomical clumsiness and the lack of an editorial voice (1986, p. 175) and Susan Robbins adds that by 'embedding letters in her narratives, [Austen] merged the presentational and assessing perspectives' (1989, p. 219). Mary Favret suggests that the letter becomes 'a character in its own right' to be tested and re-evaluated, and that 'narrative authority depends on our learning to see and read letters properly' (1993, p. 137). We are offered another layer of epistolary knowledge by the continuing discussion of letters within the novels and by assessments of their appearance and intended function. The character of Mary Crawford is as much bound up in letters as that of Mr Collins. In the teeth of discovery by John Knightley or Mrs Elton, Jane Fairfax has a parallel secret life in the reclamation of texts from the Post Office.

Refusal of closure has been identified as one factor of epistolary narrative (MacArthur 1990, p. 3) and Austen's endings often screech into view as if she has maintained all along that refusal she first explored in the unfinished Juvenilia and the added conclusion to *Lady Susan*. In the voice of the author, she corresponds with the reader. In *Northanger Abbey*, the narrator draws attention to 'the tell-tale compression of the pages . . . hastening together to perfect felicity' (p. 259). In *Sense and Sensibility* Edward leaves Barton Cottage after revealing that he is not married to Lucy but how soon 'he had walked himself into the proper resolution . . . need not be particularly told' (p. 409). The voice concluding *Mansfield Park* leaves misery to 'other pens' (p. 533) and 'purposely' abstains from dates (p. 544).

In Austen's writing, the letter is deployed as both a written commonplace and a complex overarching form. The letter's potential for communication and structural uncertainty provides a spreading arc over her life and narratives. In 'Frederic and Elfrida' (1787), her earliest surviving work, Elfrida writes to Charlotte Drummond asking her friend to buy 'a new and fashionable Bonnet, to suit the complexion of your / E. Falknor' (*J*, p. 4); Charlotte obliges and so ends the 'little adventure' (p. 5) of the bonnet. In *Pride and Prejudice*, Mr Bingley is reported, perhaps as the result of exchanged letters, to be bringing twelve ladies and seven gentlemen to the Meryton assembly but the day before the ball this is reduced to five sisters and a cousin and then to only five people including himself (p. 10). Twenty years after this potential exchange in 'First Impressions' (1796–1797), Diana Parker's mis-corresponding 'chain' (*LM*, pp. 187–200) brings only four women rather than 'two considerable families' (p. 187) to the resort of Sanditon. The epistolary form of the novel provides insight into the development of Austen as an author. Elfrida and Diana may have remained hidden from published view until the early twentieth century (Chapman 1933; Chapman 1925) but they represent Austen's own world of epistolary communication in a correspondence with the world of the novels. The epistolary in Austen's fictional publication is now bookended by Sir John Middleton offering a cottage to Mrs Dashwood and Captain Wentworth offering marriage to Anne Elliot. Her life is letter-bound by Tom Lefroy's light morning-coat (9–10 January 1796) and Catherine Prowting's petticoat (28–29 May 1817).

6

Letters and Novels

Places and Spaces

None of Austen's fictional works is set in rural Hampshire where she spent most of her life. The real places that feature in her fiction have both a grounded and contemporary reality and a role tailored to her fictional landscape. This chapter looks at these real places in the fiction – Bath, London, Lyme Regis, Portsmouth – to consider how places are embraced by the Austen social vision and become a critique of her society. Within the novels, Austen's fictional places with their basis in her own experience of both private and public spaces demonstrate a palpable engagement with her own time, suggesting that knowledge of contemporary locations in both specific and general terms is essential to a proper reading of the Austen universe. Her later novels drew attention to place – particularly *Mansfield Park* and the unfinished *Sanditon* – but there are important distinctions to be inferred about place in all Austen's fiction. Economies of presentation driven by the letters in her own life bring to life the unfurnished world identified by Richard Simpson (1870, p. 129). Austen suggested to Anna that she should not 'give too many particulars of right hand & left' (9 September 1814) but the reading of location learned from her letter-writing technique becomes a very particular and studied act for the reader of Austen the novelist.

In observing 'the slightness of the matter and the authority of the manner' in Austen's novels, Ian Watt identifies a deliberate restriction of scale (1963, p. 12). Austen's letters orientate her writing towards the same state because the situations over which she has control and the interests of her audience are the drivers of her communication. She has made a virtue out of the learned techniques of letter writing to stage and situate the plots of the novels. Although the Juvenilia still lurk in her extravagance and mockery of conventions, descriptive economy and traded detail are refined in the novels producing a layered effect that enriches a narrative without 'too many particulars'. The set viewpoints of an epistolary narrative would have made detail creaky in real time but real-life letters can train a novelist's eye to focus on shorthand description and scene setting with richer meaning. In the places and spaces of the novels, the narrators evolved from epistolary novels are given viewpoints from which to speak that encourage the reader to see and apprehend. This chapter traces the development of places and spaces as a factor in Austen criticism and reads the letters through the situations and transitions of Austen's life. The placing of spaces is then tracked within the novels offering comparisons with the descriptive economies and visioning style of the letters in life. In the novels, Austen is reading and representing the country house through oppositional discourses. She explores boundaries within the staging of the estate as well as village groupings, seaside locations, and other travel. Dialogues evolved from the letter are dramatised within Austen's topography, geography, and mental maps.

When Austen's unfinished last novel was published in 1925, the novelist E.M. Forster pronounced the fragment 'a queer taste . . . half topography, half romance' in a review reprinted in his *Abinger Harvest*: 'Topography comes to the front and is screwed much deeper than usual into the story' (1936, p. 150). In the novella, Sanditon is 'praised and puffed' (*LM*, p. 146) to 'young renown' (p. 147) by Mr Parker, so much so that the developing resort has become 'a second wife and four children to him' (p. 148). Austen writes her 'puff' in the same manner as guidebooks to Bath of the time. The new residents have been relocated from the safely 'sheltered dip' (p. 155) of the 'real village' (p. 159) to the windy cliffs but Parker insists that 'Nature had marked it out – had spoken in the most intelligible characters' (p. 143) and that Sanditon is 'the most favoured by Nature and promising to be the most chosen by man' (p. 142). Parker's choice to leave the house of his forefathers and his mistaking one Willingden for another signals a concern about man's decision-making and his place in nature that Austen did not live to explore, and *Sanditon* has been recognised as a new treatment of place, topography, and social climate (Southam 1964, p. 104).

As a novelist, Forster too had developed a shorthand symbolism of place and social status. In *A Room with a View* (1908), the house owned by the Honeychurch family Windy Corner is described by the vicar Mr Beebe as 'commonplace' and 'impertinent' albeit in a glorious situation (p. 195). Mr Honeychurch is a country solicitor but the family has come to be mistaken for 'indigenous aristocracy' (p. 129). The house, however, effectively rescues Lucy Honeychurch from her engagement to Cecil Vyse and from its 'glorious situation' Windy Corner becomes 'a beacon in the roaring tide of darkness' (p. 210). In *Howards End* (1910), the 'nine windows, the vine and the wych-elm' (p. 73) are shorthand for the fictional house. A review in the *Standard* observed that the subject of the novel is 'the all-pervading influence of place . . . Everyone is tested by the walls, the chimneys, the garden of Howards End. Do they see, do they understand, can they connect' (Gardner 1973, p. 128; *Standard* 28 October 1910, p. 5). Malcolm Kelsall has since suggested that the country house becomes a 'mystic sign' (1993, p. 176) and this surely has its origins in the shorthand realist approach Austen takes in *Mansfield Park* and *Persuasion* in which her characters are tested in terms of their responses to houses. In an early piece of criticism after the publication of the letters, Mary Lascelles draws attention to Austen's sense of place without 'concrete particularisation' (1939, p. 178). The universe of the novels is created from places with meaning emanating from selected particulars. Austen knows what places mean and can project them in the letters where she uses her visioning to add a layer of empathy with her correspondent Cassandra.

The editor of Austen's letters R.W. Chapman identified 'a framework fixed for her by small points of contact with reality' (1948, p. 122) but more recently Janet Todd traces a progression in the use of place. *Pride and Prejudice* is a 'novel of houses' (Todd, 2013, p. 88) and where '*Emma* emphasised place and traditional values, *Persuasion* is about shifting locations and people in process' (p. 123). Roger Sale sees distances imbuing a 'sense of place and placedness' (1986, p. 36). He reads 'essays of place' in *Pride and Prejudice* (p. 40) and 'saturation' of place in *Emma* (p. 53), also described as a novel of 'geographic miniaturism' (Wallace 2007, p. 67). There is, however, a darker side to any assumptions about place developed from Austen's own experience of transition and relocation. Frank Churchill appears disengaged in Highbury; he has engaged himself elsewhere in a public place but now in public he continues a secret relationship in private. In public, the Elliots are made vulnerable by snobbery and assumptions of privilege. Inheritance will subsequently mean the loss of heritage and an abandonment of the value of stability. Sir Walter's heir still intends to send in the surveyors to value Kellynch and as matters are left at the end of *Persuasion*, William Elliot will put the house 'with best advantage to the hammer' (*P*, p. 220). There is some irony, therefore, in the ultimate fate of houses that Austen knew and their contact with reality. Godmersham was sold in 1874 by Edward Knight II who had based himself at Chawton following his elopement with Mary Dorothea Knatchbull. James Edward finally inherited Scarlets 17 years after the death of the Leigh-Perrots' intended legatee James Austen, but sold the house in 1863.

Such estates are not just settings for the novels but 'indexes to the character and social responsibility of their owners' Duckworth (1971a, p. 25). This landscape in the 'service of characterisation' (Bodenheimer 1981, p. 605) reiterates Lascelles's observation that the landscape 'is coloured . . . by the mind and mood of the imagined observer' (1939, p. 1). Privacy (Hart 1975) and boundaries (Yeazell 1984) have also been studied, and James Brown's 'mental maps' suggest that for Austen place 'connotes specific relations with home and social networks' (2014, p. 23). Rituals, roles, and occasions mark the spaces in which they take place just as walking, visits, and tea-taking mark their place in the letters. Reginald Farrer notes 'an Elizabethan economy in her stage-settings' (1917, p. 251) and A. Walton Litz 'the unfurnished quality of her world' (1986, p. 111) pointed out by

Shakespeare critic Richard Simpson's review of the *Memoir* (1870). Seeing and being placed emerge from other social and economic details that build up a backdrop like a stage set. The social and economic associations that reinforce character are present also through place. The houses and the living conditions within are denoted by ownership status and income, and by activities such as eating, sewing, and socialising. Margaret Lane explained to an annual meeting of the Jane Austen Society that 'interior description is a thing that Jane Austen disciplines herself to do without' (1962, p. 229). Barbara Hardy understands that houses in the novels can be taken for granted (1975, p. 152) and of course in her letters Austen could assume Cassandra's shared knowledge of their homes and other family locations. While still providing some architectural and topographical detail, Austen merges place with character. As Hardy also points out, 'Her houses are animated, or fail to be animated, by the life led within their walls' (p. 137).

Actual houses and places have been the source of studies speculating on the appearance of suggested locations and their actual bricks and mortar. In Austen studies, architectural history (Pevsner 1968) and geography (Herbert 1991) serve to supplement 'social geography' (Doody 2015, p. 14). Constance Hill began the practice of pilgrimage to actual sites that continues today (Hill 1902; James 2012). John Wiltshire, editing *Mansfield Park*, concludes that elements of houses Austen knew were incorporated into her treatment of the houses in the novel without any strict geographical location other than a contrast with the fashionable resorts frequented by the Crawfords (*MP*, pp. xlv–xlix). Like other commentators he describes the London references as a 'precise calibration of the social significance of an address' (p. l). In addition, there have been a number of studies exploring naming and place significance that expand radically the scope of Austen's topographical associations. Janine Barchas insists on Austen's 'cartographic sensibility' (2012, p. 73) through which history blends into a 'mimetic landscape' (p. 105). In his essay collection on Austen's 'geographies', Robert Clark identifies 'concrete . . . geolocations' in terms of mileages within the novels (2017a, p. 2) and an 'elusive . . . specificity' (Clark 2017b, p. 128) evolving and made sharper in the progress through the novels (p. 151). In the same collection, Ana-Karina Schneider points out that place is about socialisation and letter writing (2017, p. 55; p. 53) and Laurie Kaplan reads the 'allusive' geography of London (2017, p. 199).

Places in Austen's novels are thus both allusive and elusive. Mental maps and social geography interact with actual spaces and actual places. Bath and London feature in the life and in the novels; fictional spaces such as the country house and parsonage are extrapolated from these actual spaces in the letters. The Steventon elms fall in the letters (8–9 November 1800) and Sotherton's timber is under threat in *Mansfield Park* (p. 65). The Southampton store closet defies Austen's housekeeping arrangements (24 January 1809) and Lady Catherine de Bourgh interferes in the closet shelves at Hunsford (*P&P*, p. 75). Austen's characters are witnesses within the space as she was a witness to spaces in her letters to Cassandra and the nieces.

It is widely believed that Austen was in search of a home for her transition into a novelist (Honan 1987, p. 156; Worsley 2017, p. 2) but there is also a sense in which the transitions of her life gave her the impetus to develop and refine her style. She left the epistolary behind while continuing to write her life in letters where suggestive sparseness and shared economy could serve the function of narrative. Letter writing was also a physical disguise for novel writing. It has been suggested that the practicalities of composition were only addressed by her arrival at Chawton in 1809 and yet some of her most famous fictional output was nonetheless dependent on a portable writing desk and the creaking hinge that alerted her to visitors (Austen-Leigh 1871, p. 96). This section of the chapter considers how Austen's life and place are addressed within the letters. It discusses the representation of these places in her letters and considers how the real places that feature in her life have come to shape perceptions of that life and her afterlife.

Austen's actual life was lived mostly in villages. The village of Steventon consisted of 30 or so families with a further 14 at Ashe and 24 at Deane forming the Reverend George Austen's parish (Honan 1987, p. 27; Collins 1993, pp. 86–87). Chawton comprised 40 houses of 347 people in 1811 and 417 people in 1821 (Collins 1993, p. 89). James Edward described Hampshire 'the cradle of her genius' (1871, p. 22) as 'tame country' (p. 19) while Chapman finds a 'Country of pleasing irregularities' (1948, p. 20). After Steventon and before Chawton, Austen had lived in lodgings in Bath between 1801 and 1806, and in a rented house in Southampton between 1806 and 1809.

In terms of real places, much of the evidence of real-time letters from Austen's residence in Bath is lost because of the gap after the initial four letters in May 1801 followed by only two more in April 1805 prior to the removal to Southampton. Before the move in 1801, Austen had possibly visited Bath in 1794 on a trip to the Adlestrop home of her mother's cousin the Reverend Thomas Leigh (Le Faye 2004, p. 86) and she visited the Leigh-Perrots in 1797. This is mentioned in a letter to Phylly from Eliza who has heard from Bath from Austen herself (11 December 1797; Le Faye 2002, p. 150). In 27–28 October 1798 Austen also writes to Cassandra: 'Tis really very kind in my Aunt to ask us to Bath again; a kindness that deserves a better return than to profit by it'. This suggests that Mrs Leigh-Perrot's offer is to be thankfully declined. The 1799 visit with Edward and Elizabeth could be enjoyed and indulged as a holiday as previously discussed but Austen's letters of January 1801 become increasingly hysterical at the thought of actually living in Bath. In 5 January 1801, Austen explains that they are only keeping six beds out of all their familiar furniture. The control over her movables is being denied her and she must now participate in the wider discussion about possible areas for renting. To compensate, Austen interests herself in the 'bustle of going away' and finds the prospect of 'future summers by the Sea or in Wales . . . very delightful'. They could have a chest of drawers made in deal and painted to look like the piece they already own because Bath is 'a place where everything may be purchased', and this may be a suggestion that the sisters are themselves being renovated and put up for sale at the resort. Austen adapts the tone of Mr Collins describing Hunsford: 'I flatter myself that for little comforts of all kinds, our apartment will be one of the most complete things of the sort in Bath–Bristol included'. This letter's very appearance promotes its hysteria. After – but textually before – the discussion of furniture and holidays comes an inverted pre-script note about tithes, bees, and the heat of South Parade, and a 'Monday' postscript below the address proposes at least two visits to Martha. Austen is planning on a calculated absence from Bath. Even though she may 'Perhaps' not write again that week, Austen does and this next letter of 8–9 January has been preserved, preserving also the desperation of a 'merciless Sister' correspondent (14–16 January 1801) who will only be silenced by their being together.

Living in Bath as a dependent spinster was a very different proposition from visiting in Edward's family party in 1799. The Georgian town was shaped by expansions in foreign trade and domestic industry; increased leisure time created consumer markets and a rise in urban sociability fuelled by press interest (Ellis 2001, p. 3). Bath provided spectacle and a recognised and busy social calendar (p. 20). David Gadd describes how it was built up as a resort by the fashionable Beau Nash harnessing the obsession of architect John Wood and the efficiency of entrepreneur postmaster Ralph Allen (1971, pp. 34–35). Civilised society was the result of being seen in public (p. 67) but by the 1780s Bath 'was becoming a caricature of itself and London began to sneer and stay away' (p. 174). Bath can also be mapped against the residence of Austen and her characters. The Elliots are in lofty Camden Place but the Dalrymples are more elevated socially and economically in Laura Place. Mrs Smith is in downgraded Westgate Buildings and the Austens would similarly find themselves in damp Green Park Buildings (21–29 January 1805) and then Gay Street (8–23 April 1805). Catherine Morland braves the 'mob' in the Upper Rooms and attends the Lower Rooms after 'regular duties' (*NA*, p. 17) suggesting that Austen was already conscious of the display and routines of life in a public place. In *Northanger Abbey*, she regards her fellow visitors with amused irony: 'a fine Sunday in Bath empties every home of its inhabitants and all the world appears on such an occasion to walk about and tell their acquaintance what a charming day it is' (p. 28). When the Austens arrived in 1801 changes had begun to take hold. The population was older and sicker, and Peter Borsay remarks that 'the line between recuperation and recreation was a thin one' (2000, p. 33). The *Life* observes that Austen liked Bath's Queen Square on her 1799 visit (17 May–19 June) 'much better than she made her Miss Musgroves like it when she wrote *Persuasion*, 16 years later' (Austen-Leighs 1913, p. 127).

The Musgroves stay in the indeterminate but sociable and busy White Hart that Austen adapts to new purposes herself as discussed in Chapter 5. Meanwhile, private parties like those of the Elliots served to undermine the original concept of public civility, driving gambling underground (Hill 1989, p. 14).

In terms of the capital, Mrs Austen wrote to Phylly's mother on 26 August 1770 that London is 'a sad place, I would not live in it on any occasion: one has not time to do one's duty either to God or man' (*AP*, p. 24) .The real-life London locations in Austen's letters are Henry-centred except for the *en route* letter from Cork Street. In it Austen alludes to the 'idle Dissipation' of 'Love and Freindship' (*J*, p. 105) when she announces to Cassandra that she is 'once more in this Scene of Dissipation & vice' (23 August 1796). The link between this phrase and Fordyce's Sermons has been discussed in Chapter 1, and continues in 28 September 1814 where Austen advises Anna not to refer to London as the 'vortex of Dissipation': 'I do not object to the Thing, but I cannot bear the expression'. By this time Fanny Price has already recorded a hope that the Crawfords will be drawn in and distracted; that 'London would soon bring its cure' (*MP*, p. 374). In the letters, Austen and Cassandra visit Henry or use the capital as a take-off point for other places while settling bills, shopping, and visiting cultural sites such as galleries and theatres. After living in Brompton from June 1808, Henry moved to more spacious 64 Sloane Street in 1811 but downsized to 10 Henrietta Street after Eliza's death before relocating to 23 Hans Place in 1814 (Watson 1955). In 20 May 1813, Austen calculates the distances to Sloane Street via Guildford and Bagshot and in the novels she makes the social calculations mapped out by Pevsner (1968, p. 413) and Laurie Kaplan (2010). The Bennet sisters' Cheapside connection will 'very materially lessen their chance of marrying men of any consideration in the world' (*P&P*, p. 40) while 'no poverty of any kind, except of conversation, appeared' in the John Dashwoods' Harley Street house (*S&S*, p. 266). For Lady Susan, 'London will be always the fairest field of action' offering 'Dissipation' after 'a 10 weeks' penance at Churchill' (*LM*, p. 57) while Mrs Bennet, 'shops and public places' notwithstanding, finds the country 'pleasanter' after an embarrassing exchange about there being 'quite as much of *that* going on in the country as in town' (*P&P*, p. 89). At Pemberley, however, the Cheapside Gardiners prove that there are other factors besides location to recommend them as 'relations for whom there was no need to blush' (p. 282).

The Austens did take advantage of travel opportunities while living in Bath and their seaside visiting seems to have encompassed Sidmouth (1801) as well as Lyme Regis and Dawlish (Fergus 1991, p. 119). Austen's own travel was to take her as far north as Hamstall Ridware in Staffordshire (1806) where her cousin Edward Cooper was rector. She went furthest south to Portsmouth during her time in Southampton, west to Dawlish (1802), and east to Ramsgate (1803; Le Faye 2004, p. 141). In 'Love and Freindship' written in 1790, the Vale of Usk is Laura's original home, and there is continuing speculation about Austen's possible visit to Tenby and Barmouth in Wales in 1801 (Southam 2011). Clark differentiates between the material sense of travel in Austen's letters and a more abstract form of movement in the novels (2017a, pp. 15, 18) and Schneider regards journeys as 'governed by the larger imperatives of social ceremonies' as opposed to the privacy of home (2017, p. 52). In *Pride and Prejudice*, for instance, Austen announces rather glaringly that it is 'not the object of this work to give a description of Derbyshire' but that a 'small part of Derbyshire is all the present concern' (p. 266). Fictional Lambton is the significantly located place as opposed to actual Oxford, Blenheim, and Birmingham (p. 266). The real places are used, however, when conversation flags and the group talk 'of Matlock and Dove Dale with great perseverance' (p. 284) to oil social wheels and cover conversational gaps.

At a transitional moment between Bath and Southampton in 1806, Mrs Austen and her daughters visited the largest house known to them with their cousin the Reverend Thomas Leigh. This visit furnished Austen with much to laugh about (*AP*, p. 247) and to reuse for fictional purposes including the Sotherton chapel in *Mansfield Park*. In an 'odd sort of Letter' from Stoneleigh on 13 August 1806, Mrs Austen describes 'a Nobel large Parlour hung round with family Pictures' (p. 246). The Leigh family home was formerly a Cistercian abbey and Austen's mother tells Mary Lloyd Austen that the house is beautiful but difficult to navigate: 'I had figured to myself long Avenues, dark rookeries, & dismal Yew Trees, but there are no such melancholy things' (p. 245). They sit in the breakfast room because it looks towards the river as does the chapel. In *Pride and Prejudice*, Mrs Philips comes to be gratified by Mr Collins's comparison of her own apartment with 'the smaller summer breakfast parlour' at Rosings when she finds out that in 'one' of the drawing rooms 'the chimney-piece alone had cost eight hundred pounds' (p. 84). Rosings clearly has more than one drawing room and potentially four breakfast parlours. At Stoneleigh, there are 45 windows and 26 bedchambers in the newer part and more in the old (*AP*, p. 246). Visiting Rosings Elizabeth is 'but slightly affected by [her cousin's] enumeration of the windows' (*P&P*, p. 182) but learns the cost of their glazing. Mrs Austen also describes 'the smaller drawing Room' and 'the old Gallery' at Stoneleigh leading into 'the State Bed chamber with a high dark crimson Velvet Bed', 'an alarming apartment' in Northanger style 'just fit for an Heroine' (*AP*, p. 246). This suggests that Mary Lloyd Austen was privy to the joke and Austen had dedicated her juvenile piece 'Evelyn', named for a fictional town in Sussex, to her when she was Mary Lloyd. Circumstantial evidence suggests, however, that she probably appreciated more her mother-in-law's accounts of Stoneleigh's brewing, kitchen garden, and dairy on site.

The important space of the first 25 years of Austen's life and of 22 of the extant letters was the dressing room/bedroom she shared with Cassandra. The *Life* claimed that the 'chocolate-carpeted dressing-room' was 'a place of eager authorship' (Austen-Leighs 1913, p. 73). The family biographers quote Anna on the 'flow of native wit' surrounded by 'scanty furniture and cheaply painted walls' in a room with 'the common-looking carpet with its chocolate ground and painted press with shelves above for books' (p. 15). The Lefroy family manuscript revisited for the updated *Family Record* differs in its reference to 'cheaply papered walls' and 'native homebred wit' (Le Faye 2004, p. 73). Victorian influences are plain in this set of recollections and the Austen sisters' Tonbridge-ware boxes make an appearance with qualifications: 'I thought them beautiful, & so perhaps in their day, & their degree, they were' (p. 73). The boxes (re)appear in an illustration to *Sailor Brothers* (Hubbacks 1906, p. 271) either through a Hubback family recollection or possibly because they have been retained as family objects demonstrating the spinsters' 'irreproachable virtue and unproblematic domesticity' (Vickery 2009, p. 283). The boxes can be safely displayed as evidence of the space that contained needlework and novels in a domestic environment. Cross-referencing with George Austen's accounts at suppliers in Basingstoke, the dressing room wallpaper was blue, the curtains blue-striped, and the press chocolate to match the 'common' carpet (Le Faye 2004, p. 73).

There are many references to reading aloud in this room but Austen had no need to describe it to Cassandra. Even absences, however, do not always provide description. On 27 August 1805 from Edward's in-laws' home Goodnestone, Austen writes to her sister: 'As you have been here so lately, I need not particularly describe the house or style of living . . . nor need I be diffuse on the state of Lady Bridges's bookcase and corner-shelves upstairs'. She is emphasising the absence of Cassandra as a component of place as she does again in 15–17 June 1808: 'I am in the Yellow room – very literally – for I am writing in it this moment. It seems odd to me to have such a great place to myself, and to be at Godmersham without you is also odd'. From London Sloane Street, Austen the published novelist is 'very snug with the front Drawingroom all to myself & would not say 'Thank you' for any companion but You' (20 May 1813).

Later that same year she is writing at '½ past 8' from Henrietta Street *en route* to Godmersham 'seated in the Breakfast, Dining, sitting room, beginning with all my might' (15–16 September 1813). Henry is planning pheasant shooting but Austen is trying to include Cassandra in arrangements to go into Oxfordshire. The plays mentioned in the letter deliberately confuse places. 'Five hours at Brighton' is a play and Edward's daughters 'revelled last night in Don Juan, whom we left in Hell at ½ past 11'. This information is put into the bank branch parcel after Austen writes at '½ past 7' and she then writes again on 16 September 'after dinner' thanking herself 'for the nice long Letter I sent off this morning'. London affords its usual shopping opportunities, and a trip to Grafton House for net, veil, and edging brings out Edward's 'wonderful patience'. While he and Henry have a 'comfortable coze' after the choice of a Wedgwood dinner set 'all four of us young ladies [are] sitting around the Circular Table in the inner room writing our Letters' (16 September 1813).

Austen shares not just physical space by means of letters. She also shares her judgement of those spaces in ways she adapts for the novels. In 3 November 1813 from Godmersham she gives a telling account of her experience of space in the library of a country house: 'At this present time I have five Tables, Eight & twenty Chairs & two fires to myself'. This is the 'formidables' letter to Cassandra in Henrietta Street recounting how she and Edward 'walked about snugly together & shopp'd' in Canterbury with Edward inspecting the Gaol. This snugness contrasts with the space in the library and the parallel confines of the 'scheme' for her return to Chawton. In 25 September 1813 from earlier in the same visit, she proposes to 'shake off vulgar cares & conform to the happy indifference of East Kent wealth'. In this sense 'vulgar' means daily or workaday, differentiating the easier financial situation of her brother. Austen observes 'a succession of small events, somebody is always coming or going' and the sheer organisation of the Knight family becomes clear when Mrs Austen later describes a visit by Edward to Chawton House comprising 28 people (27 April 1820, *AP* p. 266) including four daughters, two sons, and 19 servants. From her Godmersham vantage point, Austen is also reinventing Cassandra's life. In 26 October 1813 Austen writes to her sister in London longing to know 'whether you are buying Stockings or what you are doing . . . Edwd & I settled that you went to St Paul's Covent Garden, on Sunday'. She endeavours also to calibrate authorship with women's counterculture: 'be sure to have something odd happen to you, see somebody that you do not expect, meet with some surprise or other, find some old friend sitting with Henry when you come into the room. – Do something clever in that way'. Her vision conveys the sense of being confined by travel arrangements at the same time as insisting on control over and prior knowledge of Cassandra's movements: 'Mrs Hill will come & see you – or else she won't come and see you, & will write instead'.

For Austen in life the location where the letters are written is part of the process of communication whether in a private sociable space or on display in a public place. Austen describes herself beginning with all her might (15–16 September 1813), up two pair of stairs (24 October 1798; 5–6 May 1801) or alone with a lot of furniture (3 November 1813). The absent are made present by the situation in which they are writing. The "on the road" letters make this more evident by giving a sense of the movement between places through which London or Dartford act as points of entry or re-entry. There is more detail because Cassandra can only share in the transition letter by means of that further envisioning. The use of recollection within letters is related to place and the vision of movement in letters is written from these points of transition. More particularly travel in the letters is about the distance between the two sisters and the logistics of any (re)location from one place to another.

The outlying letter dated 23 August 1796 from Cork Street in London on the way to Rowling in Kent describes a route via Staines then Hertford Bridge and exuberantly notes their 'melancholy parting' yesterday. Austen is in London 'once more' so this is not her first visit. Her brothers have issued forth to seek their fortunes but Austen 'must leave off, for we are going out'. There is a jokey control over arrangements in 24 October 1798 from Dartford with its account of the stages of the journey with her parents, their rooms and dinner. Austen thanks her sister for her 'watchfulness with regard to the weather' on their 'accounts'. By 5–6 May 1801 going to live in Bath, Austen provides a smoothly cynical account manipulating the conventions of the letter manual: 'we changed Horses at the end of every stage, & paid at almost every Turnpike; we had charming weather, hardly any Dust, & were exceedingly agreeable, as we did not speak above once in three miles'. Control over travelling arrangements becomes even more fraught after George Austen's death. In 15–17 June 1808 Austen has been 'rather crowded' travelling to Godmersham with her boa and the three-year-old Caroline. Although feeling as if she has occupied James's place in the carriage, she pictures for Cassandra 'Our two brothers . . . walking before the house as we approached, as natural as life'. She is thus, however, at the mercy of James and Edward's travel arrangements and must shorten her visit with 'no prospect of any later conveyance'. The exuberance of the Juvenilia has been replaced by grown-up shorthand allusions as 'yesterday' passes 'quite a la Godmersham'. The prospect of Chawton has been under discussion by the end of this year and in 10–11 January 1809, Austen announces that 'the very day of our leaving Southampton is fixed' as 3 April with planned visits to Alton, Bookham, and Barton. There is the addition of Dartford in the next letter (17–18 January) before the battle with the Castle Square closet (24 January and 30 January) appears to close their residence. Other sources, however, indicate that the 'dear trio' did not reach Chawton until 7 July because of Mrs Austen's latest illness (Le Faye 2004, pp. 171–173) and no further letter survives until 18–20 April 1811 with its 'good dose of Walking & Coaching', *Sense and Sensibility* in proof, and Austen's 'Goings . . . tolerably fixed' for May. Spaces are occupied by the movables that Austen can control. The inability to control objects and transport embellishes the problem of home.

At the same time, travel with its sense of being out of place distorts the evidence of letters that are more likely to have been written on journeys or visits. The letter envisioning the absent is used, however, to demonstrate empathic communication. In 20 May 1813 from London Sloane Street, Austen has 'fancied it might then be raining so hard at Chawton as to make you feel for us much more than we deserved'. On a concentrated 12-hour journey she has been in Guildford for two hours for breakfast and, with only Henry accompanying her, 'wanted all our Brothers & Sisters to be standing with us in the Bowling Green & looking towards Horsham'. Austen also predicts that her new gloves will not be up to standard because they were too easy to buy. In 2–3 March 1814, she tells Cassandra, 'You were wrong in thinking of us at Guildford last night, we were at Cobham' and have travelled via Farnham with Henry reading *Mansfield Park*. They have breakfasted at Kingston and reached Henrietta Street by two where, Austen writes, 'I have taken possession of my Bedroom, unpacked my bandbox, sent Miss P.'s two Letters to the twopenny post, been visited by M^{de} B., – & am now writing by myself at the new Table in the front room'. Austen insists on her possession of the spaces she can control and the actions she can perform. She can later assure Cassandra of the reinstitution of home activities and involve her in her reading: 'It is Even$^{g.}$ We have drank tea & I have torn through the 3^d vol. of the Heroine'. Perhaps even more importantly Austen reports that Henry admires Henry Crawford: 'I tell you all the Good I can, as I know how much you will enjoy it'. On the same visit, Austen trims her lilac sarsenet with black satin ribbon sharing control over her wardrobe by making it 'a very useful gown, happy to go anywhere' (5–8 March 1814) but control over travel remains problematic with 'convenient Listening' to other plans essential in order to plot their meeting up at Catherine Hill's in Streatham. Cassandra is still at Chawton on 9 March but Austen sends her sister's love to Frank from Henrietta Street on 21 March suggesting that some version of their plan was possible. By 14 June, Cassandra is back in London but Austen is already planning their next move via the Cookes: 'This is a delightful day in the Country, & I hope not much too hot for Town. – Well you had a good journey I trust & all that; – & not rain enough to spoil your Bonnet'. They will travel to Bookham with help from Edward's gamekeeper rather than his carriage and the modes of transport proposed reach new heights of extravagance and danger: 'it must be such an Excess of Expense that I have quite made up my mind to it, & do not mean to care. I have been thinking of Triggs & the Chair you may be sure, but I know it will end in Posting'.

Austen has developed specific views about fictional travel by the time she is advising Anna in the letters of 1814 as also discussed in Chapter 4. In these letters Austen answers queries of detail and offers a broader perspective on place. London features in response to a query: 'Yes – Russel Square is a very proper distance from Berkeley S^{t}' (10–18 August 1814), the latter being the location of Mrs Jennings's house in *Sense and Sensibility* and the 'distance' about two miles. Another distance calls for correction within the 'last book': 'They must be <u>two</u> days going from Dawlish to Bath. They are nearly 100 miles apart' (10–18 August 1814). This is a journey Austen herself would have made in 1802. The 'Dawlish scheme' (8–9 November 1800) was under discussion when Austen was still living at Steventon before plans were disrupted by her parents' Bath scheme but Austen has already told Anna in 1814 that her reference to the library at Dawlish was consistent with Austen's own experience 12 years before. In a postscript to Anna, Austen adds that she has changed a Dorsetshire reference to Devonshire because it would be too far for Mr Griffin to travel to Dawlish and distance is put into context as part of social interaction with a further reference to a place that Austen also visited and wrote from in 1804: 'Lyme will not do. Lyme is towards 40 miles from Dawlish & would not be talked of there. – I have put Starcross indeed. – If you prefer <u>Exeter</u>, that must always be safe' (10–18 August 1814). Starcross is a village four miles north of Dawlish and the much larger Exeter is a further nine miles in the same direction.

At a broader level, Austen advises Anna not to go to Ireland with the Portmans: 'You will be in danger of false representations. Stick to Bath & the Foresters. There you will be quite at home' (10–18 August 1814). It is not only a matter of knowing 'the Manners'; Austen also raises the wider issue of a 'desultory' approach producing a 'wandering story' and in 9–18 September 1814 reiterates the situation in *Emma*, under composition at the time, by recommending '3 or 4 families . . . favourably arranged'. Austen's own descriptive style called for less minuteness and fewer 'particulars of right hand & left'. This letter also announces that Cassandra regards 'wandering' and changes of scene with less 'Latitude' than Austen who thinks 'Nature & Spirit' provide cover for such 'sins'. Indeed she suggests in a later letter that Anna should 'invent something spirited' but not 'Improbable' to take her character Egerton to York or Edinburgh (28 September 1814). The words 'in an old great Coat' are inserted superscript and may be an addition to the joke about Frederick Tilney's not being a Gothic villain (*NA*, p. 133) combined here with a retrospective allusion to the Scottish coach journey in 'Love and Freindship' (*J*, pp. 133–136). Only a few weeks before, Austen has introduced her 'own coach' between Edinburgh and Stirling into an intervening letter to Cassandra from London (23–24 August 1814).

At a chronological level, the letters offer retrospective views of place that position Austen in her various landscapes and pinpoint her locations. Austen's comment to Anna about the 'pitiful and wretched' library confirms the sisters' 1802 Dawlish visit (10–18 August 1814) and Austen takes time out of Godmersham news to remind Cassandra 'It will be two years tomorrow since we left Bath for Clifton, with what happy feelings of Escape' (30 June–1 July 1808). In the same letter, Austen attributes an improvement in the weather to her having written about it and envisions Cassandra 'on the Water & at 4 in the morn^g' because of 'amiable' Frank's return. In 15–17 June 1808 Austen recollects that there was more animation at Godmersham three years before when Miss Sharp, now a correspondent, was governess. She also tells Cassandra, 'Our first eight miles were hot; Deptford Hill brought to my mind our hot journey into Kent 14 years ago' and the Austens find the same 'bad butter' at the Bull in Dartford as in 1794. Austen has even written on 24 October 1798 from this same inn when leaving Cassandra behind at Godmersham after the birth of William Knight. In 9 December 1808 she reports dancing in the same room in Southampton as in 1793 'with thankfulness that I was quite as happy now as then' but by this time the sisters plan to be living at Chawton by the following spring. The 18-year-old Austen is recalled at a pivotal moment by the author about to be 33 and in renewed control of her manuscripts.

Austen's places in the novels have been identified and mapped as locations in relation to each other and to real places. The geography of the novels emerges from a combination of the real and imaginary pressed into the service of realism and plot development. The buildings themselves may not be minutely described but they exist as spaces in which the events of the novels would, could, and probably should take place. Spaces are created by social situation and by the character-driven elements of the plot but are reinforced by a geographical specificity of location. Austen's life revolves around real places with now historical associations and her letters provide a sense of how such places impacted on her life and works. In the letters and the novels, location is about logistics, accessibility, and control over the space, and places are created in relation both to location and to each other. Evidence from the letters demonstrates how fictional places and spaces might become social geography and a functioning mental map within the novels.

Although completed in 1790, Laura's warning to Isabel in 'Love and Freindship' encapsulates real places from the whole of Austen's life. Austen enjoyed varying relationships with the three locations listed as 'Stinking', 'unmeaning', and 'insipid' (*J*, p. 105). Having nearly died of typhus among 'the Stinking fish of Southampton' in 1783, Austen lived in the seaport in a joint household with Frank and his wife Mary for three years (1806–1809). Austen enjoyed 'the unmeaning luxuries of Bath' on holidays in the 1790s but was relieved to escape their life of lodgings in 1809. She visited London to see Henry and Eliza but found pleasure in its 'insipid Vanities and idle Dissipation' and the city played a key role in her professional authorship. 'Love and Freindship' was, of course, originally dedicated to Eliza who was often on the move from London to fashionable resorts both for enjoyment and for the treatment of her invalid son Hastings. On 3 July 1797, Eliza tells their other cousin Phylly that she has 'a variety of rural Plans' but has yet to leave London. She alludes to Henry's potential ordination as opposed to his current profession in the army but Brighton in this year of 'First Impressions' was for sea bathing rather than officers. Eliza will 'neither climb the Welsh mountains, retire into the embowering shades of the Rectory or quarter myself near a Camp but rather hearken to the dashing Billows on the Sussex coast' (Le Faye 2002, p. 140). In reality Eliza went to Cheltenham for health and then to Lowestoft which was suitably placed to meet Henry at Great Yarmouth in the months leading up to their marriage in December 1797. The evidence of Austen and Cassandra's being in Bath in the same month comes from a parallel correspondence with Austen (p. 150). If this was conducted in a similar tone to that with Phylly, the travels surviving into *Pride and Prejudice* have an identifiable inspiration.

Extravagant geography is part of the exuberance of many of the surviving Juvenilia but Eliza's 'embowering shades' may also have referred to the Bower in 'Catharine' (1792) which is both safe and secret. Place is becoming more realistic and suggestive of character. For Kitty 'her Bower alone could restore her to herself' (*J*, p. 243). It is an 'arbour . . . formed' in 'those days of happy childhood' (p. 243): a reminder of past friendships and a refuge for reading in freedom from social responsibilities. In the context of duty, this space is seen as threatening rather than soothing by Kitty's tediously cautious aunt and the triangulation here between a private house with visitors, a public ball for display, and the women's countercultural bower begins an exploration of space and places continued in the later novels. This is a space without the jokey and jerky movements in place and time indulged by earlier pieces. 'Lesley Castle', written earlier in the same year as 'Catharine', controls time through letters and confines its exaggerations to eating and drinking across the farther reaches of Scotland with correspondents in London and Bristol. When Austen returns after 'Catharine' to the relative safety of the epistolary form, *Lady Susan* (1794–1795) will explore a town and country theme dually located in London and Churchill.

J. David Grey describes Austen as 'scrupulous' in the service of realism in her use of real and imagined localities Grey (1986, p. 380). In *Sense and Sensibility*, Norland is near the Sussex coast as indicated by the furniture's being 'sent round by water' (*S&S*, p. 30) to Barton which is four miles north of Exeter (p. 29). Plymouth and Dawlish are on the same road for Thomas's encounter with the newly married Lucy Ferrars (pp. 299–301, 413). London is 170 miles away and a three-day journey via Honiton (p. 182) with the Palmer's home Cleveland 80 miles distant to break the return journey and Willoughby's Combe Magna estate 30 miles south east of it. The location of Longbourn, one mile from Meryton in Herfordshire (*P&P*, p. 31) has been much discussed (Clark 2017b, pp. 132–151) but from here it is three miles to Netherfield (*P&P*, p. 35) and 24 miles to Gracechurch Street (p. 172). Hunsford in Kent is near Westerham (p. 69), a place Austen would have known from journeys into Kent, four hours by coach from Longbourn and a walkable half mile from Rosings (p. 182). Lambton is five miles from Pemberley via 'Blenheim, Kenelworth, Birmingham' (p. 266), and the Gardiners and Elizabeth cover 150 miles 'expeditiously' (p. 315) back to Longbourn in two days. Brighton, Newcastle, and Ramsgate also feature in the novel and suffer by their associations with Wickham,

Mansfield Park is four miles north of Northampton. The White House abode of Mrs Norris is a quarter of a mile away and there is a view of both it and the parsonage from the main house if Fanny walks a short way from the hall door (*MP*, pp. 78–79) which she must do to observe Mary Crawford monopolising her horse-riding opportunities. Edmund's rectory at Thornton Lacey is eight miles from Mansfield (p. 288) and Sotherton is ten miles distant on another road; Portsmouth can be reached via Oxford and Newbury (120 miles) or via London (140 miles), the route of Fanny's first journey. Henry Crawford's Everingham estate is a little apart in Norfolk to the east but the southern sites of Brighton, Richmond, and Twickenham are all associated with his pursuit of Maria Rushworth. *Emma* meanwhile is the most geographically concentrated of the mature novels. Emma has never seen the sea or been to London even though her sister is mobile between these locations. Isabella lives in Brunswick Square (*E*, p. 8) and has spent a summer in Southend for sea air on the recommendation of Mr Wingfield (p. 113). Highbury is situated 16 miles from London (p. 5), positioned for Frank Churchill's notorious haircut, with Donwell a mile away in another parish (p. 8). Randalls is only half a mile from Hartfield (p. 5) and it is seven miles to the real location of Box Hill, sufficient, however, for a disruption in manners. Weymouth, offstage on the south coast, is the scene for Frank Churchill's secret courtship of Jane Fairfax as Mr Woodhouse innocuously informs everyone when Isabella arrives, like Edward at Chawton, with her 'five children and a competent number of nursery-maids' (p. 99). Mr Woodhouse cannot fully recall the previously discussed 'hand-some letter' except that it was 'written from Weymouth, and dated Sept. 28th' (p. 103). Northanger Abbey is 30 miles from Bath (*NA*, p. 159) and Henry Tilney's rectory at Woodston a further 20 miles away (p. 218). Catherine proves that she is a heroine in daily living when she manages the journey of 70 miles back from the Abbey to Fullerton alone (p. 233).

Taking a closer look at *Persuasion*, composed when Austen had a settled life, the transitions within the novel demonstrate to Anne Elliot 'the art of knowing our own nothingness beyond our own circle' (*P*, p. 45). In the novel, Kellynch is three miles from Uppercross (p. 45) which is 17 miles from Lyme Regis (p. 101). Unlike *Pride and Prejudice* where letters between Elizabeth and her sister and aunt create a bridge between family spaces, Anne relocates from Kellynch after her strange duties of removal to discover that 'every little social commonwealth' dictates 'its own matters of discourse' and that 'it was highly incumbent on her to clothe her imagination, her memory, and all her ideas in as much of Uppercross as possible' (p. 46). As at Godmersham, the men have 'game to guard, and to destroy; their own horses, dogs and newspapers to engage them; and the females were fully occupied in all the other common subjects of house-keeping, neighbours, dress, dancing and music' (p. 46). When leaving, however, Anne 'persisted in a very determined, though very silent, disinclination for Bath . . . And looked back, with fond regret, to the bustles of Uppercross and the seclusion of Kellynch' (p. 147). Anne's 'imprisonment of many months' (p. 148) echoes Austen's 'happy escape' letter of 1808. Austen builds on her own experiences to offer telling observations of the comparison between Kellynch and the Elliot's Bath lodgings in Camden Place. The single character trait of 'vanity . . . vanity of person and situation' (p. 5) has disconnected Sir Walter from his own property which he must leave because of the (over)expenditure he thinks reflects his proper station. When Bath is pronounced 'a much safer place for a gentleman in his predicament' where the baronet can be 'important at comparatively little expense', this is a dual condemnation of place and character subtly conveyed by the 'skilful' Mr Shepherd (p. 15). On seeing Kellynch as a visitor, Anne has already admitted feeling no need to acknowledge the 'ancient family . . . driven away' (p. 136) and learns again the art of her own nothingness in Bath. She has, however, a new family and newly fit custodians for the family home in the Crofts. She 'could not but in conscience feel that they were gone who deserved not to stay and that Kellynch-Hall had passed into better hands than its owners' (p. 136). In the Bath setting, Austen opposes 'the duties and dignity of the resident land-holder' with Sir Walter's vanity 'in the littlenesses of a town' (p. 149). Elizabeth his daughter opens her folding doors 'boasting of their space . . . that woman, who had been mistress of Kellynch Hall, finding extent to be proud of between two walls, perhaps thirty feet asunder' (p. 149). This puts the four-foot width of the '16 feet square' Barton Cottage sitting rooms into perspective (*S&S*, p. 33).

The Crofts are, of course, only tenants and Kellynch remains under threat. Ownership status and occupancy count towards character as do the layouts and relative distances that were factors within Austen's own life too. Income makes a huge difference in the calibration of the Austens' move to Bath. Laura Place is 'above our price' and 'Gay Street' 'too high' but favoured Charles Street leads to the potentially damp 'Green park-Streets' (3–5 January 1801). Chawton Cottage later proves close enough to Chawton Manor for the Austen household to act in Edward's stead at the great house. In terms of controllable spaces, Austen and Cassandra occupy a shared dressing room at Steventon, the (large) yellow room at Godmersham, and an economically intermediate space 'up two pair of stairs' at the Leigh Perrots' number one Paragon. In *Pride and Prejudice*, Mrs Bennet considers four potential houses for her daughter Lydia having rejected many 'as deficient in size and importance' (*P&P*, p. 342). The four houses in themselves, although fleetingly discussed, give some indication of the significance of house choices in the novels as a whole. Ashworth is 'too far off', the Stoke drawing room is too small, Purvis Lodge has 'dreadful attics', and Haye Park is inconveniently tenanted by the Gouldings. Mrs Bennet's arguments are, however, resoundingly undermined first by Mr Bennet's determination neither to contribute nor even to allow the couple to enter Longbourn but also by her failure to take the Wickhams' income into account.

Places and the means of inhabiting them are pinpointed in the novels as in life by income and the style of one's carriage. In *Sense and Sensibility*, the Dashwoods' household of two maids and a man reinforces their income of £500 and on leaving Norland they must dispose of the carriage (p. 30). Austen tells Cassandra that their parents will have a similar establishment in Bath with the addition of a 'steady Cook, & a young giddy Housemaid', reflecting their larger income of £600 (3–5 January 1801) in George Austen's lifetime. Their briefly owned carriage has already been given up. In the novel, Colonel Brandon's Delaford has five sitting rooms and 15 bedrooms (p. 331) and, as in Steventon, the parsonage is close to the mansion house (p. 329). Brandon's income from the estate of £2,000 a year (*S&S*, p. 82) makes him considerably less prosperous than Mr Bingley but his rival Willoughby is reported to be living above his means of £600 to £700 (p. 83) with a curricle and hunters. In their debate over wealth and competence, Elinor who rates 'wealth' at £1,000 observes to herself that Marianne's expense headings sound like those of Combe Magna and Margaret meanwhile looks forward to a 'large fortune apiece' (p. 106) like Austen in quest of a 'Legacy' (26 June; 30 June–1 July 1808). Marianne echoes Mary Stanhope in 'The Three Sisters' when she proposes a competence as £2,000 because a 'proper establishment of servants, a carriage, perhaps two, and hunters, cannot be supported on less' (*S&S*, p. 106). Her 'competence' will therefore be granted at her marriage to Brandon. By comparison, the Delaford living offered to Edward Ferrars generates income of £200 a year (p. 320) and is not enough to marry on even with the further £150 income from his own capital of £2,000 and Elinor's of £1,000 (p. 418). Austen herself observed of her brother Edward's brother-in-law Edward Bridges 'Marriage is a great Improver . . . As to Money, that will come you may be sure, because they cannot do without it' (21 November 1808) but in the novel 'they were neither of them quite enough in love to think that 350 pounds a year would supply them with the comforts of life' (*S&S*, p. 418). Edward Ferrars's income is finally augmented by the grudging Mrs Ferrars who gives them a further £250 to marry on (p. 424). For a comparison, George Austen's income rose from £110 to £900 (Collins 1993, p. 58) with additions from farming and multiple livings. Austen comments in the letters on her brother James's income (27–28 December 1808). She would also have been able to assess the place/income realities of her godfather at Great Bookham, the Leighs at Adlestrop, the Fowles at Kintbury, and the Bullers at Colyton. In the novels, James Morland's despised living that means waiting for marriage is £400 a year (*NA*, p. 144) while Dr Grant can afford to eat himself into apoplexy on £1,000 (*MP*, p. 3) at which point Edmund Bertram can add this income, or at least a large part of it, to his £700 a year from Thornton Lacey (p. 264).

The buildings in the novels maintained by these incomes have been subject to examination and dating although the architectural historian Pevsner observes that most of Austen's heroines might be living in the same 'handsome' house (1968, p. 406). Like Godmersham, Mansfield Park is Palladian and newly built; Northanger and Donwell are dispossessed monasteries and Sotherton Court is Elizabethan with a late seventeenth-century chapel like that at Stoneleigh (Lamont, 2005, pp. 226–227). Pevsner describes Godmersham as 'a plain house' and Stoneleigh as 'a monumental ensemble in the tradition of Chatsworth' (1968, p. 405) but this is a convenient marker because of the regular identification of fictional Pemberley with the Derbyshire estate. At Pemberley, we are invited to read the stream 'of some natural importance . . . neither formal nor falsely adorned' (*P&P*, p. 271) and the 'refreshing view' over the lawn to 'high woody hills . . . beautiful oaks and Spanish chestnuts' (p. 295). The established estate with a 10-mile boundary wall (p. 280) reflects its guardians and the testimony of the housekeeper. The likeness is, of course, in no way straightforward: Austen lists Chatsworth separately on Elizabeth's tour of the Peak District (p. 265) in order to use the famed house as a placeholder and point of reality within the plot. Pemberley is Elizabethan or Jacobean, Uppercross is from the time of William and Mary, and Delaford from the time of Wren (Honan 1987, p. 113).

Despite such dating, these are domestic rather than architectural spaces. The houses function as markers of their owners and occupants, and as spaces over which the characters have identifiable degrees of control and responsibility. It is the ability to inhabit a place rather than its design or appearance that counts. As in the letters, places contain space with emotional connections such as the Bower and Fanny's east room, and women's management of spaces is significant. At Hunsford Parsonage 'the paling of Rosings Park was their boundary on one side' (*P&P*, p. 176), reflecting Mr Collins's dependence on patronage. When Elizabeth visits with the Lucases, 'The garden sloping to the road, the house standing in it, the green pales and the laurel hedge, everything declared they were arriving' (p. 176). More significant is the female organisation, 'neatness and consistency' of the space in which Mr Collins can be 'often forgotten' (p. 178).

Fictional landscapes provide a larger context for their fictional houses. In *Persuasion*, Uppercross is 'a moderate-sized village, which a few years back had been completely in the old English style' (*P*, p. 38). It is laid out like the villages Austen knew: 'the mansion of the 'squire, with its high walls, great gates and old trees, substantial and unmodernised – and the compact, tight parsonage, enclosed in its own neat garden, with a vine and a pear-tree trained round its casements' (p. 39). The designation of the 'farmhouse elevated into a cottage' (p. 39) built for Charles and his wife suggests the snobbery of Mary's justification for her change of residence from Kellynch and prepares for her downright view of the Hayter farm at Winthrop (p. 92). The whole is a more substantial description and reflection of the family dynamic explained after Anne's arrival: 'The Musgroves, like their houses were in a state of alteration, perhaps of improvement. The father and mother were in the old English style, and the young people in the new' (p. 43). The migration through the generations has created the hospitable and fatly sighing Mrs Musgrove (p. 73) and her daughters with their harp (p. 43) but the 'improvement' is in doubt. The Musgroves welcome Anne but fail to appreciate her in ways different from the neglect of her father and sisters. The family habits of communicating everything 'however undesired and inconvenient' (p. 89) are observed in the context of proximity, and in sociable Bath, 'good' Mrs Musgrove's 'open-hearted communication' is without 'taste or delicacy' (p. 250).

Mansfield Park sits in a broader and more overtly threatening landscape. The house is seen through the eyes of Mary Crawford assessing her marriage prospects with regard to Tom Bertram with 'almost everything in his favour': 'a park, a real park five miles round, a spacious modern-built house so well-placed and well-screened as to deserve to be in any collection of engravings or gentlemen's seats in the kingdom and wanting only to be completely new furnished' (*MP*, p. 55). Godmersham appears in just such a collection (Figure 6.1). For Mary, the house is an acquisition for display. She seeks control through refurnishing without valuing the existing fabric and relies on 'the true London maxim that everything is to be got with money' (p. 69). The related location of Mansfield Parsonage is described because Fanny the observer must walk out to comprehend that she has been deprived of her exercise by Mary's use of her horse. Although 'scarcely half a mile apart', the houses are 'not within sight of each other' (p. 78) suggesting the difference between the secular and spiritual locations. The discrepancies are not, however religious. Not only is Mary Crawford herself resident in the parsonage. Its previous occupant Mrs Norris is a bully and a skinflint and the current incumbent Dr Grant is greedy and lazy. The parsonage represents other facets of the same

Figure 6.1 Godmersham Park in John Preston Neale, Views of the Seats of Noblemen and Gentlemen in England, Wales, Scotland and Ireland, second series, Volume 2 (London: Sherwood and Johnson, 1826), p. 62. The British Library.

social geography and Fanny must look beyond it to find her place: 'by walking 50 yards from the hall door she could look down the park and command a view of the parsonage and all its demesnes, gently rising beyond the village road' (pp. 78–79). The physical situation of the house and parsonage reflects the situation of Austen's actual villages of Steventon and Chawton from which Austen has herself become an observer.

The more substantial comparison in *Mansfield Park* is with Sotherton Court, a 'capital freehold mansion and ancient manorial residence' (*MP*, p. 96). Sotherton is designated by these words as being owned by the Rushworths and acting as their principal home. Maria's 'Rushworth-feelings' betray her attitude to the Elizabethan house which is a 'large, regular brick building – heavy but respectable looking' with 'a good many rooms' but 'ill-placed' in terms of improvement (p. 66). Edmund is set in opposition to his sister and incidentally to Mary Crawford when he identifies himself as Mansfield's future guardian by opposing improvement for its own sake. He declines to put himself 'in the hands of an improver and will make his own "blunders"'; he 'would rather have an inferior degree of beauty', of his 'own choice, and acquired progressively' (p. 67). Through his sister Maria's eyes, Sotherton village has disgraceful cottages, a 'tidy looking' parsonage, and a church spire 'reckoned remarkably handsome' (p. 96). The observations are about her prestige; fine timber, family-built almshouses and a respectable steward add to her impression of her own consequence (p. 96). The downhill approach for half a mile spoils her appreciation of the house itself. Fanny meanwhile describes it out loud as 'a sort of building which she could not look at but with respect' (p. 96) and Austen adds that it is 'amply furnished in the taste of 50 years back' (p. 99) revisiting Mary's views of Mansfield. Mrs Rushworth has learned from the housekeeper and 'was now almost equally well qualified to show the house' (p. 99) demonstrating that ownership of the house has passed into the realms of touristic display. Most significant in terms of the onward plot is the untidy schema of walks that demarks the groups of visitors observed by Fanny from her resting place at the locked iron gate: 'they had all been walking after each other' and it was 'too late for re-establishing harmony' (p. 121).

Emma offers similar if lower-key contrasts between inside and outside, village and beauty spot. At Randalls on Christmas Eve there is indoor agreement in disagreement: 'Poor Mr Woodhouse was silent from consternation; but every body else had something to say; every body was either surprized or not surprized, and had some question to ask, or some comfort to offer' (p. 136). This is the prelude to Mr Elton's awkwardly unwelcome marriage proposal in transit to Highfield. Later at Box Hill after another transition, the visitors are 'separated too much into parties'; there is silence and a lack of social interaction 'a languor, a want of spirits, a want of union which could not be got over' (p. 399). When Henry Crawford recalls the separate parties on the Sotherton visit in *Mansfield Park*, he uses the very same words from earlier in the novel that 'it was a hot day and we were all walking after each other and bewildered' (p. 285) and this reminder does not promote his cause when he tries to persuade Fanny to marry him.

The starkest comparison, of course, is between Mansfield Park and Portsmouth: the 'abode of wealth and plenty', 'elegance, propriety, regularity and harmony' (*MP*, p. 425, 453) opposed to 'the abode of noise, disorder and impropriety' (p. 450). Fanny's 'review of the two houses' (p. 454) concludes with a resounding reference to Dr. Johnson, that the pains of Mansfield Park are as nothing to the lack of pleasure in Portsmouth. This recapitulates the outcome at Sotherton where 'to determine whether the day had afforded most pleasure or pain, might occupy the meditations of almost all' (p. 124). The recurrence of the word 'abode' in the novel suggests a new and particular emphasis that has evolved in the novels and letters. The word derives from 'abiding' or waiting and came to mean a habitual residence from the 1570s. In Austen's letters it occurs four times and always in a joking context. In 15–16 September 1796 from Rowling, Austen tells Cassandra she has passed by 'the abode of Him, on whom I once fondly doated' on the way to a dinner. In 8–9 January 1801, Sidmouth is proposed as their 'summer abode' in the mounting hysteria sequence discussed above. By its very existence this letter undermines the postscript 'Perhaps' used by Austen to negotiate more frequent communication. In 9 December 1808, Austen wishes Mary Gibson Austen's potentially troublesome cousin Miss Curling a 'long & happy abode' in Portsmouth but hopes in 16 February 1813 to Martha that Miss Benn, given notice to quit, will find something to replace 'her present wretched abode'.

In *Northanger Abbey*, Catherine's 'passion for ancient edifices was next in degree to her passion for Henry Tilney' (p. 143) and she is surprised at the Tilneys lack of elation about their home. Henry's later Abbey jokes make clever use of Catherine's reading and lack of experience (pp. 161–165). Austen names all the potential living spaces and concludes with her own jokey 'abode'. 'With all the chances against her of house, hall, place, park, court, and cottage, Northanger turned up an abbey' (p. 143) but, for the Tilneys themselves, '[t]heir superiority of abode was no more to them than their superiority of person' (p. 144). In *Sense and Sensibility* 'abode' is used of Sir John Middleton, Edward, and Colonel Brandon in the sense of impermanent habitation in London, Plymouth, and Cleveland respectively (pp. 194, 285, 386) but an exception to this usage is made for the 'future abode' (p. 32) of Mrs Dashwood. Barton Cottage is 'comfortable and compact' fairly new and in good repair 'but as a cottage it was defective, for the building was regular, the roof was tiled, the window shutters were not painted green, nor were the walls covered with honeysuckles' (p. 33). There are two sitting rooms, four bedrooms, and two garrets but the cottage is 'poor and small indeed' (p. 33) by comparison with Norland so recently and extravagantly mourned by Marianne (p. 32). In *Pride and Prejudice*, the term 'abode' is specifically reserved for Mr Collins.

Seven of the eight occurrences of the word in the novel refer to his 'humble abode' and in *Emma* the only reference is through Emma to 'the blessed abode' (*E*, p. 89) of Mr Elton, mocking both its occupant and Harriet Smith. Sir Walter Elliot is persuaded to a 'change of abode' (*P*, p. 14) as a substitute for retrenchments at home but in *Mansfield Park* all uses of the word are deployed and weighted with greater seriousness.

Henry Crawford, for instance, inherits a tendency to wander from the Juvenilia: 'To anything like a permanence of abode, or limitation of society, [he] had unluckily a great dislike' (*MP*, p. 47). Mrs Norris changes her 'abode' to interfere in the theatricals, increase her own consequence, and save money (p. 152). In 'the ceaseless tumult of [Fanny's] present abode' (p. 454) in Portsmouth, 'nobody was in their right place' (p. 450), and 'the stairs never at rest' (p. 454), resonating with the comings and goings of Godmersham. The contrasting (im)propriety and (dis)order have actually taken up their 'abode' in the houses at Portsmouth and Mansfield.

The abode as a joke is the more prevalent idea to which Austen returns at the end of the novel when Fanny and Edmund are finally installed in closer proximity to 'the paternal abode' (*MP*, p. 547). Mansfield guardian Edmund gains the Mansfield living and Fanny finds perfection in the parsonage and its demesne after her previously painful sensations 'of restraint and alarm' (p. 548) under the Norrises and Grants. Other places have been rejected or controlled to achieve this stasis but there is a particular significance in the stance taken against the performance within the house of 'Lovers' Vows'. The proposed theatricals with their reorientated space represent a more dangerous and prolonged version of the bounds broken at Sotherton. Mansfield Park is threatened from within by the abodeless Crawfords who test bounds both in Northamptonshire and in southern resorts. Although Edmund at first opposes amateur acting with 'all the disadvantages of education and decorum to struggle through' (p. 146), it is Fanny who resists more strenuously when the threat from that hot day of walking is replayed within the bounds of Mansfield Park itself.

A further variation on this manipulation of locations within and without bounds is carried on in *Emma* where the allegory of threatened spaces is more oblique. Frank Churchill has been gifted an abode by his adoptive mother but his inheritance is in danger from his choice of wife and he masks his true objectives with his surface charm and his letters. Jane Fairfax is in a vaguely defined social relationship with the Campbells and Dixons, and is threatened with a future foreshadowed by the degraded situation of her own aunt. Jane's position without a home is further complicated by her Churchill encounter in a socially indefinable holiday location. In this case it is not an open theatrical experience but an offstage seaside place that represents alternative society and allows the pair to form 'a league in secret to judge us all' (p. 435). Emma protests that Frank has 'come among us with affection and faith engaged and manners so *very* disengaged' (p. 432). In this case the 'paternal abode' is secured by an unacknowledged actor managing his appearances in Highbury, and exploiting the bounds of social responsibility.

Austen demonstrates her understanding of the lack of bounds in her Lyme letter where she provides a bridge between resorts and seaside societies and incidentally with the future inheritance of her displaced naval characters. The reported lack of ice on Cassandra's visit to Weymouth with Henry and Eliza provokes her into declaring it 'altogether a shocking place I perceive, without recommendation of any kind, & worthy only of being frequented by the inhabitants of Gloucester' (14 September 1804). By this she appears to mean the Royal Family who lodge at Gloucester House. She thanks Cassandra for her letter from Weymouth *en route* to Ibthorpe imagining her travelling via Blandford and reports that she (Austen) is fashionable enough to have a cold. The letter also allows future readers to discover that Austen likes sea bathing and is familiar with the 'Cobb' and with Charmouth. She reports the 'usual order' at their new smaller lodgings and also assesses the family of an Irish viscount 'just fit to be Quality at Lyme'. In the letter she identifies the 'ease' of the Irish and when she transfers Lyme itself to *Persuasion*, this thought is put into the mouth of an English viscountess. In conversation with the sycophantic Sir Walter at a concert, Lady Dalrymple observes that Captain Wentworth has '[m]ore air than one often sees in Bath. – Irish I dare say' (*P*, p. 204).

The novels confirm their sense of place and take control of both fictional and factual locations. Bath is a public place with its own boundaries and regulations and London locations are specifically chosen as facets of characterisation. The Dashwood sisters are reconfigured from Norland to Delaford via Exeter and Berkeley Street. The Bennets are given control because they can choose to walk to Meryton but Bingley's sisters are scandalised when Elizabeth walks three miles to Netherfield. Pemberley appears to be out of bounds because of the location of Cheapside but is nonetheless accessible through the sociable, touristic agency of the Gardiners. *Mansfield Park* concerns the placing of Mansfield Park in oppositional dialogues with Sotherton, the theatre, and Portsmouth, and *Emma* has its confines dangerously broadened by offstage Weymouth. In *Persuasion*, Kellynch is displaced first for Uppercross but then by less stable tourist locations at Lyme and Bath. Sanditon is finally in the process of becoming without the structural benefits of longevity and social norming so that 'everybody must now "move in a circle" – to the prevalence of which rotatory motion, is perhaps to be attributed the giddiness and false steps of many' (*LM*, p. 203).

Austen's sense of place was honed by the practice of letter writing. The representation of space and places in her novels develops from life-written letters into the narrative and descriptive economies of her fictional style. The considered and proof-read texts of the novels present the vortex, the abode, and the carpet as pre-texts for Forster's roaring tide, wych-elm, and windows. Her letters supply evidence of places stored for use in fiction such as Bath or Stoneleigh Abbey or Godmersham but her spaces also represent the lived sociability of the inhabitants. This is a significant feature of any topographical display. London and Chatsworth may literally be placeholders but it is the interaction between locations and the lives lived in them that drives plots with the benefit of the letterly conversation of the absent.

Austen's life is structured through place because letters assume geographical separation and a shared knowledge of the spaces from which those letters are composed. Henry Austen might have reduced his sister to 'a life of usefulness, literature and religion' but the letters reprise a life of waiting, transition, and habitation. Places and spaces emerge because Cassandra reads and characters see. The letters can also be reread in the context of randomised accidental fragments preserved from that life as the next chapter demonstrates. Mapped onto incidentally preserved evidence, the letters embellish a biographical kaleidoscope of paper, fabric, pounds, shillings, and pence.

7

Letters and Patchwork

Scraps in the Life

The letters that provide the biographical detail of Austen's life are part of a patchwork pieced together. Patchwork uses scraps to construct new patterns and a newly practical whole, and letters act as biographical connections or threads between other extant scraps of both Austen's life and that of adjacent family members. This chapter considers textual as well as textile scraps in relation to the letters in order to explore the life and to reconfigure its connections. The scraps and letters reconstruct a life for Austen from missing or incomplete records including account books and household and personal documents in addition to the family quilt (or coverlet) preserved at Chawton. The letters are inflected against financial memoranda, recipes, sewing projects, and an extended family record. The chapter considers other networks within letters suggested by inter-familial relationships that impacted on the family as lower gentry. Sisterhood in letters is revisited in an extended footnote piecing together the lives of three women lost and found within Austen's letters: Austen's benefactor Catherine Knatchbull Knight, her neighbour Elizabeth Papillon, and her distant cousin/sister-in-law Eleanor Jackson Austen.

It is perhaps only because we have the luxury of 'compacted obscurity' (Mullan 2001, p. 23) allied with unfathomable depths of interpretation and ownership that it becomes permissible to speculate on the lost documents of the Jane Austen life. Maria Tambouku observes that 'the letter in the archive has to be read with the letter that was lost or burnt in mind' (2011, p. 4) and Claudia Johnson draws attention to the cult of 'Austenian things' (2012, p. 156) with 'memorialised' scraps becoming 'proxies of Austen herself' (p. 172). The surviving letters reinvigorate these surviving scraps and provide keys to the rereading and realignment of the evidence. Previous chapters have drawn on the letters as life writing and as novel writing. Instead of existing between the gaps, the letters can also regain their value as evidence of a life by filling up the gaps left by preservation.

In addition to the letters and manuscripts, two valuable scraps in Austen's hand record financial transactions and both are in the Pierpont Morgan Library. One is

The Life of the Author: Jane Austen, First Edition. Catherine Delafield.
© 2023 John Wiley & Sons Ltd. Published 2023 by John Wiley & Sons Ltd.

'Memorandums at the end of the year 1807' in the *Collected Reports of the Jane Austen Society* (Piggott 1980, p. 147); the other is the overall 'Profits of my Novels' visible online with the other manuscripts (Sutherland 2010). These financial statements present Austen at very different moments in her life: dependent in Southampton and a published novelist at Chawton. Both, however, have ghostly existence within the letters and combine to illuminate other facets of the biographical kaleidoscope.

'Profits' has been the subject of detective work to uncover the source of Austen's holding of £600 in the annuities dubbed 'Navy Fives'. Jan Fergus calculates this purchase to have been an investment of £531 representing the profits from the first published novels and the inferred £310 to £347 profits of *Mansfield Park* (1991, pp. 191–192). The letters record clearly the £110 received for the copyright of *Pride and Prejudice* (29–30 November 1812) and £140 from self-publishing *Sense and Sensibility* (15–16 September 1813). Of the other 'profits' recorded, Austen wrote to Caroline on 14 March 1817 specifying £19.13.0 from the second edition of *Sense and Sensibility* following on from an annual payment of £13.15.0 for the same publication in March 1816 (*C*, p. 531). The £13.7.0 residue from *Mansfield Park* recorded in 'Profits' was the sum lost when Henry's bank failed (Clery 2017, p. 300). The second edition of this novel was notably unsuccessful and its losses were offset by John Murray against *Emma* leaving only £38.18.0 profit from the later work that was the last published in Austen's lifetime (Gilson 1982, p. 69). Austen mentions the 'hazard' of a second edition of *Mansfield Park* to Fanny when she expresses her desire for 'Pewter' as well as praise (30 November 1814). This carries on Austen's discussion of the edition and of her own greed 'for more' in her previous letter contrasted with Fanny's indifference to the sources of wealth (18–20 November 1814). For Austen, the financial memorandum was a summary if not a letter to herself, capturing the 'Pewter' on offer and perhaps making ready to approach the market with the novels in hand.

The 1807 memorandum is altogether on a different scale but nonetheless fascinating for its insights into Austen's life. During her thirty-second year Austen has summarised her expenditure on the pages provided at the end of a diary or pocketbook of which this is the only surviving leaf. The year begins with £50.15.0 in hand and ends with £6.4.6. The extant letters for this year begin with Mrs Austen reiterating to Austen, and Austen to Cassandra, that the year also begins with '30l. in her [Mrs Austen's] favour' (7–8 January 1807). On the second day of writing this letter Austen must clarify the figures at Mrs Austen's insistence: 'My mother is afraid I have not been explicit enough on the subject of her wealth; she began 1806 with 68l., she begins 1807 with 99l., and this after 32l. purchase of stock'. It seems likely that the Austens were in the habit of keeping accounts even though this is the only evidence of Jane's that survives. In *Sense and Sensibility* Mrs Dashwood with her similar income to that of Mrs Austen talks about making up her accounts in spring (p. 85). It could be that Austen kept her own accounts every year as represented by the fragment or that the specific situation in 1807 made the record significant. In January the question of living expenses relates to the rental of the house in Castle Square. Austen tells Cassandra that 'Frank too has been settling his accounts and making calculations' for the joint household on which Frank has set a limit of £400 a year at the current rental (7–8 January 1807). Austen also expresses their joint caution, with 'each party' feeling 'quite equal to our present expenses' but wary of any increase in rent.

In the event, the combined household moved in on 10 or 11 March with Cassandra leaving Godmersham on 16 March to arrive at Southampton in early April in time for the birth of Frank's first child Mary Jane on 27 April (*C*, pp. 338–339). Only three Austen letters in total survive for 1807, all from January and February. Apart from the memorandum, the only specific expenditure mentioned for the year is thus in 8–9 February when Austen sends 'four pair of small Soals' to Kintbury at a cost of six shillings. Through an unidentified 'Booking', this transaction leaves Cassandra 18 pence or 1/6 in Austen's debt. This too would suggest more detail in reckoning than is apparent from the overall evidence in the documents of Austen's life. At the highest level Austen refers obliquely in 7–8 January 1807 to the 'family treaty' concerning James Leigh-Perrot's agreement to relinquish his interest in Stoneleigh Abbey in return for £24,000 and an annuity of £2,000 (Le Faye 2004, p. 156). In February, Austen records her sister's 1/6 indebtedness to her with amusement because the Stoneleigh settlement under negotiation was an unimaginable sum for the Austen women entertained by the Abbey when Thomas Leigh took them there in 1806. Another 10 years on from that gift of 'Soals', Uncle Leigh-Perrot's failure to make provision for Mrs Austen at his death in 1817 causes Austen to have a relapse in her ongoing illness when she confesses to Charles that she has had to 'press' for Cassandra's earlier return from the funeral (6 April 1817).

The 1807 memorandum uses 10 broad headings that furnish additional detail of the events lost because of missing or non-existent letters between March 1807 and June 1808. Austen's cash outlay seems to have been about £1.12.0 more than her accounted spend of just under £43. She claims to have actually paid out £44.10.6 so further miscellaneous items are undocumented. On the record, 'Waterparties and plays' cost 17/9 and an unspecified 'Journey' £1.2.10 meaning that Austen has travelled at her own expense during the year and paid for her own theatre trips. The Austen women were at Chawton House from 1 to 11 September according to Fanny's pocketbook that also records visits and plays (Le Faye 1986b), and Austen and Cassandra went to Manydown for a visit around Christmas returning on 4 February 1808 (*C*, pp. 347–349). Austen has also had to tip the 'Servants &c' 13/9 on visits and this is a subhead under anxious debate in the letters. A very early reference concerns Austen agonising over a tip for the servants at Rowling

(5 September 1796). In 24 August 1805 she describes herself as 'a Sister sunk in poverty' when she 'cannot afford more than ten shillings for Sackree', nursemaid at Godmersham for 58 years. In 1807 Austen has also paid £2.13.6 to hire a piano which is a considerable expense compared with her later proposal that an instrument '<u>will</u>' be bought for Chawton Cottage for 30 guineas (27–28 December 1808). In 23 January 1817 Austen writes to Caroline in a prescript that she is the 'constant Theme' of the piano at Chawton 'in various keys, tunes & expressions' albeit not the 'Anna with variations' of her half-sister. In the same letter, Austen enrols her niece in the women's travel conundrum because Caroline cannot so easily visit as James Edward.

Unsurprisingly, given the discussion of fashion economies and consequent laundry in the letters, 'Cloathes and Pocket' at £13.9.3 is the largest outlay in 1807 at over 30% of spend; £9.5.11½ (or 20%) is spent on 'Washing'. Among various laundry references in the letters, Austen proposes to send a parcel 'mostly dirty Cloathes' via the Collier coach in 17–18 October 1815 to 'be paid for on my own account'. This aligns washing with postage which is usually an invisible cost within the letters unless significantly higher to her as recipient. In 1807 £3.17.6½ was spent on 'Letters & Parcels' about 9% of the total for the year. At that period there was no convenient postal transmission through Henry's bank branch. Austen comments in 14–16 January 1801 that eight pence was due in postage on a Cassandra letter rather than the usual sixpence and she later debates value for money with Frank whose letter from the Baltic has cost her 2/3 compared with her 'scratch of a note' (25 September 1813). In 26 November 1815 amidst news of the proofs of *Emma*, a parcel costing 2/10 is declared 'a certain saving' possibly from laundering as the four pairs of silk stockings need not be washed.

Bringing clothes expenditure to account is more furious when Austen takes her opportunities in London and in Bath but remaining references in the letters may fairly represent the composition of her 1807 outlay. There are frequent occasions for fabric purchase both for herself and on behalf of others. While waiting for her mother to see the physician Mr Lyford in Basingstoke, Austen has visited Mrs Ryder's and bought ink to dye a hat and flannel at 2/3 a yard (27–28 October 1798). Netting silk may have been bought but was at that time in short supply at the draper's. The following month, a doorstep salesman called the Overton Scotchman calls at the rectory and 'rids' Austen of her money in return for six shifts and four pairs of stockings (25 November 1798). She debates the quality of the Irish linen she also buys at 3/6 a yard. The holiday in Bath in 1799 yields a cloak at just under £2 as well as Austen's lace sketch to assist Cassandra in defining her commission (2 June). There are further dyeing discussions in the quest for economy with four shillings paid for a blue gown that subsequently disintegrates (7–9 October 1808) and money owing to Henry for silk dyeing. This prompts the comment that dyers are wicked, 'dipping their own Souls in scarlet sin', because her 'poor old Muslin' has been overlooked (2–3 March 1814). Gloves at four shillings (20 May 1813), a six-shilling silk handkerchief with plaiting lace at 3/4 (16 September 1813), and a cap from Mrs Hare to cost £1.16.0 at most (15–16 September 1813) suggest headings within the clothes outlay for any given year. For 18–20 April 1811 Austen is in London to proofread *Sense and Sensibility* and is perhaps feeling more extravagant when she spends 2/4 on 'Bugle Trimming', 36 shillings on three pairs of silk stockings, and 17 shillings on a pelisse although she comments that the buttons are expensive. In fact she has effectively spent her whole quarterly allowance in one morning.

In 1807, Austen paid 11 shillings for her pew at church benefiting Dr Mant the incumbent of All Saints in Southampton who was the subject of her teasing of Martha (17–18 January; 24 January 1809). Combined with 'Charity' at £3.10.3½, this was another 9% of Austen's outlay perhaps reflecting a tithe on her income. References to charitable giving in the letters usually refer to gifts in kind except when the Austens are disbursing charity at Chawton on Edward's behalf. 'Presents' at £6.4.4 may include the 'Soals' noted above. On 18 June 1807, Fanny records the gift of 'a long strip of beautiful work as a present from Aunt Jane' (*C*, p. 340) but if this is a handmade item, its costs may have been accounted for elsewhere under 'Pocket' money. Cassandra has given Fanny a pair of bracelets on her birthday on 23 January (p. 336) so perhaps Austen had a share in these. The sisters certainly shared in the 16-shilling cost of a veil bought in Bath for Mary Lloyd Austen (11 June 1799) and in 30 June–1 July 1808 Austen proposes to spend half a guinea on a 'Broche' or silver knife for Mary Gibson Austen. She also gives 18 shillings for a 'neat & plain' locket on commission for Cassandra (24 May 1813) but its recipient is unknown and there are words cut out of the original text at this point.

In terms of recorded income to service this expenditure, the year 1807 may itself have been anomalous for Austen. Although Park Honan suggests that her £50 received for the year would have originated from her 20-guinea annual allowance supplemented by presents from Mrs Knight and Edward (1987, p. 245), Deirdre Le Faye believes that £50 was a bequest from their Bath acquaintance Mrs Lillingston (2004, p. 163). Mrs Lillingston appears fleetingly in the letters from Bath (5–6 May; 21–22 May; 26–27 May 1801) and died there on 30 January 1806 (*C*, p. 325). Austen had previously received a bequest of £50 in 1794 from Edward's adoptive father Thomas Knight (Le Faye 2004, p. 87). Austen records that she has £7 in hand in her desk when it is accidentally carried off from Dartford towards 'the West Indies' (24 October 1798) and this also may be the residue and accumulation of her allowance of five guineas a quarter. The allowance is noted as due at the end of December 1798 (24–26 December) after a gift of £10 has also been paid to her (18–19 December 1798). Fanny Knight records in her pocketbook that Austen won 17 shillings in a raffle on 19 September 1805 when they were staying in Worthing (*C*, p. 318) thus augmenting her quarterly allowance by a sixth during the period of transition between her residence at Bath and Southampton.

The settling of debts and acknowledgement of transactions can thus be pieced from the letters under the headings of the memorandum. Despite Austen's being in receipt of her novel profits, 20 May 1813 opens, 'Before I say anything else, I claim a paper full of Halfpence on the Drawingroom Mantlepiece; I put them there myself & forgot to bring them with me'. The dissipation of London and its potential dangers is the subtext and she adds, 'I cannot say that I have yet been in any distress for Money, but I chuse to have my dues as well as the Devil'. Austen is scrupulous in return, sending 18 pence 'due' to her mother with 16 September 1813 although this may be the return from settling their Twining account for tea mentioned in March 1814. Women especially must receive their due. Austen is insistent on paying Madame Perigord, daughter of Henry's housekeeper, a shilling for hat-making willow and she transfers £6.15.0 to Mrs Austen after it has been erroneously placed in her (Austen's) own account (2–3 March 1814). Austen tells Cassandra that she is grateful for £5 from 'kind, beautiful Edward' in 15–16 September 1813 but adds 'I shall save what I can of it for your better leisure in this place'. From this London visit, Austen then travels on to Godmersham but writes from Kent four times to Cassandra in London, where the residue of the gift could have been spent, between 21 October and 7 November. In contrast with her paper of halfpence, she later sends Cassandra 'five one pound notes, for fear you should be distressed for little Money' on 24 November 1815. The catalogue entry for the 1807 memorandum in the Pierpont Morgan Library quotes from the first page of the document before a further expenditure on washing, 'Medecine' (1/1½) and 'Pocketbooks' (1/4) totalling 13 shillings is carried over onto the second page, possibly the result of the end-of-year absence at Manydown. The pocketbook purchase suggests that further records would have been kept and are now missing, and the continued existence of this fragmentary document in Austen's hand has indeed the fugitive biographical quality of Edmund's note to Fanny begun and unfinished in the east room of Mansfield Park.

Pocketbooks, of course, had uses other than as records of accounts, and Cassandra's initialled memorandum dating Austen's published novels is perhaps a summary made from annual pocketbooks such as the ones kept by Fanny Knight.

> First Impressions begun in Oct 1796/Finished in Aug[t] 1797. Published/ afterwards, with alterations & contractions/under the title of Pride & Prejudice/Sense & Sensibility begun Nov 1797/I am sure something of this/ same story & character had been/written earlier & called Elinor & Marianne/ Mansfield Park begun sometime/about Feby 1811 – Finished soon after/June 1813/Emma begun Jan[y] 1814, finished/March 29th 1815/ Persuasion begun Aug[t] 8th 1815/finished Aug[t] 6th 1816/North-hanger Abbey was written/about the years 98 & 99/C.E.A.
>
> *(Chapman 1954, facing p. 242)*

This information could have been extracted from the records of either sister although evidence confirms that the final form of the memorandum is dependent on Cassandra herself because she uses the published titles of the novels that appeared after Austen's death. Austen herself called *Persuasion* 'The Elliots' and *Northanger Abbey* was sent off to Crosby as 'Susan' and later referred to as 'Miss Catherine' (13 March 1817). The dates may also have been gleaned from other drafts of the novels since the completion of *Emma* is dated exactly and the dates of *Persuasion* equate to dates in the surviving manuscript of the cancelled chapters. Such dates weave threads across the life and novels. Among Austen's very exactly dated remembrances is one written in 8–11 April 1805 from Bath where they have seen Miss Chamberlayne 'look hot on horseback. – Seven years & four months ago we went to the same Ridinghouse to see Miss Lefroy's performance'. This is a reference to their stay with the Leigh-Perrots in November/December 1797. In 1805 Austen is writing from lodgings in Gay Street in the months after her father's death. She will later lodge the Crofts in Gay Street in *Persuasion* but will relocate Anne's reconciliation with Captain Wentworth from the Crofts' first-floor sitting room to the street via the White Hart, dating her own authorial movements exactly in the cancelled chapters. She originally concludes with the word 'Finis' and dates this 16 July 1816 before adding a new 'Finis' to a new section dated 18 July. It has been observed that the manuscript chapters like the scraps allow Austen to be 'caught in the act of drudgery as well as of genius' (Harris 2007, p. 38). The revision and substitution of three chapters for these two originally drafted was then completed as per the memorandum on 6 August.

Despite the illumination of this extant scrap, any knowledge of the novel-writing process is fugitive and fleeting. Information about the novels may also be scanty in the letters themselves as discussed in Chapter 1 but the content of Austen's communications offers insight into the daily lives plotted by her fiction and adds pieces and other scraps to the picture of Austen's own life in recipes, needlework, and letters.

Letters were incorporated into domestic duty and linked with household tasks, and Austen would have been familiar with texts exhorting pride in such duties. She read Thomas Gisborne's *An Enquiry into the Duties of the Female Sex* at Cassandra's recommendation (30 August 1805) to be told that in addition to being 'completely versed in the sciences of pickling and preserving, and in the mysteries of cross stitch and embroidery', a woman must be 'thoroughly mistress of the family receipt-book and of her needle' (Gisborne 1797, p. 18). Science, mystery – or possibly *métier* – and mastery suggest knowledge, skill, and control that elevate these duties and distract from some of the drudgery entailed in the days before the sewing machine and refrigerator. Austen might have translated Gisborne's catalogue into Miss Bingley's definition of the accomplished woman with her 'thorough knowledge of music, singing, drawing, dancing and the modern languages'

(*P&P*, p. 85). James Edward was later keen to promote Austen's skills as a needle-woman in his memoir but, in describing the household at Steventon from his own Victorian rectory, he was 'sure that the ladies there had nothing to do with the mysteries of the stew-pot or the preserving-pan' (Austen-Leigh 1871, p. 37).

The 'mysteries' of women's lives were, however, becoming elided in the letter manuals such as *The Young Woman's Companion or Frugal Housewife* (1811), an early nineteenth-century publication that contained 'the most approved methods of pickling, preserving, potting, collaring and confectionary etc.' This was perhaps an acknowledgement of useful information that might also form the acceptable contents of a letter. In an 'Advertisement' to the volume, the compiler explains that arithmetic has been excluded because the aim of the volume is to promote an 'immediate tendency to cultivate the mind'. They apologise for any improper inclusions from moral writers past: 'it is presumed that nothing has been inserted which could wound the feelings of young females, for whose instruction and edi-fication this volume is principally designed' (1811, 'Advertisement'). The text of pages 388 to 392 reuses sections of earlier guides word-for-word (*The Complete Letter-Writer* 1776, pp. 38–39). There are the customary recommendations about writing 'like a conversation' and producing elegant and proper words with the also customary warnings against perverting the end by obvious labour (1811, p. 389). It is clearly essential to balance elegance with the 'familiar' and to reject 'all pomp of words'. Correction after perusal, evidenced in Austen's superscript additions to her letters, is also acceptable because 'a blot is by no means so bad as a blunder' (p. 390) but a 'dirty, ill-folded letter bears marks of illiteracy upon the face of it' (p. 392). James Edward was equally quick to reassure his readers of Austen's dex-terity in letter-folding (Austen-Leigh 1871, p. 93) while Austen makes the ill-written direction of Jane Bennet's letter a plot device (*P&P*, p. 301) and piles further anguish onto Fanny Price when Mary Crawford hesitates in her folding of a letter in order to add more evidence of her brother's doubleness (*MP*, pp. 503–504).

There is no Austen 'receipt book' to demonstrate her adherence to Gisborne's advice but items that featured in the *Frugal Housewife* compilation occur in the letters particularly when Austen is in charge of the housekeeping and pleasing her own appetite (17 November 1798). Meat products are often mentioned such as 'ragout veal' and 'haricot mutton' (17 November 1798), 'Chicken boiled perfectly tender' (27 November 1798), sparerib (1 December 1798), and duck with 'pease' (31 May 1811). Preserved foods such as cold souse made of pickled pigs' ears or brawn (14 January 1798), black butter made of spiced apples (27 December 1808), and pickled cucumbers (16 December 1816) are on the menu in Steventon, Southampton, and Chawton respectively. Although exact dating is not possible, Martha Lloyd's surviving 'Household Book' must have been at the Austen sisters' disposal and this compilation includes 'A Harrico of Mutton', and

'A Pease Soup' as well as Austen's reported favourite toasted cheese (27 August 1805) along with a version of the white soup thought essential for the Netherfield ball (*P&P*, p. 100). A request for a piece of Catherine Biggs's wedding cake on the part of Mrs Dundas (7–9 October 1808) is echoed in the Perry children's cake-eating at the outset of *Emma* (p. 18) and Martha also included 'Mrs Dundas's Biscuits' in her 'Book'. This is a far plainer recipe than most others suggesting that Martha's friend and relation needed something dry for her digestion but also that recipes were being shared and recorded. Mrs Austen sent her recipe for potato cakes to her half-sister-in-law Mrs Walter (12 December 1773; *AP* p. 30) and in 1795 Edward Cooper's mother-in-law Caroline Lybbe Powys garnered recipes from Austen's cousin Jane Williams née Cooper and Mrs Leigh-Perrot (*C*, p. 171). In collected form, the *Frugal Housewife* provides not only letter-writing tips but also printed recipes for souse (1811, p. 49), veal 'ragoo' (p. 241) and 'harrico' mutton (p. 275) in addition to the homemade beverages such as mead (p. 126) and orange wine (pp. 93–94) mentioned to Cassandra and other correspondents. After the journey via Dartford in 1798, Mrs Austen must also have a personalised recipe for dandelion tea with a chaser of 12 drops of laudanum (27–28 October 1798). Austen carries 'the keys of the Wine & Closet' about with her (27–28 October 1798) and professes herself proud of her 'experimental housekeeping' such as ox cheek with dumplings 'that I might fancy myself at Godmersham' (17 November 1798). The dumplings would accompany this cheap cut of meat required by the economies of country living. At Godmersham, however, there are ices and French wine (30 June–1 July 1808) and later the 'douceur' of 'being a sort of Chaperon for I am put by the Fire & can drink as much wine as I like' (6–7 November 1813).

Food was also a variant of location and dependence. Austen's letters indicate how Godmersham supplied game for the family's consumption after the move to Bath that cut them off from their own fresh supplies. Austen has specifically mentioned the slaughtering of animals at Steventon but writes to Cassandra about the price of actual meat in Bath (5–6 May 1801) and even comments on it to Frank in the Baltic albeit in the letter where she conforms 'to the happy Indifference of East Kent wealth' (25 September 1813). The economics of dependence and debility are highlighted through food in *Emma*. The Bates household is grateful for gifts from Donwell (pp. 255–258) and Hartfield (pp. 184–186) about which Miss Bates elaborates at length while incidentally providing cover for Frank Churchill (p. 259). At the same time Mr Woodhouse advises less salt for the Hartfield pork and more baking of the Donwell apples, and his guests are constrained by his advice on eating boiled eggs and apple tart (p. 24) leaving Emma to the 'honours' of minced chicken and scalloped oysters (p. 23). In 'Frederic and Elfrida' Charlotte and her aunt eat a hare, two partridges, three pheasants, and a dozen pigeons after Charlotte agrees to marry two men simultaneously (*J*, p. 9) but the apogee of eating comes in 'Lesley Castle'. Charlotte Lutterell draws up a 'Devouring Plan'

(*J*, p. 147) to deal with the beef sirloin, mutton, soup, ham, and chicken remaining from her sister's cancelled wedding and yet a pigeon pie, turkey, and six aspic jellies must still be taken to Bristol to be 'got rid of' over two days by their landlady's family (p. 153). At home the servants and charwomen have been eating 'as hard as they possibly could' to clear the pantry (p. 153). In 5 September 1796, Austen writes from Rowling that two Mr Harveys will 'devour' venison from Godmersham 'and on friday or Saturday the Goodnestone people are to finish their Scraps'.

After this juvenile eating, a third Charlotte is maliciously alleged in *Pride and Prejudice* to be 'wanted about the mince pies' (p. 48) and, at the Netherfield ball, her mother Lady Lucas is left by a preening Mrs Bennet 'to the comforts of cold ham and chicken' (p. 112). Mrs Bennet has earlier exclaimed 'with some asperity that they were very well able to keep a good cook, and that her daughters had nothing to do in the kitchen' (p. 73) as James Edward claimed of his aunts. Mrs Bennet's own housekeeping and 'anxious designs' on Mr Bingley require a dinner of two courses (p. 374) that later consists of venison, soup, and partridges (p. 379). Having already written 'First Impressions', Austen is happy with the dinner supplied for Mr Lyford in exchange for his dandelion tea receipt: 'I was not ashamed at asking him to sit down to table, for we had some pease-soup, a sparerib, and a pudding' (1–2 December 1798). Austen is not, however, always so content with this housekeeping role, normally undertaken by Cassandra. A visit from the James Austens causes her regret and she welcomes being left to the 'comfortable disposal' of her time after 'the torments of rice puddings and apple dumplings' and underdone mutton (7–8 January 1807). A visit from James Edward with its 'Joints of Mutton & doses of rhubarb' inhibits the composition of 8–9 September 1816 and causes Austen to reflect with thanks on Cassandra's work caring for the house.

In the unfinished *Sanditon* yet another Charlotte (Heywood) witnesses the complexity of seaside vegetable economics when the new resort severs family relationships with the land as the move to Bath did for the Austens. The Parkers have left behind an established garden and the retained servant old Andrew must toil uphill to harvest from it. Any shortfall can be bought from stingy Lady Denham's gardener or from the newly established Stringers whom Mr Parker wants to support as part of his enterprise (*LM*, p. 158). Austen finished this fragment on 18 March 1817 and was perhaps thinking of vegetables arriving from their old home at Steventon. She wrote to Caroline along with news of her income from *Sense and Sensibility*: 'the Seacale will be extremely acceptable . . . the future only relates to our time of dressing it, which will not be until Uncles Henry & Frank can dine here together' (14 March 1817).

Having banished his aunts from the kitchen, James Edward wanted Austen safely confined to her needlework through the craft of stitching and the mastery of her needle. Despite the later evidence of the letters and his sisters' firsthand experience, he pronounced Austen and Cassandra 'scarcely sufficiently regardful of the fashionable, or the becoming' (Austen-Leigh 1871, p. 82). He describes Austen's needlework 'both plain and ornamental' as 'excellent, and might almost put a sewing machine to shame' (p. 93). Since she 'was considered especially great in satin stitch' this may have been the form of the 'beautiful work' sent to Fanny in 1807. James Edward seems relieved to find that Austen 'spent much time in these occupations' rather than in writing novels and emphasises that 'some of her merriest talk was over clothes which she and her companions were making, sometimes for themselves, and sometimes for the poor' (p. 93). He describes the carefully unused housewife or needlecase made by Austen, and given to his mother on the Lloyds' removal from Deane, as 'a curious specimen' made by 'some benevolent fairy' (p. 93). At this point the object had been kept for 70 years and was still accompanied by the verses that gifted it to Mary:

> This little bag, I hope, will prove
>> To be not vainly made;
> For should you thread and needles want,
>> It will afford you aid.
> And, as we are about to part,
>> 'T will serve another end:
> For, when you look upon this bag,
>> You'll recollect your friend.
>
> *(p. 93)*

These items have been frozen in time along with the scraps, letters, and other manuscripts. Although the housewife is dedicated as the contemporaneous Juvenilia are, the verses express sympathy for separation rather than any underlying joke. James Edward, however, presents his information without commenting on the unavoidable fact that Mary Lloyd Austen will later hasten the Austens out of Steventon and be married to the man who has hastened the Lloyds out of Deane. She will take her place at Austen's side on her deathbed having preserved both text and textile despite her renowned economy and practicality. Is the housewife pristine because it was highly valued or because Mary never looked on it as a remembrance? Like the physically preserved letters that are epistolary gifts, textile becomes text in the recovery of biographical information. A sewing project from daily record presents in miniature the hazardous piecing together of letters and objects into a life.

Constance Hill described this particular object as a 'tiny housewife of fairy-like proportions' (1902, p. 231) but she had already made a statement about Austen's textile duties of home when she announced that the text of *Homes and Friends* is bound in 'a facsimile of embroidery upon a muslin scarf worked in satin stitch by Jane Austen' (p. xiv). Hill has chosen to surround her account of a novelist's places with evidence of her domesticity or mastery of the craft described by James Edward. Hill refers also to a 'large chintz patchwork counterpane of most elaborate design' (p. 177) probably the one now on show at Jane Austen's House and available in simplified kit form for ambitious quilters to copy. It is technically a coverlet rather than a quilt because it has a cotton backing without wadding. The central panel of the original is formed, by the English paper piecing method, of 249 small diamonds and there are more than 2,500 smaller diamonds pieced together as the border with tiny stitches at a concentration of 12 per inch. Those not able to emulate this feat of piecing even with improved twenty-first-century lighting can also create designs matched to Austen's novels and even buy the requisite fat quarters of material printed with facsimiles of her letters. This takes communing with the author to new levels of devotion beyond even that of Hill and her sister.

The housewife declares its provenance. The coverlet is on an altogether different scale and Austen may not necessarily have worked on it. When loaned by the family, it was reported to have been finished about 1810 by Mrs Austen (Report 1950, p. 15) but perhaps the then newly-formed Jane Austen Society did not wish to associate Austen with handicrafts that have subsequently undergone a revival. The coverlet was a larger household item than those worked on in company but its composition was a communally sociable task demonstrating both creativity and industry. Needlework could be conducted or performed in public like letter writing, and eighteenth-century patchwork reflects economies in the home as well as a condoned leisure activity for women. At the same time the need to sew was a household necessity and it has been described as a 'charged activity' (Ford 2008, p. 218) especially when acting as social camouflage. In *Pride and Prejudice*, Elizabeth uses 'work' for observation firstly at Netherfield (p. 59). She sits 'intently at work, striving to be composed' (p. 370) when Bingley and Darcy come to visit Longbourn again. This is her excuse for speaking as 'little to either as civility would allow' before sitting down 'to her work, with an eagerness which it did not often command' (pp. 370–371). Darcy pretends to admire her work when he sends her to speak to Mr Bennet about his renewed proposal (p. 417) and this re-echoes the earlier occasion when Elizabeth is disturbed at work with Mrs Bennet and Kitty by Mr Collins's offer (p. 118). Mrs Austen later wrote to Charles that she was spending time on patchwork despite her other infirmities and constraints: 'I can manage a needle better than a pen or your quilt would not be worth acceptance' (Honan 1987, p. 405). James Edward wrote to Anna on 3 April 1822 about a 'magnificent piece of Patchwork' Mrs Austen was making for Henry 'as an emblem of his own conduct through life – the colours are brilliant, various & strongly contrasted' (*C*, p. 618). The siblings who sought to place Austen with her needle were seeing this patchwork enterprise as their own character commentary with more irony than they will apply to the *Memoir*.

In a modern work designed to provide examples of potential Austen stitching projects, Jennie Batchelor describes Austen as 'a talented stitcher' but also reveals that the muslin scarf or shawl employed as binding by Hill and her publishers is only a legend after all (2020, p. 7). The medallion coverlet has greater provenance within the family as reported by the Jane Austen House Museum website. There are reportedly pieces from 64 fabrics of both dress and furnishing cottons but the 1810 dating suggests that the letter evidence, when Austen writes to request more 'peices for the Patchwork' in 31 May 1811, refers to another project. Following Hill's lead, the coverlet forms the actual cover of the Jane Austen Society Annual Report in 1962 and of the 1989 Boston Hall edition of *Family Record*. Other recorded stitching jobs were more practical, plain, and mundane however merry James Edward sought to make them. In 1 September 1796, Austen is the 'neatest worker of the party' on Edward's shirts and in 20 February 1817 she has 'contributed the marking to Uncle H's shirts'. After her return from Northanger Abbey, Catherine Morland neglects to work on her brother Richard's cravats and her mother reproves her for having 'no greater inclination for needle-work' despite three night's rest (*NA*, p. 249). Needlework was part of character and camouflage, gifting and sisterliness. Although household sewing is ordinarily done for rather than by men, wood-turning captain Frank is reported making 'a very nice fringe for the Drawingroom-Curtains' in 20–22 February 1807 and William Knight's footstool for Chawton Cottage (17–18 January 1809) is embroidered during an illness. Frank was also 'disabled' by a cough suggesting that men's handicraft is only for those less able to be manly. Given Austen's concerns about Edward's indulgence of her nephews, her remark about William – 'What a comfort his Cross-stitch must have been!'(10–11 January 1809) – may have been two-edged for Cassandra's and her own benefit.

The patchwork of Austen's income is recoverable from the existing documents but its substance is frequently related to family connections that lead into the complexities of gentry inheritance in which the Huguenot family of Papillon are entwined. Cross-stitch interweaves strands to make a new reading of a whole, and from the knotting silk and patchwork pieces in Austen's letters it also is possible to read new facets of a sisterhood of letters in the lives of Catherine Knight, Elizabeth Papillon, and Eleanor Austen.

Edward Austen Knight's adoptive father Thomas (1735–1794) was related to both the Austens and the Papillons. Thomas bequeathed Edward the combined estates of Godmersham and Chawton as well as an income of £8,000 a year (Clery 2017, p. 220) exceeding that of Mr Bingley but falling short of Mr Darcy's. Austen's own relationship with Edward's adoptive mother Catherine née Knatchbull has a fiscal quality to it and, although the older woman seems to have meant kindly by her interventions, references to Mrs Knight stress the dichotomy of dependence discussed throughout this book. In 20–22 June 1808 'the usual Fee, & all the usual Kindness' is acknowledged along with an invitation to visit which Austen accepts: 'I wrote without much effort; for I was rich – & the Rich are always respectable, whatever be their stile of writing'. As a result, Austen tells Cassandra in 30 June–1 July 1808 that 'Mrs Knight is kindly anxious for our Good, & thinks Mr L. P. <u>must</u> be desirous for his <u>Family's</u> sake to have everything settled'. This was the Stoneleigh settlement discussed above and this is the letter in which Austen is casting around for their 'Legacy'. It is evident that Mrs Knight is party to Austen's first publication (25 April 1811) but she died aged 59 before the appearance of *Pride and Prejudice*. In 29–30 November 1812 Austen tells Martha that Mrs Knight has left £20 to the parish so, along with the 'very pleasant' Christmas duty of 'laying out Edward's money for the Poor', the 'Sum that passes through our hands this year is considerable.'

It is Mrs Knight who begins the fiction spun by Austen herself that Austen should marry John Papillon rector of Chawton. Austen observes that this is part of a debt when she writes to Cassandra, 'I owe her much more than such a trifling sacrifice' (9 December 1808). She asks her sister to pass on a message to Mrs Knight that 'she may depend upon it that I <u>will</u> marry Mr Papillon, whatever may be his reluctance or my own'. John Rawstorn Papillon was the fourth surviving son of David Papillon of Huguenot descent and two of his older brothers were also rectors. He shared a common ancestor with Thomas Knight as indicated on the chart (Figure 7.1) and this is one of the ways in which the Papillon family is entwined in matters of Austen finance. John was vicar of Tonbridge from 1791 to 1804 and rector of Chawton from 1802 to his death in 1837. At the death of Thomas Knight in 1794, he declined to give up the future living of Chawton despite Edward's offering £1,200 to buy it for his brother Henry (Le Faye 2004, p. 87) and Papillon was wealthy enough to rebuild the rectory in 1803 (p. 176). Even in the last year of Austen's life the joke about their potential marriage was ongoing presumably because the likelihood was so small. In 16–17 December 1816, Austen wrote to James Edward that the rector 'will soon make his offer, probably next Monday, as he returns on Saturday'.

The Papillons were very distantly related to the Austens through their common ancestor John Austen III so that when Henry married John Papillon's niece Eleanor Jackson he was once again married to a cousin, and a succeeding generation thus fulfilled a version of Mrs Knight's proposal. As shown on the chart (Figure 7.1), Jane Papillon née Brodnax, great-great-grandmother to John Papillon, is the pivotal family connection, described as a 'worthy consort' (Papillon 1887, p. v) in the memoirs of her husband published late in the nineteenth century. The Brodnax-Papillon alliance demonstrates how women's letters act counter-culturally, puncturing the more formal correspondence of political men. Jane Papillon's letters, presented in an appendix to the memoirs, temper a fraught life including her husband's long absences and the early deaths of her first three children (p. 46). On 25 May 1668 she concludes in her sympathising letter-manual style: 'Excuse my long scrawl; for methinks I am talking with thee, and very loth to conclude' (p. 406).

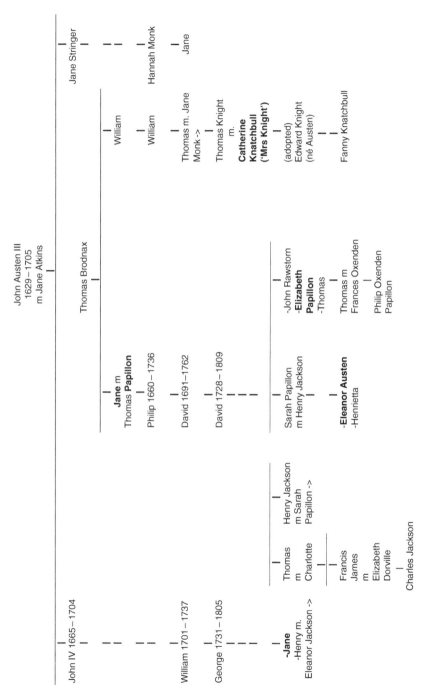

Figure 7.1 The Papillon connection: a selected family tree.

John Papillon and his sister Elizabeth remained unmarried and feature in Austen's letters from Chawton where they demonstrate both their wealth (Elizabeth) and bad temper (Rector John). In 24 January 1813 Elizabeth is reported to be in the book society and Austen has been observing her brother with Patience Terry, sister of Anna's original fiancé. Austen has also been visiting the poor of the parish with Miss Papillon, calling on the Garnets 'very pleasantly . . . I was quite as entertaining as she was'. Austen supplies the family with an old shift and some linen; 'my Companion left some of her Bank Stock'. A Papillon party in the same letter is 'not unagreeable, tho' as usual we wanted a better Master of the House, one less anxious & fidgety, & more conversible'. Cassandra is intended to understand these references to their neighbours and in 9–18 September 1814 Austen is perhaps relieved that Anna's characters Mr L. L. and his sister Rachael are 'not so much like the Papillons' as expected. Austen later reports that brother-in-law Henry Jackson is 'fond of eating & does not much like M^r or Miss P'. (17–18 October 1815). At the risk of this chapter's becoming as 'foolishly minute' as Austen fears for her letter, the Miss Papillons enlisted for a ball in Kent (6–7 November 1813) are probably the eldest daughters of John and Elizabeth's brother Thomas of Acrise Place and Crowhurst. Thomas Papillon had 14 children, 12 of whom survived to adulthood and his son Thomas, the younger brother of these Misses Papillons, had a further 11 with Frances Oxenden. This expands the Austen connection further. Frances Margaret Oxenden was sister to the Mary Graham Hammond already 'growing old by confinements & nursing' in Austen's 13 March 1817 letter to Fanny.

The female Papillons are representative of a variable pattern in the socio-economic dependence of gentry women at this period. Elizabeth acts as housekeeper to her brother but becomes independent through an inheritance from their father's cousin Ann who, despite the enormous potential range of other Papillons in Kent, inherits the Lexden estate in Essex in her own right. Austen reports to Cassandra in 8–9 September 1816 that the Papillons 'have been hurried off into Essex to take possession – not of a large Estate left them by an Uncle – but to scrape together all they can I suppose of the effects of a Mrs Rawstorn a rich old friend & cousin, suddenly deceased, to whom they are joint Executors'.

This is an aside on 'Uncle' James Leigh-Perrot who will disappoint his family the following year but John Papillon's middle name suggests he was always to be the future inheritor from Jane Brodnax Papillon's granddaughter Ann Rawstorn, unmarried despite the title of 'Mrs'. After John Papillon's death in 1837 aged 74, his sister Elizabeth, owner of 'Bank Stock', was allowed a lifetime interest in the manor at Lexden inherited in 1816. She was termed 'Lady of the Manor' in the census of 1851 and lived to the age of 88 without apparently suffering the spinsterly fate of Miss Bates or the Austen sisters. She was able to transfer her stock to the eight daughters of her brother Thomas and to Eleanor Austen and her sister

Henrietta although the investment will not pass to failed banker Henry in the event of Eleanor's earlier death. Lexden will pass next to Philip Oxenden Papillon, nephew of Fanny's friend Mrs Hammond. In 8–9 September 1816, the 'scraping together' suggests some bitterness accumulating from Mrs Knight's 'Fee' and the non-legacy from Uncle James, and Austen is bitter too in her dismissal when she adds: 'So, there is a happy end of the Kentish Papillons coming here'. Austen writes to Alethea Bigg (24 January 1817) in the last months of her life about Henry assisting Mr Papillon as his curate but Henry is never rector himself. When the family returns from Lexden, Austen is too ill to go to church but she tells Fanny rather cryptially, 'I cannot hear, however, but that they are [the] same Mr P. and his sister they used to be' (23–25 March 1817). Fanny notes as usual in her pocketbook 'A letter fm. At.JA' (*C*, p. 562) not realising that this is the last letter she will receive from Austen – or at least the last she will preserve.

Elizabeth Papillon was one of four daughters born to David Papillon and his first wife Bridget née Turner who was also descended from Jane Brodnax Papillon. Elizabeth's eldest sister Anna Maria died in 1769 aged 15 and her youngest in infancy in 1770 at the same time as their mother. In Austen's life the available sisters in addition to Cassandra, Martha, and Fanny include cousins and in-laws to whom Austen was often related more than once. Cousin Eliza was also a sister-in-law; Cassandra's fiancé Tom Fowle was cousin to Mary Lloyd Austen whose sister had herself married her cousin Fulwar, Tom's brother. In addition to missing accounts and missing recipes, it is well-known that Austen's brother George is missing from her letters and there is some evidence also of a missing sister like the Jane Papillon who died in 1770. There is an unaccustomed gap between pregnancies just after the Austen family's removal to Steventon in 1768 when Mrs Austen was reported to be unwell (Le Faye 2004, p. 20). James, George, and Edward had been born at very regular intervals after her marriage to George senior but the gap of three years eight months to the birth of Henry might suggest the loss of a child or even children as the regularity of births resumed thereafter with the births of Cassandra, Frank, and Jane. Austen's arrival seemed late because of her parents being 'bad reckoners' in their old age according to the Reverend Austen writing to Mrs Walter (*AP*, p. 32). Mrs Austen was 40 when Charles was born after a further three and a half years. When they befriended the Lloyd and Bigg sisters who lived in communities populated by more women, Austen and Cassandra may have been in search for a sister in a house full of brothers and pupils. There were five Bigg sisters even after the death of third sister Dorothy in 1793 and three Lloyds. The Austens also regarded sisters-in-law as sisters but these were familial acquisitions dependent on brothers. Austen herself declined to make sisters of the Biggs by marriage despite Harris Bigg-Wither's offer in 1802 and the cultivation of Martha as a wife for Frank only succeeded after Mrs Austen's death. Elizabeth Papillon was a sister only in poor-visiting.

The Papillon thread, however, also links a further sister to the Austens. Elizabeth's only adult sister Sarah was mother to Henry Austen's second wife Eleanor. Although Austen met Eleanor, the marriage did not take place until 1820 so the only Eleanor reference in Austen's letters tells us that she was, at the age of 17, a 'Rejected Addresser' (24 January 1813) on a visit to the Chawton Papillons. Eleanor's father Henry (1757–1823) who enjoyed eating was great uncle to Charles Jackson who succeeded Henry Austen as Perpetual Curate of Bentley in 1844. Charles was a beneficiary of Eleanor Austen's will after the subsequent death of her sister Henrietta (Barlow 2018, p. 76) but was also present at Cassandra's funeral in 1845 making him the subject of some undefined scorn in a letter from James Edward Austen-Leigh to his half-sister Anna. Cassandra's nephew wrote about the windy conditions at the service where emblematic 'withered beech leaves' strewed the coffin as if the older generation were being swept away. James Edward also expressed his 'utter astonishment' that 'Mr Charles Jackson . . . was invited to join in the procession & was come for that purpose, there being no more reason for his presence on the occasion than for that of Bentley Church itself' (*AP*, p. 294). It may be that there had been some competition for donations to church improvements previously announced by Henry to James Edward in 1835 (Austen-Leigh and Knight 1911, p. 61). James Edward's account was otherwise respectful but his resentful tone does not reflect Cassandra's own sisterly regard for Eleanor expressed in her letters. Mrs Austen wrote to Mary Lloyd Austen on 27 April 1820 that Cassandra with Edward was visiting her 'new Sister' Eleanor at Steventon and that the Papillons had also travelled there from Chawton on a day trip (*AP*, 267). Whatever the cause of displeasure at the funeral in 1845, Cassandra's gift to Eleanor of Austen's turquoise ring was scrupulously returned as another memorial object to James Edward's sister Caroline in 1863 (*C*, p. 681).

These are scraps of lives hidden in the archives and managed into existence by family record. As a novelist Austen was a compiler of both her own manuscript work and the reported works of others as part of the shared and inter-pieced language of her letters. Her more structured pocketbook now in only one extant scrap may have been supplemented by some form of commonplace book holding references for shared consumption. For Cassandra, Austen was able to conjure nearly exactly the 'Casks' quotation from Mrs Piozzi (9 December 1808) and she also regularly adapts lines from novels and plays. In 14–16 January 1801 she quotes Flutter in Hannah Cowley's *The Belle's Strategem*: 'Mr Doricourt has travelled; he knows best' (1780, III. 3), and there are at least two references to Burney's *Evelina*. In 8–9 February 1807, 'What a Contretems! – in the language of France; What an unluckiness in that of M^{de} Duval' (Burney 1778b, p. 40) and in 26 November 1815, 'Like Capt. Mirvan to M^{de} Duval "I wish it well over with him"' (Burney 1778a, p. 149). It has been assumed when Austen concludes 3 November 1813 from Godmersham with the Deedes' visit that this is an allusion to a piece of music

(Le Faye 2011, p. 641) but 'we shall end with a flourish the last Canto' seems to suggest another shared joke about a play or poem.

More significantly, Austen compiled her own work into bound notebooks that have themselves become both archives and objects (Byrne 2013, p. 53) as well as being the source of reversionary quotations in the letters. The preservation and appearance of these scraps sheds instructive light on the life, like letters being written back to biography. 'Lesley Castle' with its pairs of sisters, eating, drinking, and letter writing appears on pages 67 to 152 of Volume the Second, and the novella's epistolary exuberance is in visual contrast with the neatness of another 'scrap' calmly copied onto pages numbered 245 to 247. In 'A Letter from a Young Lady', three women are triangulated briefly in a sisterhood of letters when a note to her 'beloved Ellinor' concludes 'I am now going to murder my Sister./Y^{rs} Ever, Anna Parker' (*J*, p. 223). At the time this letter-crafted fiction was being copied in 1793, Anna Lefroy was just born but the name of Parker would not be applied to a man careless of vegetable economy until 1817. A wide range of other sisters and sisters-in-law among the gentry were waiting to be compiled and pieced into future archives. Within the next three years Austen would write social murderess *Lady Susan* in letters and the epistolary 'Elinor and Marianne'. Austen's actual sister was both preserved from being murdered and happy to preserve the pieced contents of Volume the Second, and to retain the ghostly outlines of other life evidence. It is with Cassandra's help that we 'know how interesting the purchase of a sponge-cake is' to the author (15–17 June 1808). We know also that, while publisher Murray is a civil 'Rogue' (17 October 1815), 'Good apple pies are a considerable part of our domestic happiness.'

Conclusion: Letters and Biography

Prisms, Kaleidoscopes, 'Elephants & Kangaroons'

In 1939 Virginia Woolf famously suggested that 'Biography will enlarge its scope by hanging up looking-glasses at odd corners' (1939, p. 121). This biography has used Austen's letters to angle the mirror. As Julian North has observed, biography for the Victorians was caught between art and commerce, 'selling illusions of intimacy with genius' (2019, p. 184). Letters as biography might then appear to be reconstitutions of an epistolary relationship that never existed. The letters of women are about intimacy as absence, shared places and spaces, and planning for presence. Austen's letters of the author are deceptively complex as evidence of a life because her methods constructed a correspondent who could barely be differentiated from herself: in the words of Lord Brabourne, an 'other self'. The letter as a viewing device demonstrates its biographical value not just as a reflection in a mirror but as a prism focused by correspondent and as a kaleidoscope distributed in fragments.

The final task for Austen's letters could have been to address the puzzle of her early death. Evidence of Addison's disease (tuberculosis of the adrenal glands) and of Hodgkin's lymphoma (a form of cancer) has been found (Cope 1964; Tomalin 1997, pp. 289–290; Upfal 2005) but the letters inevitably come up short. Cassandra was too often present in the final years, and Austen's changes in complexion (23–25 March 1817), ear infections (1–2 and 7–9 October 1808), fatigue, and conjunctivitis are not absolutely conclusive except of immune system problems. It seems likely that these symptoms could have been at least controlled by modern medicine and also that stress, such as that over Henry's bankruptcy in 1816 and the Leigh Perrot 'Legacy' as confided to Charles (6 April 1817), was a contributing factor. The thought that longer gestation as a child signalled in the Reverend George Austen's letter to Mrs Walter (17 December 1775; *AP*, pp. 32–33) may have already sealed Austen's fate (Upfal 2005, p. 4) is sad and beyond control. After the final resort to 'Dandelion Tea' and laudanum, Austen sought help in Winchester from Giles Lyford, the nephew of her mother's Basingstoke surgeon who had been happily fed 'pease-soup, a sparerib, and a pudding' (1–2 December 1798). Austen tells Anne Sharp that her 'sad complaint' has kept her in bed for five weeks (22 May 1817), since just after the reading of Uncle James Leigh Perrot's will, and that the journey to Winchester demonstrates her to be 'a very genteel, portable sort of an Invalid'. She has been resorting to the sofa more than she wishes and uses a donkey carriage if not the actual donkey for transport where she was once such a 'Desperate Walker'. In private, she has, of course, made her own will on 27 April and has also given up writing *Sanditon* on 18 March. There is a sense of resignation about the letter to Anne Sharp although Austen jokes that Mary Gibson Austen's parallel confinement has been more productive: of a baby. Austen also predicts that the potential acquisition of Scarlets about to be postponed still further will not make Mary Lloyd Austen more 'liberal-minded' despite their gratitude at the 'accommodation' of James's coach for the imminent last journey.

This is not, of course, a conclusion to the life of the author. Austen's final hours are reported by letter and in letters kept by their recipients. Cassandra's letters to Fanny (Le Faye 2011, pp. 359–364) give Cassandra a voice and demonstrate how seriously the role of correspondent should be taken. Familiar letters have gained more traction in their emergence from Victorian definitions. They have been rescued from a dense foliage of excuse and explanation, family rivalry, and obfuscation if not concealment. Austen's letters have emerged with revised credentials but are also in need of annotation to analyse family relationships and to work their allusive textures into a narrative 'fit for a heroine'. Unless of course it is Cassandra who emerges as the heroine in need of rescue from years of accusatory scorn aimed at her for doing her job. It is Cassandra who has given us the remnants of epistolary confidences; it is Cassandra who preserved through multiple house moves and many duty visits the records of Jane Austen's life that were threatened with flames in the early 1840s. Cassandra's distribution of the letters as keepsakes has occasionally been overtaken by the actions of her descendants but in the absence of any surviving correspondence with Edward or Henry, one letter to Charles and evidence of only eight more to Frank, Cassandra's restraint over letters to herself seems astonishing. The neglect of Fanny Knight Lady Knatchbull was ultimately an act of preservation, perhaps guessed by her 'Aunt Cass[a]'; and we must be very grateful that Austen's early hankering after authorship meant that her three volumes of manuscript early work circulated and survived as memorial objects.

Melanie Bigold suggests that letters are 'a version of literary manuscript performance' (2013, p. 7) and in Austen's case manuscript circulation and letter circulation remained concurrent. In her 23–24 August 1814 letter she refers to 'Love and Freindship' when a journey puts her 'in mind of my own Coach between Edinburgh & Sterling'. In the 1790 novella, Laura mounts this coach in the dark and only discovers later that by ludicrous coincidence its passengers and driver are her surviving relations and friends. Austen's journey from Chawton to Hans Place in August 1814 was 'not crouded' because the other passengers inside were 'of a reasonable size' but passing through Bentley and then Farnham, Egham, and Holybourne, she has discovered, as Laura does, that several people she knows are on board. Through the letter written to Chawton, Cassandra was thus able to share the fictional memory and the factual journey 24 years after Austen's original composition.

The letters indeed demonstrate that the contents of any coach are significant for the pace of recovery from a transition, and stages on the road are recorded with care or imagined for the sister-correspondent *alternée*. Trunks and letters are expected to go astray and aunts to be held up at the behest of family. In 24 October 1798, the precious writing desk was carried off to a potential fate in the West Indies only to be rescued before the end of the letter. The desk was restored to a grateful author along with the 'treasure' of £7 Austen admitted to, leaving future editor Cassandra to imagine the averted loss of writing in progress. Rereading the letters and extrapolating the life from them leaves us conscious of the amount of ink and paper expended on thus negotiating and controlling current and future locations. The mode and timing of travel arrangements are minutely revisited together with the logistics of packing and washing, and forwarding letters, recipes, patchwork, and sides of meat. Parcels are not just footstools or bonnet trimmings but aunts themselves. In order to be conveyed back to Southampton for a visit from Catherine and Alicia Bigg in 1808, Austen must anxiously reveal to Edward and Elizabeth at Godmersham that she has turned down a comfortable future home for herself and Cassandra (26 June 1808). She urgently wishes to retain her own 'honour' and 'affection' along with the sisterhood of her good 'Friends' who are sisters also of Harris Bigg-Wither, the disappointed suitor of 1802.

A life based on letters must learn how to embrace not just travel but gaps and silences, and to understand the public/private boundary mapped by a letter's lay-out and contents. An open-ended correspondence is ended by presence (or by a final absence) but letters can be reread by unlicensed readers and preservation affects proportion. If 'no private correspondence could bear the eye of others' (*P*, p. 221), that too has to be accommodated. In Austen's life, the letters maintained connections that were ritually broken by duty visits and aunt concerns. In the letters, sisterhood could be invoked over responsibility to parents or to uncles who might question expenditure on correspondence. Letters from Jane Austen might appear to give access to the author but the woven detail and allusive nature of most of the letters create further distance from the woman writer whilst reiterating the nature of the ordinary woman apparently going about her necessary business: brewing mead, trimming a bonnet, and trying to make herself invisibly portable.

Austen the author offers a lesson in reading a life through the realities of famil-iar letters and not through the grand vision of the public correspondence. This is 'familiar chat', 'important nothings', and a life hidden in plain sight. Despite the need for economy and frugality with materials and costs, she regulates her final inscriptions. At one remove, letters are the ultimate marginalia where Austen has some control of space. It is in the letters that the anarchic contrivance and descriptive economy of her manuscripts survive. Letters can be and will be finished and started again; they are most akin to her burlesque work in that their frantic competition for news is unsustainable at greater length, and yet Austen learned from her regulation of this medium to represent brutally comic plots with economy and style.

The author of 'Love and Freindship' would have appreciated the amusing pitfalls of wishing for more suggested by the recent discovery of wholly new material. Austen's letter to Cassandra of 15–16 September 1813 was rediscovered in the Honresfield Collection in 2021 but its detached ending had already been found in an autograph collection in 2017. The letter appeared in Brabourne's edition (1884b, pp. 145–154) but a report of 1931 confirms that the manuscript was missing its final lines and signature (Le Faye 2011, p. 369). The version in *Letters* ended 'You will take your walk this afternoon and ...' (p. 154). This designedly longer letter was originally transmitted through Henry's banking connections meaning it would be post-free to the recipient. Austen is 'seated in the Breakfast, Dining, sitting room, beginning with all my might' and waiting for Fanny to join her to write her own letter. The communal sociability of women's letter writing is emphasised as well as the size of Henry's accommodation over the bank in London contrasting with the library, billiard room, and plentiful servants at Godmersham. Austen is recounting their journey, its costs, timings, and food choices and her excitement at a potential trip to the theatre. It is unclear how the last lines of the letter became detached. It is possible that their contents were found unworthy, and therefore expendable, by either Fanny or her son. In the fragment recovered in 2017, Austen sends blessings to the rest of Edward Knight's family now at Chawton but her main concluding message is not about how to write a novel or to negotiate with a publisher. It is about Henry's 'Storeplaces' managed by Madame Bigeon and in it the author of *Pride and Prejudice* celebrates the addition of two roller towels to her linen inventory. There is so far no extant inventory in Austen's hand other than that found by Catherine Morland at Northanger Abbey. The letter merely provides, as Austen termed it in 11 February 1801, news worthy of London: 'Wit, Elegance, fashion, Elephants & Kangaroons'.

Bibliography

Adkins, L. and Adkins, R. (2013). *Eavesdropping on Jane Austen's England*. London: Little Brown.

Alexander, C. (ed.) (2014). *Jane Austen's 'Love and Freindship' and Other Youthful Writings*. London: Penguin.

Alexander, C. and McMaster, J. (2005). *The Child Writer from Austen to Woolf*. Cambridge: Cambridge University Press.

Alexander, C. and Upfal, A. (ed.) (2009). *Jane Austen's 'The History of England' & Cassandra's Portraits*. Sydney: Juvenilia Press.

Altick, R.D. (1966). *Lives and Letters: A History of Literary Biography in England and America*. New York: Knopf.

Altman, J.G. (1982). *Epistolarity: Approaches to a Form*. Columbus: Ohio State University Press.

Altman, J.G. (1986). The letter book as a literary institution 1539–1798: towards a cultural history of published correspondences in France. *Yale French Studies* 71: 17–62.

American works of fiction (1843). *The Foreign and Colonial Review Quarterly* 2: 458–488.

Austen, C. (1952). *My Aunt Jane: A Memoir*. London: Jane Austen Society.

Austen, H. (1818). Biographical notice of the author and postscript. In: *'Northanger Abbey' and 'Persuasion' by the Author of 'Pride and Prejudice', 'Mansfield Park' &c*, v–xix. London: Murray.

Austen, H. (1833). Memoir of Miss Austen. In: *Sense and Sensibility Standard Novels 23*, v–xv. London: Bentley.

Austen, J. (1818). *'Northanger Abbey' and 'Persuasion' by the Author of 'Pride and Prejudice', 'Mansfield Park' &c*, vol. 1. London: Murray.

Austen-Leigh, J.E. (1870). *A Memoir of Jane Austen, by her nephew*. London: Bentley.

Austen-Leigh, J.E. (1871). *A Memoir of Jane Austen, by her nephew*, 2e. London: Bentley.

Austen-Leigh, J. (1989). My aunt Jane Austen. *Persuasions* 11: 28–36.

The Life of the Author: Jane Austen, First Edition. Catherine Delafield.
© 2023 John Wiley & Sons Ltd. Published 2023 by John Wiley & Sons Ltd.

Austen-Leigh, M.A. (1922). *Personal Aspects of Jane Austen*. London: Murray.

Austen-Leigh, R. (ed.) (1942). *Austen Papers, 1704–1856*. Colchester: Spottiswoode Ballantyne.

Austen-Leigh, W. and Austen-Leigh, R. (1913). *Jane Austen: Her Life and Letters: A Family Record*. London: Smith Elder.

Austen-Leigh, W. and Knight, M.G. (1911). *Chawton Manor and its Owners: A Family History*. London: Smith Elder.

Austen-Leigh, W., Austen-Leigh, R., and Le Faye, D. (1989). *Jane Austen: A Family Record*. London: The British Library.

Ballard, M. (2017). Tales of inheritance from West Kent. In: *Jane Austen's Geographies* (ed. R. Clark), 68–94. Abingdon: *Routledge*.

Bannet, E.T. (2005). *Empire of Letters: Letter Manuals and Transatlantic Correspondence, 1688–1820*. Cambridge: Cambridge University Press.

Bannet, E.T. (ed.) (2008). *British and American Letter Manuals. Volume 4 The Art of Correspondence 1770–1810*. London: Pickering and Chatto.

Barchas, J. (2012). *Matters of Fact in Jane Austen: History, Location and Celebrity*. Baltimore: Johns Hopkins University Press.

Barchas, J. (2017). How celebrity name-dropping leads to another model for Pemberley. In: *Jane Austen's Geographies* (ed. R. Clark), 203–219. Abingdon: Routledge.

Barlow, A. (2018). Eleanor Jackson, the second Mrs Henry Austen. *The Jane Austen Society Report for 2018:* 63–79.

Barton, D. and Hall, N. (ed.) (1999). *Letter Writing as Social Practice*. Amsterdam: John Benjamins.

Batchelor, J. and Larkin, A. (2020). *Jane Austen Embroidery*. London: Pavilion.

Beizer, J. (2009). *Thinking Through the Mothers: Reimagining Women's Biographies*. Ithaca: Cornell University Press.

Bender, B.T. (1967). Jane Austen's use of the epistolary method. University of Richmond Masters Thesis, Paper 258.

Benton, M.J. (2009). *Literary Biography: An Introduction*. Chichester: Wiley-Blackwell.

Benton, M. (2011). Towards a poetics of literary biography. *The Journal of Aesthetic Education* 45 (3): 67–87.

Bigold, M. (2013). *Women of Letters, Manuscript Circulation and Print Afterlives in the Eighteenth Century*. Basingstoke: Palgrave Macmillan.

Black, M. and Le Faye, D. (1995). *The Jane Austen Cookbook*. London: British Museum.

Bodenheimer, R. (1981). Looking at the landscape in Jane Austen. *Studies in English Literature* 2 (4): 605–623.

Borsay, P. (2000). *The Image of Georgian Bath 1700–2000*. Oxford: Oxford University Press.

Bossis, M. (1986). Methodological journeys through correspondences. *Yale French Studies* 71: 63–75.

Brabourne, E., Lord (ed.) (1884a). *Letters of Jane Austen*, vol. 1. London: Bentley.

Brabourne, E., Lord (ed.) (1884b). *Letters of Jane Austen*, vol. 2. London: Bentley.

Bradford, R. (2019). Introduction. In: *A Companion to Literary Biography* (ed. R. Bradford), 1–6. Chichester: Wiley-Blackwell.

Bradley, A.C. (1929). *A Miscellany*. London: Macmillan.

Brant, C. (2006). *Eighteenth-Century Letters and British Culture*. Basingstoke: Palgrave Macmillan.

Bray, B. (2001). Letters. In: *Encyclopedia of Life Writing: Autobiographical and Biographical Forms*, vol. 2 (ed. M. Jolly), 551–553. Chicago: Fitzroy Dearborn.

Bray, J. (2003). *The Epistolary Novel: Representations of Consciousness*. London: Routledge.

Bree, L., Sabor, P., and Todd, J. (2013). *Jane Austen's Manuscript Works*. Peterborough, ON: Broadview.

Brown, J. (2014). Jane Austen's mental maps. *Critical Survey* 26 (1): 20–41.

Burney, F. (1778a). *Evelina*, vol. 1. London: Lowndes.

Burney, F. (1778b). *Evelina*, vol. 2. London: Lowndes.

Butler, M. (1975). *Jane Austen and the War of Ideas*. Oxford: Oxford University Press.

Butler, M. (1981). *Romantics, Rebels and Reactionaries: English Literature and its Background 1760–1830*. Oxford: Oxford University Press.

Butler, M. (1985). Introduction. In: *Jane Austen: Selected Letters 1797–1817* (ed. R.W. Chapman), ix–xxvi. Oxford: Oxford University Press.

Butler, M. (1998). Simplicity. *London Review of Books* 20 (5): 3–6.

Byrde, P. (1999). *Jane Austen Fashion*. Ludlow: Excellent Press.

Byrne, P. (2013). *The Real Jane Austen: A Life in Small Things*. London: Harper.

Byrne, P. (2017). *The Genius of Jane Austen*. London: William Collins.

Castle, T. (1995). Sister-sister. In: *London Review of Books* (3 August 1995), 3–6.

Cecil, D. (1980). *A Portrait of Jane Austen*. Harmondsworth: Penguin.

Chapman, R.W. (ed.) (1925). *Fragment of a Novel by Jane Austen*. Oxford: Oxford University Press.

Chapman, R.W. (ed.) (1932). *Jane Austen's Letters to her sister Cassandra and Others*. Oxford: Oxford University Press.

Chapman, R.W. (ed.) (1933). *Volume the First*. Oxford: Oxford University Press.

Chapman, R.W. (1948). *Jane Austen: Facts and Problems*. Oxford: Clarendon Press.

Chapman, R.W. (ed.) (1954). *Minor Works: The Works of Jane Austen*, vol. 6. Oxford: Oxford University Press.

Chorley, H.F. (1870). *A memoir of Jane Austen* and *a life of Mary Russell Mitford*. *Quarterly Review* 128: 196–218.

Clark, R. (2017a). Introduction. In: *Jane Austen's Geographies* (ed. R. Clark), 1–27. Abingdon: Routledge.

Clark, R. (2017b). 'Slight and fugitive indications': some locations in *Sense and Sensibility* and *Pride and Prejudice*. In: *Jane Austen's Geographies* (ed. R. Clark), 128–155. Abingdon: Routledge.

Clery, E.J. (2017). *Jane Austen: The Banker's Sister*. London: Biteback.

Collins, I. (1993). *Jane Austen and the Clergy*. London: Hambledon.

Cook, E.H. (1996). *Epistolary Bodies: Gender and Genre in the Eighteenth Century Republic of Letters*. Stanford: Stanford University Press.

Cope, Z. (1964). Jane Austen's last illness reprinted from the *British Medical Journal 18 July 1964, vol. ii, pp. 182–183. Collected Reports of the Jane Austen Society* I: 267–272.

Copeland, E. and McMaster, J. (ed.) (1997). *The Cambridge Companion to Jane Austen*. Cambridge: Cambridge University Press.

Corbett, M.J. (2008). *Family Likeness: Sex, Marriage and Incest from Jane Austen to Virginia Woolf*. London: Cornell University Press.

Culley, A. (2014). *British Women's Life Writing, 1760–1840: Friendship, Community and Collaboration*. Basingstoke: Palgrave Macmillan.

Davidson, H. (2017). Jane Austen's pelisse-coat. In: *Jane Austen: Writer and the World* (ed. K. Sutherland), 56–75. Oxford: Bodleian Library.

Dawson, W.R. (ed.) (1958). *The Banks Letters: A Calendar of the Manuscript Correspondence of Sir Joseph Banks*. London: British Museum.

Decker, W.M. (1998). *Epistolary Practices: Letter Writing in America Before Telecommunications*. Chapel Hill: University of North Carolina Press.

Delafield, C. (2020). *Women's Letters as Life Writing 1840–1885*. New York: Routledge.

Dillon, B. (1992). Circumventing the biographical subject: Jane Austen and the critics. *Rocky Mountain Review of Language and Literature* 46 (4): 213–221.

Doody, M.A. (ed.) (1993). *Jane Austen: 'Catharine' and Other Writings*. Oxford: Oxford University Press.

Doody, M.A. (2015). *Jane Austen's Names, Riddles, Persons, Places*. London: University of Chicago Press.

Dow, G. and Hanson, C. (2012). Introduction. In: *Uses of Austen: Jane's Afterlives* (ed. G. Dow and C. Hanson), 1–18. Basingstoke: Palgrave Macmillan.

Duckworth, A.M. (1971a). Mansfield Park and estate improvements: Jane Austen's grounds of being. *Nineteenth Century Fiction* 26 (1): 25–48.

Duckworth, A.M. (1971b). *The Improvement of the Estate: A Study of Jane Austen's Novels*. Baltimore: Johns Hopkins University Press.

Duncan-Jones, E.E. (1995). Correspondence and English matters. *Review of English Studies* 46 (183): 380.

Earle, R. (1999). Introduction. In: *Epistolary Selves: Letters and Letter-Writers, 1600–1945* (ed. R. Earle), 1–12. Aldershot: Ashgate.

Edgeworth, M. (1795). Letters of Julia and Caroline. In: *Letters for Literary Ladies*. London: Johnson.

Ellis, J.M. (2001). *The Georgian Town 1680–1840*. Basingstoke: Palgrave.

Epstein, J. (1985). Jane Austen's Juvenilia and the female epistolary tradition. *Papers in Language and Literature* 21: 399–416.

Epstein, J. (1986). Fanny Burney's epistolary voices. *Eighteenth Century* 27 (2): 162–179.

Ewing, J.S. (2019). As the wheel turns: horse-drawn vehicles in Jane Austen's novels. *Persuasions On-Line* 40 (1): https://jasna.org/publications-2/persuasions-online/volume-40-no-1/ewing/ (accessed 6 May 2022).

Farrer, R. (1917). Jane Austen *ob* July 18, 1817. *Quarterly Review* 452: 246–272.

Favret, M.A. (1993). *Romantic Correspondence: Women, Politics and the Fiction of Letters*. Cambridge: Cambridge University Press.

Fergus, J. (1991). *Jane Austen: A Literary Life*. London: Macmillan.

Fergus, J. (ed.) (1993). *'Amelia Webster' and 'The Three Sisters'*. Edmonton: Juvenilia Press.

Fergus, J. (ed.) (1998a). *Love and Freindship*. Edmonton: Juvenilia Press.

Fergus, J. (ed.) (1998b). *Lesley Castle*. Edmonton: Juvenilia Press.

Fergus, J. (2005a). Biography. In: *Jane Austen in Context* (ed. J. Todd), 3–11. Oxford: Oxford University Press.

Fergus, J. (2005b). 'The whinnying of harpies'? Humour in Jane Austen's letters. *Persuasions: The Jane Austen Journal* 27: 13–30.

Flynn, C.H. (1997). The letters. In: *The Cambridge Companion to Jane Austen* (ed. E. Copeland and J. McMaster), 100–114. Cambridge: Cambridge University Press.

Ford, S.A. (2008). 'To be above vulgar economy': thrifty measures in Jane Austen's letters. *Persuasions: The Jane Austen Journal* 30: 216–221.

Fordyce, J. (1766). *Sermons to Young Women. Volume 1*. London: Millar, Cadell, Dodsley, and Payne.

Forster, E.M. (1908;1987). *A Room with a View*. London: Penguin.

Forster, E.M. (1910;2000). *Howards End*. London: Penguin.

Forster, E.M. (1936). *Abinger Harvest*. London: Arnold.

Gadd, D. (1971). *Georgian Summer: Bath in the Eighteenth Century*. Bath: Adams and Dart.

Galperin, W.H. (2003). *The Historical Austen*. Philadelphia: University of Pennsylvania Press.

Gardner, P. (ed.) (1973). *E. M. Forster: The Critical Heritage*. London: Routledge and Kegan Paul.

Gerson, C. (2001). Locating female subjects in the archives. In: *Working in Women's Archives: Researching Women's Private Literature and Archival Documents* (ed. H.M. Buss and M. Kader), 7–22. Waterloo Ontario: Wilfred Laurier University Press.

Gilbert, S.M. and Gubar, S. (1979). *The Madwoman in the Attic: The Woman Writer and the Nineteenth Century Literary Imagination*. New Haven and London: Yale University Press.

Gilroy, A. and Verhoeven, W.M. (2000). Introduction. In: *Epistolary Histories: Letters, Fiction, Culture* (ed. A. Gilroy and W.M. Verhoeven), 1–25. Charlottesville: University Press of Virginia.

Gilson, D. (1982). *A Bibliography of Jane Austen*. Oxford: Clarendon Press.

Gisborne, T. (1797). *An Enquiry into the Duties of the Female Sex*. London: Cadell.

Gleadle, K. (2018). Silence, dissent, and affective relations in the juvenile diaries of Eva Knatchbull-Hugessen (1861–1895). In: *19: Interdisciplinary Studies in the Long Nineteenth Century*, 27. https://19.bbk.ac.uk/article/id/1648/ (accessed 6 May 2022).

Gover, M. (2006). 'A very pretty hand': the questionable value of using Jane Austen's letters as a means of knowing Austen. *Lifewriting Annual* 2: 1–25.

Grey, J.D. (1986). Topography. In: *The Jane Austen Handbook* (ed. J.D. Grey), 380–388. London: Athlone.

Grey, J.D. (ed.) (1989). *Jane Austen's Beginnings: The Juvenilia and 'Lady Susan'*. Ann Arbor: U.M.I. Research Press.

Hall, N. (1999). The materiality of letter-writing: a nineteenth-century perspective. In: *Letter Writing as Social Practice* (ed. D. Barton and N. Hall), 88–107. Amsterdam: John Benjamins.

Harding, D.W. (1940). Regulated hatred: an aspect of the work of Jane Austen. *Scrutiny* 8: 346–362.

Harding, D.W. (1965). Introduction to *A Memoir of Jane Austen*. In: *Persuasion* (ed. D.W. Harding), 267–270. Penguin: Harmondsworth.

Harding, D.W. (1993). The supposed letter form of *Sense and Sensibility*. *Notes and Queries* 40 (4): 464–466.

Harding, D.W. (1998). *Regulated Hatred and other essays on Jane Austen*. London: Athlone Press.

Hardy, B. (1975). *A Reading of Jane Austen*. London: Owen.

Harman, C. (2009). *Jane's Fame: How Jane Austen Conquered the World*. Edinburgh: Canongate.

Harris, J. (2007). *A Revolution Almost Beyond Expression: Jane Austen's 'Persuasion'*. Newark: University of Delaware Press.

Hart, F.R. (1975). The spaces of privacy: Jane Austen. *Nineteenth Century Fiction* 30 (3): 305–333.

Herbert, D. (1991). Place and society in Jane Austen's England. *Geography* 76: 193–208.

Hill, C. (1902). *Jane Austen: Her Homes and Friends*. London: Bodley Head.

Hill, B. (2001). *Women Alone: Spinsters in England 1660–1850*. New Haven: Yale University Press.

Hill, M.K. (1989). *Bath and the Eighteenth-Century Novel*. Bath: Bath University Press.

Holden, P. (2014). Literary biography as a critical form. *Biography* 37 (4): 917–934.

Honan, P. (1986). Biographies. In: *The Jane Austen Handbook* (ed. J.D. Grey), 18–23. London: Athlone.

Honan, P. (1987). *Jane Austen: Her Life*, reprint, 1997. Phoenix: London.

Honan, P. (1990). *Authors' Lives: On Literary Biography and the Arts of Language.* New York: St Martin's Press.

Hubback, J.H. and Hubback, E.C. (1906). *Jane Austen's Sailor Brothers*. London: Lane.

Hudson, G.A. (1992). *Sibling Love and Incest in Jane Austen's Fiction*. London: Palgrave.

Huff, C. (2001). Women's letters. In: *Encyclopedia of Life Writing: Autobiographical and Biographical Forms*, vol. 2 (ed. M. Jolly), 952–954. Chicago: Fitzroy Dearborn.

Hughes-Hallett, P. (ed.) (1990). *Jane Austen: 'My Dear Cassandra'*. London: Collins and Brown.

Hurst, J. (2010). Aunt Cassandra – 'a very great loss to us all.'. *Jane Austen Society Annual Report*: 110–115.

Jack, I. (1961). The epistolary element in Jane Austen. In: *English Studies Today: Second Series* (ed. G.A. Bonnard), 173–186. Winterthur: Gemsberg-Druck Der Geschwister Ziegler.

James, P.D. (1998). Emma considered as a detective story. *Collected Reports of the Jane Austen Society V*: 189–200.

James, F. (2012). At home with Jane Austen: placing Austen in contemporary culture. In: *Uses of Austen: Jane's Afterlives* (ed. G. Dow and C. Hanson), 132–153. Basingstoke: Palgrave Macmillan.

Jane Austen (1882). *Temple Bar* 64: 350–365.

Jarvis, W.A.W. (1986). Jane Austen and the Countess of Morley. *Collected Reports of the Jane Austen Society IV*: 6–14.

Jenkins, E. (1938). *Jane Austen: A Biography*. London: Gollancz.

Jewesbury, M. (1831). Literary women II: Jane Austen. *Athenaeum* 200 (27 August): 553–554.

Johnson, C. (1779). *The Complete Art of Writing Letters*, 6e. London: Lowndes and Evans.

Johnson, C.L. (1988). *Jane Austen: Women, Politics and the Novel*. London: University of Chicago Press.

Johnson, C.L. (2012). *Jane Austen's Cults and Cultures*. London: University of Chicago Press.

Johnson, C.L. and Tuite, C. (2009). *A Companion to Jane Austen*. Chichester: Wiley-Blackwell.

Johnson, R.B. (ed.) (1912). *The Letters and Novels of Jane Austen (12 vols)*. Edinburgh: John Grant.

Johnson, R.B. (ed.) (1925). *The Letters of Jane Austen*. London: Lane.

Jolly, M. and Stanley, L. (2005). Letters as/not a genre. *Life Writing* 2 (2): 91–118.

Jones, V. (2004). Introduction. In: *Jane Austen Selected Letters*, ix–xxxv. Oxford: Oxford University Press.

Juhasz, S. (1987). Bonnets and balls: reading Jane Austen's letters. *Centenniel Review* 21 (1): 84–104.

Kaplan, D. (1984). The disappearance of the woman writer: Jane Austen and her biographers. *Prose Studies* 7 (2): 129–147.

Kaplan, D. (1987a). Female friendship and the epistolary form: Lady Susan and the development of Jane Austen's fiction. *Criticism* 29 (2): 163–178.

Kaplan, D. (1987b). Henry Austen and John Rawstorn Papillon. *Collected Reports of the Jane Austen Society IV*: 60–64.

Kaplan, D. (1988). Representing two cultures: Jane Austen's *letters*. In: *The Private Self: Theory and Practice of Women's Autobiographical Writings* (ed. S. Benstock), 211–219. Chapel Hill: University of North Carolina Press.

Kaplan, D. (1992). *Jane Austen Among Women*. London: John Hopkins University Press.

Kaplan, L. (2010). *Sense and Sensibility*: 3 or 4 country families in an urban village. *Persuasions: The Jane Austen Journal* 32 (2010): 196–209.

Kaplan, L. (2017). Jane Austen's allusive geographies: London's streets, squares and gardens. In: *Jane Austen's Geographies* (ed. R. Clark), 175–202. Abingdon: Routledge.

Kavanagh, J. (1863). *English Women of Letters*, vol. 2. London: Hurst and Blackett.

Kebbel, T. (1885). Jane Austen at home. *Fortnightly Review* 37: 262–270.

Kelsall, M. (1993). *The Great Good Place: The Country House and English Literature*. Brighton: Harvester.

Kerhervé, A. (2010). *The Ladies Complete Letter-Writer (1763)*. Newcastle: Cambridge Scholars.

Keymer, T. (2017). Teenage writings: amusement, effusion, nonsense. In: *Jane Austen: Writer and the World* (ed. K. Sutherland), 16–35. Oxford: Bodleian Library.

Kirkham, M. (1983a). *Jane Austen: Feminism and Fiction*. Brighton: Harvester.

Kirkham, M. (1983b). The Austen portraits and the received biography. In: *Jane Austen: New Perspectives* (ed. J. Todd), 29–38. New York: Holmes and Meier.

Knatchbull-Hugessen, S.H. (1960). *Kentish Family*. London: Methuen.

Knuth Klenck, D.J. (2005). Fun and speculation: *Sense and Sensibility* and *Pride and Prejudice* as revisions. *Persuasions: The Jane Austen Journal* 27: 39–53.

Lamont, C. (2005). Domestic architecture. In: *Jane Austen in Context* (ed. J. Todd), 225–233. Oxford: Oxford University Press.

Lane, M. (1962). Address given at AGM. *Collected Reports of the Jane Austen Society I*: 224–234.

Lane, M. (1995). *Jane Austen and Food*. London: Hambledon Press.

Lane, M. (2005). Food. In: *Jane Austen in Context* (ed. J. Todd), 262–268. Oxford: Oxford University Press.

Langbauer, L. (2016). *The Juvenile Tradition: Young Writers and Prolepsis 1750–1835*. Oxford: Oxford University Press.

Lanser, S.S. (1985). No connections subsequent: Jane Austen's world of sisterhood. In: *The Sister Bond: A Feminist View of a Timeless Connection* (ed. T.A.H. McMahon), 51–67. New York: Pergamon.

Lascelles, M. (1939). *Jane Austen and her Art*. Oxford: Clarendon Press.

Laslett, P. (1976). The wrong way through the telescope: a note on literary evidence in sociology and historical sociology. *British Journal of Sociology* 27 (3): 319–342.

Le Faye, D. (1986a). Fanny Knight's diaries: Jane Austen through her niece's eyes. *JASNA Persuasions: On-Line Occasional Papers* 2: 5–27.

Le Faye, D. (1986b). Journeys, Waterparties & Plays. *Collected Reports of the Jane Austen Society IV*: 24–30.

Le Faye, D. (1988). Anna Lefroy's original memories of Jane Austen. *Review of English Studies, ns* 39 (155): 417–421.

Le Faye, D. (1992). Jane Austen's letters. *Persuasions: The Jane Austen Journal* 14: 76–88.

Le Faye, D. (2000). *Fanny Knight's Diaries: Jane Austen Through Her Niece's Eyes*. Winchester: Jane Austen Society.

Le Faye, D. (2001). Anna Lefroy and her Austen family letters. *The Princeton University Library Chronicle* 62 (3): 519–562.

Le Faye, D. (2002). *Jane Austen's 'Outlandish Cousin': The Life and Letters of Eliza de Feuillide*. London: British Library.

Le Faye, D. (2004). *Jane Austen: A Family Record*, 2e. Cambridge: Cambridge University Press.

Le Faye, D. (2005a). Letters. In: *Jane Austen in Context* (ed. J. Todd), 33–40. Oxford: Oxford University Press.

Le Faye, D. (2005b). Memoirs and biographies. In: *Jane Austen in Context* (ed. J. Todd), 51–58. Oxford: Oxford University Press.

Le Faye, D. (ed.) (2011). *Jane Austen's Letters*. Oxford: Oxford University Press.

Le Faye, D. (2013). *A Chronology of Jane Austen and her Family*, 2e. Cambridge: Cambridge University Press.

Le Faye, D. (2017). Updates on Jane Austen's letters. *Jane Austen Society Annual Report*: 26–30.

Leduc, G. (2015). Letters and letter-writing in *Sense and Sensibility* (1811). *Études Anglaises* 68 (3): 296–315.

Lee, H. (2009). *Biography: A Very Short Introduction*. Oxford: Oxford University Press.

Lee, W.A. (2010). Resituating 'regulated hatred': D.W. Harding's Jane Austen. *ELH* 77 (4): 995–1014.

Leffel, J.C. (2011). 'Everything is going to sixes and sevens': governing the female body (politic) in Jane Austen's 'Catharine; or the Bower' (1792). *Studies in the Novel* 43 (2): 131–151.

Lefroy, F.C. (1883). Is it just? *Temple Bar* 67: 270–284.

Letters of Jane Austen (1884). *Saturday Review* 58: 637–638.

Levin, A.K. (1992). *The Suppressed Sister: A Relationship in Novels by Nineteenth- and Twentieth-Century British Women*. London: Associated Presses.

Levy, M. (2010). Austen's manuscripts and the publicity of print. *ELH* 77 (4): 1015–1040.

Levy, M. (2020). *Literary Manuscript Culture in Romantic Britain*. Edinburgh: Edinburgh University Press.

Litz, A.W. (1986). Criticism, 1939–1983. In: *The Jane Austen Handbook* (ed. J. D. Grey), 110–117. London: Athlone.

Lodge, D. (1986). Jane Austen's novels: form and structure. In: *The Jane Austen Handbook* (ed. J.D. Grey), 165–178. London: Athlone.

Lutz, D. (2015). *The Brontë Cabinet: Three Lives in Nine Objects*. New York: Norton.

Lynch, D.S. (2005). Cult of Jane Austen. In: *Jane Austen in Context* (ed. J. Todd), 111–120. Oxford: Oxford University Press.

Lynch, D. (2017). The art of the letter. In: *Jane Austen: Writer and the World* (ed. K. Sutherland), 76–93. Oxford: Bodleian Library.

MacArthur, E.J. (1990). *Extravagant Narratives: Closure and Dynamics in the Epistolary Form*. Princeton, NJ: Princeton University Press.

Macaulay, T.B. (1843). Diary and letters of Madame d'Arblay. *The Edinburgh Review* 76: 523–570.

Macdonagh, O. (1991). *Jane Austen: Real and Imagined Worlds*. New York: Yale University Press.

May, W. (2012). Letters to Jane: Austen, the letter and twentieth-century women's writing. In: *Uses of Austen: Jane's Afterlives* (ed. G. Dow and C. Hanson), 115–131. Basingstoke: Palgrave Macmillan.

McMaster, J. (1996). 'Laura and Augustus' and 'Love and Freindship'. *Thalia* 16: 16–26.

McMaster, J. (1999). 'Amelia Webster' and 'Love and Freindship'. *Eighteenth Century Fiction* 11 (3): 339–346.

McMaster, J. (2000). The Juvenilia: energy versus sympathy. In: *A Companion to Jane Austen Studies* (ed. L.C. Lambdin and R.T. Lambdin), 173–189. Westport, CT: Greenwood.

McMaster, J. (2017). *Jane Austen: Young Author*. London: Routledge.

McVeigh, J. (2017). *In Collaboration with British Literary Biography: Haunting Conversations*. Basingstoke: Palgrave Macmillan.

McVeigh, J. (2019). Concerns about facts and form in literary biography. In: *A Companion to Literary Biography* (ed. R. Bradford), 143–158. Chichester: Wiley-Blackwell.

Milne, E. (2010). *Letters, Postcards, Email: Technologies of Presence*. New York: Routledge.

Mitchell, L.C. (2016). Entertainment and instruction: women's roles in the epistolary tradition. *Huntingdon Library Quarterly* 79 (3): 439–454.

Modert, J. (1986). Letters/correspondence. In: *The Jane Austen Handbook* (ed. J.D. Grey), 271–278. London: Athlone.

Modert, J. (ed.) (1990). *Jane Austen's Letters in Facsimile*. Carbondale: Southern Illinois University Press.

Monaghan, D. (1980). *Jane Austen: Structure and Social Vision*. London: Macmillan.

Morgan, S. (2000). Adoring the girl next door: geography in Austen's novels. *Persuasions On-Line* 21 (1): https://jasna.org/persuasions/on-line/vol21no1/morgan.html (accessed 6 May 2022).

Mudrick, M. (1952). *Jane Austen: Irony as Defense and Discovery*. Princeton, NJ: Princeton University Press.

Mullan, J. (2001). Malice. *London Review of Books* 23 (16): 20–23.

Mullan, J. (2012). *What Matters in Jane Austen*. London: Bloomsbury.

Murphy, O. (2016). 'A partial, prejudiced' and precocious historian: Jane Austen's 'History of England'. *Clio* 46 (1): 51–72.

Nadel, I.B. (1984). *Biography: Fiction, Fact and Form*. Basingstoke: Macmillan.

Narain, M. (1998). A prescription of letters: Maria Edgeworth's *Letters for Literary Ladies* and the ideologies of the public sphere. *Journal of Narrative Technique* 28 (3): 266–286.

Neale, R.S. (1981). *Bath 1680–1850: A Social History, or a Valley of Pleasure and Yet a Sink of Iniquity*. London: Routledge and Kegan Paul.

Neale, R.S. (1990). Bath: ideology and utopia, 1700–1760. In: *The Eighteenth Century Town: A Reader in Urban History 1688–1820* (ed. P. Borsay), 223–242. London: Longman.

Nixon, C.L. and Penner, L. (2005). Writing by the book: Jane Austen's heroines and the art and form of the letter. *Persuasions On-Line* 26 (1): https://jasna.org/persuasions/on-line/vol26no1/penner_nixon.htm (accessed 6 May 2022).

Normandin, S. (2014). Jane Austen's epistolarity. *ANQ* 27 (4): 158–165.

North, J. (2019). How to be an author: Victorian literary biography c. 1830–1880. In: *A Companion to Literary Biography* (ed. R. Bradford), 45–62. Chichester: Wiley-Blackwell.

Nussbaum, F. (1989). *The Autobiographical Self: Gender and Ideology in Eighteenth-Century England*. Baltimore: John Hopkins University Press.

Oliphant, M. (1862). The lives of two ladies. *Blackwoods Edinburgh Magazine* 91: 401–423.

Oliphant, M. (1870). Miss Austen and Miss Mitford. *Blackwoods Edinburgh Magazine* 107: 290–313.

Page, N. (1972). *The Language of Jane Austen*, reprint, 2011. Abingdon: Routledge.

Papillon, A.F.W. (1887). *Memoirs of Thomas Papillon, London Merchant (1623–1702)*. Reading: Bancroft.

Park, J. (2013). 'What the eye cannot see': interior landscape in *Mansfield Park*. *The Eighteenth Century* 54 (2): 169–181.

Parker, R. (1984). *The Subversive Stitch: Embroidery and the Making of the Feminine.* London: Women's Press.

Percents and sensibility: personal finance in Jane Austen's time (2005). *The Economist* (24 December), pp. 105–106.

Pevsner, N. (1968). The architectural setting of Jane Austen's novels. *Journal of the Warburg and Courtauld Institute* 31: 404–422.

Piggott, P. (1980). Jane Austen's Southampton piano. *Collected Reports of the Jane Austen Society III:* 146–149.

Piozzi, H.L. (ed.) (1788). *Letters to and from the Late Samuel Johnson, LLD*, vol. 1. London: Strahan and Cadell.

Pocock, D.C.D. (1981). Place and the novelist. *Transactions of the Institute of British Geographers* 6 (3): 337–347.

Poovey, M. (1984). *The Proper Lady and the Woman Writer: Ideology as Style in the Works of Mary Wollstonecraft, Mary Shelley and Jane Austen.* Chicago: University of Chicago Press.

Porter, C.A. (1986). Foreword to Men/Women of Letters. *Yale French Studies* 71: 1–14.

Poster, C. and Mitchell, L.C. (ed.) (2007). *Letter-Writing Manuals and Instruction from Antiquity to Present.* New York: Columbia University Press.

Rees, J. (1976). *Jane Austen: Woman and Writer.* London: St Martin's Press.

Report for the Period 1st October 1949–31st December 1950 (1950). *Collected Reports of the Jane Austen Society I:* 15–17.

Report of Her Majesty's Commissioners Appointed to Enquire into the State (1852). *Discipline, Studies, and Revenues of the University and Colleges of Oxford.* London: Clowes.

Review: Northanger Abbey and Persuasion (1818). *Edinburgh Magazine and Literary Miscellany* 2: 453–455.

Ritchie, A.T. (1865). Heroines and their grandmothers. *Cornhill Magazine* 11: 630–640.

Ritchie, A.T. (1871). *Jane Austen. Cornhill Magazine* 24: 158–174.

Ritchie, A.T. (1883). *A Book of Sibyls.* London: Smith Elder.

Robbins, S.P. (1989). Jane Austen's epistolary fiction. In: *Jane Austen's Beginnings: the Juvenilia and 'Lady Susan'* (ed. J. David Grey), 215–233. Ann Arbor: U.M.I. Research Press.

Sabor, P. (2002). Jane Austen. In: *Censorship: A World Encyclopedia* (ed. D. Jones), 129–130. London: Routledge.

Sabor, P. (2006). Introduction. In: *Jane Austen, Juvenilia* (ed. P. Sabor), xxiii–lxvii. Cambridge: Cambridge University Press.

Sabor, P. (2011). Good, bad and ugly letters in *Sense and Sensibility. Persuasions On-Line* 32 (1): https://jasna.org/persuasions/on-line/vol32no1/sabor.html (accessed 6 May 2022).

Sale, R. (1986). *Closer to Home: Writers and Places in England, 1780–1830.* London: Harvard University Press.

Sales, R. (1994). *Jane Austen and Representations of Regency England*. London: Routledge.

Salwak, D. (2019). Literary biography in the twentieth century. In: *A Companion to Literary Biography* (ed. R. Bradford), 107–120. Chichester: Wiley-Blackwell.

Sawtell, G. (1984). Neither rich nor handsome. *Collected Reports of the Jane Austen Society III*: 304–311.

Schneider, A.-K. (2017). Emotional and imperial topographies: mapping feeling in 'Catharine, or the Bower'. In: *Jane Austen's Geographies* (ed. R. Clark), 52–67. Abingdon: Routledge.

Schofield, M.A. and Macheski, C. (ed.) (1986). *Fetter'd or Free? British Women Novelists 1670–1815*. Athens: Ohio University Press.

Selwyn, D. (2010). *Jane Austen and Children*. London: Continuum.

Shattock, J. (2001). The construction of the woman writer. In: *Women and Literature in Britain 1800-1900* (ed. J. Shattock), 22–34. Cambridge: Cambridge University Press.

Shaw, M. (1999). *The Clear Stream: A Life of Winifred Holtby*. London: Virago.

Shields, C. (2001). *Jane Austen*. London: Phoenix.

Simpson, R. (1870). Jane Austen. *North British Review* 52: 129–152.

Smith, G.B. (1885). More views of Jane Austen. *Gentleman's Magazine* 258: 26–45.

Smith, G. (1890). *Life of Jane Austen*. London: Scott.

Southam, B.C. (1962). The manuscript of Jane Austen's Volume the First. *The Library, 5th Series* 17: 231–237.

Southam, B.C. (1964). *Jane Austen's Literary Manuscripts*. Oxford: Oxford University Press.

Southam, B.C. (ed.) (1968). *Jane Austen: The Critical Heritage*. London: Routledge and Kegan Paul.

Southam, B.C. (1986). Juvenilia. In: *The Jane Austen Handbook* (ed. J.D. Grey), 244–255. London: Athlone.

Southam, B.C. (ed.) (1987). *Jane Austen: The Critical Heritage 1870–1940*, vol. 2. London: Routledge and Kegan Paul.

Southam, B.C. (2000). *Jane Austen and the Navy*, reprint, 2005. London: National Maritime Museum.

Southam, B.C. (2010). Jane Austen beside the seaside: an introduction. *Persuasions* 32: 167–172.

Southam, B.C. (2011). Jane Austen beside the seaside: Devonshire and Wales 1801–1803. *Persuasions* 33: 125–147.

Spacks, P.M. (1989). Female resources: epistles, plot and power. In: *Writing the Female Voice: essays on epistolary literature* (ed. E.C. Goldsmith), 61–76. Boston: Northwestern University Press.

Spence, J. (2003). *Becoming Jane Austen*, reprint, 2006. New York: MJF.

Spencer, J. (2005). *Literary Relations: Kinship and the Canon 1660–1830*. Oxford: Oxford University Press.

Stanley, L. (2004). The epistolarium: on theorizing letters and correspondences. *Auto/biography* 12: 201–235.

Stanley, L. (2011). The epistolary gift, the editorial third-party, counter-epistolaria: rethinking the epistolarium. *Life Writing* 8 (2): 135–152.

Stanley, L. (2013). Documents of life and critical humanities in a narrative and biographical frame. In: *Documents of Life Revisited: Narrative and Biographical Methodology for Twenty First-Century Critical Humanities* (ed. L. Stanley), 3–14. Farnham: Ashgate.

Stanley, L., Salter, A., and Dampier, H. (2012). The epistolary pact: letterness and the Schreiner epistolarium. *a/b Auto/Biography Studies* 27 (2): 262–293.

Stott, R. (2003). *Darwin and the Barnacle.* London: Faber and Faber.

Sutherland, K. (ed.) (2002). *A Memoir of Jane Austen and Other Family Recollections.* Oxford: Oxford University Press.

Sutherland, K. (2005a). *Jane Austen's Textual Lives: From Aeschylus to Bollywood.* Oxford: Oxford University Press.

Sutherland, K. (2005b). Chronology of composition and publication. In: *Jane Austen in Context* (ed. J. Todd), 12–22. Oxford: Oxford University Press.

Sutherland, K. (2009). Jane Austen's life and letters. In: *A Companion to Jane Austen* (ed. C.L. Johnson and C. Tuite), 13–30. Oxford: Wiley Blackwell.

Sutherland, K. (ed.) (2010). *Jane Austen's Fiction Manuscripts: A* Digital Edition.

Sutherland, K. (2013). Jane Austen's dealings with John Murray and his firm. *Review of English Studies* 64 (263): 105–126.

Sutherland, K. (2017a). Introduction. In: *Jane Austen: Writer and the World* (ed. K. Sutherland), 6–13. Oxford: Bodleian Library.

Sutherland, K. (ed.) (2017b). *Jane Austen: Writer in the World.* Oxford: Bodleian Library.

Sutherland, K. (2017c). Introduction. In: *Jane Austen: Teenage Writings* (ed. K. Sutherland and F. Johnston). Oxford: Oxford University Press.

Sutherland, K. (ed.) (2018). *Jane Austen: The Chawton Letters.* Oxford: Bodleian Library.

Tambouku, M. (2011). Interfaces in narrative research: letters as technologies of the self and as traces of social forces. *Qualitative Research*, 11 (5): 625–641.

Tambouku, M. (2017). Reassembling documents of life in the archive. *The European Journal of Life Writing* 6: 1–19.

Tambouku, M. (2020). Epistolary lives: fragments, sensibility, assemblages in auto/biographical research. In: *The Palgrave Handbook of Auto/Biography* (ed. J. Parson and A. Chappell), 157–164. Basingstoke: Palgrave Macmillan.

Tanner, T. (1986). *Jane Austen.* Basingstoke: Macmillan.

Tavela, S. (2017). 'I have unpacked the gloves': accessories and the Austen sisters. *Persuasions On-Line* 38 (1): https://jasna.org/publications-2/persuasions-online/vol38no1/tavela/ (accessed 6 May 2022).

Taylor, J. (2015). Texts and textiles: Jane Austen's gifting to Catherine Bigg and the Lloyd sisters. *Women's Writing* 22 (4): 472–484.

The British Letter-Writer: or Letter-Writer's Complete Instructor (1760). London: J. Cooke.

The Complete Letter-Writer containing Familiar Letters on the Most Common Occasions in Life (1776). 5th Edition. Paterson: Edinburgh.

The New Bath Guide (1762). Bath: Pope.

The Young Woman's Companion or Frugal Housewife containing the most approved methods of pickling, preserving, potting, collaring, confectionary etc. (1811). Manchester: Russell and Allen.

Todd, J. (2013). *Jane Austen: Her Life, Her Times, Her Novels*, reprint. London: Deutsch, 2019.

Tomalin, C. (1997). *Jane Austen: A Life*. London: Viking.

Tristram, P. (1998). Jane Austen and the changing face of England. In: *The Georgian Country House: Architecture, Landscape and Society* (ed. D. Arnold), 139–151. Stroud: Alan Sutton.

Tytler, S. (1880). *Jane Austen and her Works*. London: Cassell, Petter & Galpin.

Uglow, J. (1993). *Elizabeth Gaskell: A Habit of Stories*. London: Faber and Faber.

Upfal, A. (2005). Jane Austen's lifelong health problems and final illness. *Journal of Medical Ethics: Medical Humanities* 31: 3–11.

Vickery, A. (2009). *Behind Closed Doors: At Home in Georgian England*. New Haven: Yale University Press.

Vickery, A. (2016). No happy ending? At home with Miss Bates. *Jane Austen Society Annual Report:* 70–83.

Voskuil, L. (2014). Sotherton and the geography of empire: the landscapes of *Mansfield Park. Studies in Romanticism* 53 (4): 591–615.

Wallace, T.G. (2007). 'It must be done in London': the suburbanization of Highbury. *Persuasions: The Jane Austen Journal* 29: 67–78.

Wallace, B.K. (2017). Travelling shoe roses: the geography of things in Austen's work. In: *Jane Austen's Geographies* (ed. R. Clark), 115–127. Abingdon: Routledge.

Ward, M.A. (1884). Style and Miss Austen. *Macmillan's Magazine* 51: 84–91.

Warner, S.T. (1951). *Jane Austen*, revised 1964. London: Longman.

Watson, W. (1955). Jane Austen's London homes. *Collected Reports of the Jane Austen Society I*: 74–78.

Watt, I. (1963). Introduction. In: *Jane Austen: A Collection of Critical Essays* (ed. I. Watt), 1–14. Englewood Cliffs, NJ: Prentice Hall.

Whately, R. (1821). Modern novels: a review of 'Northanger Abbey' and 'Persuasion'. *Quarterly Review* 24: 352–376.

Whealler, S.C. (1993). Prose and power in two letters by Jane Austen. In: *Sent as a Gift: Eight Correspondences from the Eighteenth Century* (ed. A.T. Mackenzie), 173–200. London: University of Georgia Press.

Wheeler, D. (1998). The British postal service, privacy and Jane Austen's *Emma. South Atlantic Review* 63 (4): 34–47.

Wilkes, J. (2010). *Women Reviewing Women in Nineteenth-Century Britain: The Critical Reception of Jane Austen, Charlotte Brontë and George Eliot.* Farnham: Ashgate.

Wilson, M. (1990a). Lord Brabourne and Jane Austen's letters. *Collected Reports of the Jane Austen Society IV*: 175–179.

Wilson, M. (1990b). *Almost Another Sister.* Maidstone: Kent Arts and Libraries.

Woolf, V. (1939). The art of biography. In: *Selected Essays* (ed. D. Bradshaw), 116–123. Oxford: Oxford University Press 2009.

Worsley, L. (2017). *Jane Austen at Home.* London: Hodder and Stoughton.

Yeazell, R.B. (1984). The boundaries of Mansfield Park. *Representations* 7: 133–152.

Index

Note: Page numbers in italic type indicate figures. 'JA letters' indicates occurrences in Austen's letters.